Neal-Schuman

ELECTRONIC CLASSROOM HANDBOOK

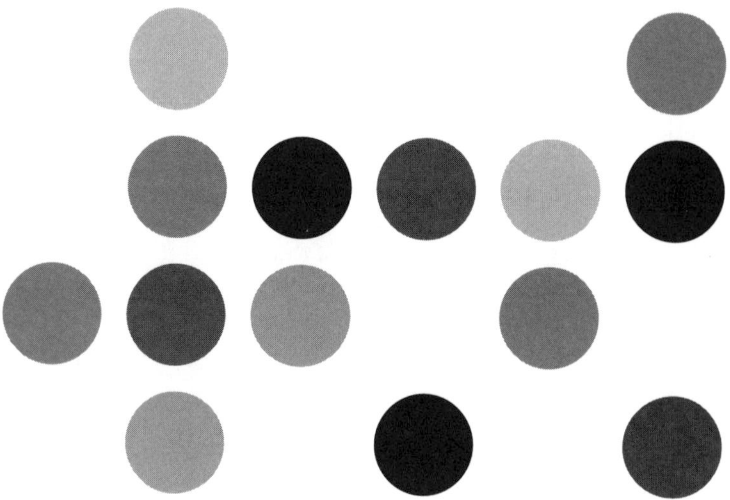

Lisa Janicke Hinchliffe

Neal-Schuman Publishers, Inc.
New York London

Published by Neal-Schuman Publishers, Inc.
100 Varick Street
New York, NY 10013

Printed and bound in the United States of America.

The paper used in this publication meets the minimum requirements of American National Standard for Information Sciences—Permanence of Paper for Printed Library Materials, ANSI Z39.48–1992. ∞

Library of Congress Cataloging-in-Publication Data

Hinchliffe, Lisa Janicke.
Neal-Schuman electronic classroom handbook / Lisa Janicke Hinchliffe.
p. cm.
Includes bibliographical references and index.
ISBN 1-55570-407-7 (alk. paper)
1. Library architecture—United States. 2. Libraries—United States—Automation—Planning. 3. Libraries—United States—Automation—Equipment and supplies. 4. Computer-assisted instruction—United States—Planning. 5. Computer-assisted instruction—United States—Equipment and supplies. I. Title:
Electronic classroom handbook. II. Title.

Z679.5 .h56 2001
022'.3—dc21

00-051958

Contents

Figures

Foreword

By Lizabeth Wilson

I have eagerly anticipated the publication of the *Neal–Schuman Electronic Classroom Handbook* since I first learned from Lisa Janicke Hinchliffe that it was under way. For the past three years, I have talked about the publication around the country even before I saw the manuscript, got a glimpse at the table of contents, or knew its title. This *Handbook* is a great idea whose time has come.

As someone concerned with promoting excellence in teaching and learning in libraries, I know that the field lacks a comprehensive manual for designing electronic classrooms. The need is palpable. Wherever I have lectured or conducted workshops on designing educational programs, I have been met with similar and recurring questions. "How do I build an electronic classroom? Do you know of any good models? Where can I find floor plans? Do drop down computer monitors really work? What is it going to cost? Who makes furniture that allows for groups to work together?" I often receive panicked phone calls. "My library just got a grant for an electronic classroom. Now what do I do?"

In the past, I routinely suggested that individuals consult "Resources for Designing Library Electronic Classrooms," [1] an invaluable annotated bibliography compiled by Hinchliffe. "That's a start," the desperate practitioner would indicate. "But, I need real advice, not just a list of references."

When Lisa Janicke Hinchliffe shared her plans with me for a primer that would answer all these questions and more, I encouraged her to move expeditiously. I knew first hand what a huge information void needed to be filled. Across the nation, our libraries are retrofitting library space or building new rooms to accommodate burgeoning instruction and training programs. The *Handbook* couldn't come fast enough, as far as I and hundreds of other practitioners were concerned.

Electronic classrooms are highly visible investments. Not only do these classrooms contend for scarce capital and operating funds, but they require space. Some would say that space is our most precious resource on campus. When an electronic classroom is opened, it can be simultaneously scrutinized, envied, and publicized by campus administrators, leaders, and educators.

If we do not design electronic classrooms that enable good teaching and learning, we run the risk of building the pedagogical equivalents of Potemkin Villages. Creation of these technological edifices gives the illusion that all is well in the hinterlands. But if we look closer, we often find an educational sham—showcase electronic classrooms that are not designed for learning. This *Handbook* helps us move beyond ill–conceived electronic classrooms and "bolted–on" technology to environments that support effective learning.

The *Neal-Schumann Electronic Classroom Handbook* is a comprehensive guide for individuals, particularly those in libraries, designing or teaching in an electronic classroom. The *Handbook* brings together, for the first time, in one volume, solid research, practical advice, and capital processes for use by the classroom designer, program coordinator, and library administrator.

The *Neal-Schuman Electronic Classroom Handbook* ensures that libraries avoid the mistakes of others and make the most of their resources. By consulting the *Handbook*, educators and administrators will design electronic classrooms that enhance teaching and learning in our libraries.

Now, go build that classroom.

Lizabeth (Betsy) A. Wilson
Director of University Libraries
University of Washington
Seattle, Washington

1. Hinchliffe, Lisa Janicke. 1998. "Resources for Designing Library Electronic Classrooms" *MC Journal: The Journal of Academic Media Librarianship*, 6, no. 1 (Spring). *<http://wings.buffalo.edu/publications/mcjrnl/v6n1/class.html>*

Preface

The *Neal–Schuman Electronic Classroom Handbook* was written for librarians or other professionals who are designing, managing, or teaching in an electronic classroom. Although my perspective is that of an academic librarian, the *Handbook* should also interest public and school librarians offering instruction programs, and corporate librarians with training programs, as well as administrators, classroom designers, computing staffs, and activities planners. Electronic classrooms are increasingly moving from being a luxury to becoming a necessity.

I designed the *Neal–Schuman Electronic Classroom Handbook* as a working resource manual encompassing the relevant theory, essential information, and practical solutions professionals need to maximize the potential of their facilities. The *Handbook* is organized to parallel the way most readers approach electronic classroom projects: the planning process, design and construction, and management and teaching. It is divided into these three parts with sections within the chapters arranged to allow the reader to quickly find relevant details on any particular topic. Throughout the text, numerous worksheets offer the opportunity for hands-on instruction. To encourage this approach to learning, electronic copies of the worksheets are available and can be downloaded from the Web site for the *Handbook* at *www.neal-schuman.com/eclassroom.html*.

Chapter One starts by defining the electronic classroom relative to its purpose — teaching and learning — and then uses that definition to explore the two types of electronic classrooms: demonstration and hands-on. Suggestions for ways in which to justify the expenditures required for an electronic classroom, such as benchmarking and the relationship of an electronic classroom to improved student learning, conclude the chapter. Planning is examined in Chapter Two by discussing the planning process, paying particular attention to identifying a project leader, establishing a planning team, involving other relevant individuals, and determining whether to hire an external consultant. Chapter Three, "Gathering and Analyzing Information" continues the discussion of the planning process. The planning team is guided through an instructional needs assessment aimed at determining the current status of the library's instructional programs and identifying the preferred future for those programs. A situational analysis of financial, library, institutional, and educational variables determines the larger context in which planning for the electronic classroom will occur. Finally, the planning team is directed through the processes of identifying assumptions, establishing priorities, and creating a timeline.

The next six chapters detail the technical, architectural, interior design, budgetary, and building considerations for an electronic classroom. Chapter Four, "Space" investigates issues related to location, size, layout, walls, ceilings, windows, doorways, and flooring, as well as storage, security, and aesthetics. Seven diagrams depicting common classroom layouts and the discussion of the advantages and disadvantages of each of the layouts highlights this chapter. Chapter Five, "Infrastructure" identifies needed decisions with respect to the data network in the electronic classroom as well as electrical, lighting, and heating, ventilation, and air conditioning systems.

Chapter Six, "Software" and Chapter Seven, "Equipment and Furnishings" together detail considerations at the heart of electronic classroom design. Chapter Six covers operating systems, library resources, personal productivity, data analysis, accessories, and control/collaboration software systems, as well as issues related to security, licensing agreements, and remote access. Equipment and furniture for student and instructor workstations, as well as projection, sound, and printing systems, are discussed in Chapter Seven. Other areas examined in this chapter include assessments and recommendations for writing surfaces, assistive technologies, ergonomics, distance learning, and accommodations for print materials.

Chapter Eight, "Budgets and Expenditures" takes an honest look at estimating the cost of an electronic classroom. Suggestions for grants and other external funding are included, as are budget limitations and the potential for overcoming limited budgets through phased implementation. Finally, Chapter Nine, "Construction and Occupancy" summarizes the processes involved in the actual building of an electronic classroom. Architectural drawings, schedules, the bidding process, awarding the contract, construction, and moving in are discussed.

The last chapters of the book provide advice and support for those who use, manage, and support the electronic classroom after it is built. Chapter Ten, "Classroom Administration" discusses issues related to personnel, continuing expenses, maintenance, policies and procedures, marking, scheduling, and statistical recordkeeping. Multiple real-world examples of related documents are included. Chapter Eleven, "Teaching and Learning Strategies" focuses on the purpose of an electronic classroom — teaching and learning. Encouragement, as well as a few words of warning, suggestions for teaching methods, teaching competencies, management of an instruction session, and developing instructional materials are all discussed. Chapter Twelve, "Evaluation" identifies multiple methods for investigating the success of an electronic classroom. Included in the chapter are suggestions for how to gather data using a logbook, observation, focus groups, student evaluation forms, and instructor surveys. Finally, Chapter Thirteen, "The Future" examines the future of instruction programs in libraries and what they mean for electronic classrooms.

The appendices for the *Neal–Schuman Electronic Classroom Handbook* are extensive. Appendix A provides reproducible cut-out figures which can be used by the planning team to consider various room layouts. Appendix B offers the codes, regulations, standards, guidelines, and laws you will need to know. Appendix C: Directory of Suppliers provides contact information for all of the companies and products mentioned in the text of the *Handbook*. Appendix D lists classroom Web sites useful in making design decisions. Appendices E and F offer sample instructional materials related to the research process and evaluating information which were developed for use in an electronic classroom. The final appendix demonstrates how the information provided in the book can be applied in school, public, and special library settings through case studies. The extensive References section provides a multitude of options for further reading and study.

The *Neal–Schuman Electronic Classroom Handbook* is a valuable resource for those who are just beginning to plan for an electronic classroom or others who are already managing multiple instructional spaces. The handbook is intended to have something for everyone. For the novice, practical and basic information is there to get you started. For the more experienced planner, the techniques and strategies suggested can be used to further investigate cutting-edge design options and to evaluate the effectiveness of existing classrooms. It is my hope that the *Handbook* responds to the needs of librarians who work daily to improve the classroom environments at their libraries in the hope of improving student learning.

I have attempted to create a practical manual for librarians designing and using electronic classrooms. I hope that it will be useful to both front-line librarians as well as library administrators and facilities planners. I would welcome any suggestions of ways that the *Neal–Schuman Electronic Classroom Handbook* might be improved. All the best to you as you design, construct, and use your electronic classroom — all the best to you in teaching and learning.

Look for the forms featured in the Neal–Schuman Electronic Classroom Handbook at *www.neal-schuman.com/eclassroom.html*

Acknowledgments

I wish to thank my colleagues at Milner Library and Illinois State University for their support and encouragement. Special thanks is due to Cheryl Asper Elzy, Jan Johnson, Beth Schobernd, Sharon Naylor, Sharon Wetzel, and Jackie Frank. I also thank my "virtual" colleagues on the BI-L listserv for their ideas and experience so willingly shared each time the topic of electronic classrooms is raised. I am grateful to Michael Kelley, a charming individual and helpful editor, at Neal-Schuman, as well as the other staff at Neal-Schuman who contributed to the production of this book.

I am thankful to Beth S. Woodard for her continuous support. It was Beth who encouraged me to submit a proposal to Neal-Schuman and reviewed the initial outline of the text. I am especially indebted to Beth for the mentoring that prompted me to begin this study during library school and see it through to the completion of this book. Never has any one had a better mentor and colleague. Gratitude also goes to Janice Kragness who got me started in librarianship through a simple observation.

Finally, I am ever-grateful to my husband, Joseph Hinchliffe, who listened and supported me through the long hours of researching and writing this text. I am a lucky individual to be loved by such a kind and caring man.

Part One

Preparation and Planning

Imagine what could be done with better facilities!
Evan Farber (1984: 13)

"We're getting an electronic classroom!" You can almost hear an instruction librarian's excitement in the printed words. Finally, the opportunity to demonstrate electronic resources, to coach learners through hands-on practice exercises, and to do so in the privacy of a separate room rather than at the computer clusters in the reference area or in borrowed space in another building on campus!

Or, at particularly fortunate institutions, maybe this is a second or even third classroom, approved for construction because of the overwhelming demands placed on the existing instructional facilities. No more negotiating who gets to use the room at 10:00 next Wednesday or at 1:00 on Tuesday—well, at least for a little while!

Chapter One

Background

Electronic classrooms have also been called accessing classrooms, collaboratories, computer-assisted classrooms, computer-mediated classrooms, e-classrooms, enhanced classrooms, enriched classrooms, hands-on computer classrooms, high-tech classrooms, Internet rooms, master classrooms, media-enhanced classrooms, media-equipped classrooms, multimedia classrooms, multipurpose classrooms, smart classrooms, smarter classrooms, teaching theaters, technology classrooms, technology-enhanced learning environments, virtual classrooms, and wired classrooms.

Whew!

So, just what is an electronic classroom? Hmmm...good question.

DEFINITION

For our purposes here, an electronic classroom will be operationally defined as a separate room equipped with electronic devices for instructional purposes. The focus on instructional purposes distinguishes the electronic classroom from a computer laboratory and from the computer clusters "out on the floor" in the library. Not the most exciting definition but it is straightforward and will provide a foundation for the rest of this book.

FOR TEACHING AND LEARNING

What is exciting about the definition is its implications. A separate room with equipment—that is good. What is great, though, is that the electronic classroom is for instructional purposes. Instructional purposes being, of course, teaching and learning—the two primary activities that the electronic classroom is designed to facilitate. Librarians teaching, students learning—what a nice picture for the mind!

But, there is more to this than a pleasing mental picture. Information literacy is a critical, foundational, and lifelong skill. Society, employers, and everyday life demand that individuals know how to navigate resources, select relevant information, and evaluate and apply that information to solve problems, make decisions, and manage personal life events. Librarians have long acknowledged the importance of information literacy and attempted to impart needed skills to students in whatever environments were available. Consider even, for example, Samuel Green's 1876 statement that librarians should give users "as much assistance as they need, but try at the same time to teach them to rely upon themselves and become independent" (80). While the phrase "information literacy" was not yet in use, the spirit of lifelong information skills clearly shone through early on in the profession.

What librarians have lacked are appropriate facilities for instruction. A hallway turned into a demonstration space, a corner of the reference area, and a difficult-to-find room in the basement—all have been used by librarians desperate for teaching space. As Evan Farber once observed, "for the most part, academic library buildings have not been designed with bibliographic instruction (BI) in mind" (1984: 5). Fortunately, the tide has turned and most libraries have or are seeking space in which to create a teaching and learning facility that is designed to support the library's instructional programs. The electronic classroom provides the appropriate venue for librarians to teach information searching, retrieval, and evaluation skills in a supportive and adequately equipped environment. Today, the electronic classroom is critical to the instructional efforts aimed at user attainment of information literacy.

CLASSROOM TYPES

There are essentially two types of electronic classrooms: *demonstration* and *hands-on*.

Demonstration Classrooms

Demonstration classrooms have an instructor workstation equipped with electronics. Just which electronics will depend on what is being taught and will be discussed in detail in later chapters. In general though, librarians might use the instructor workstation to demonstrate the use of a particular library resource, such as the online catalog, or display various media-based products, such as a videotape discussing search strategy. In demonstration classrooms, students are seated at ordinary tables or desks and do not have access to their own workstations.

Demonstration classrooms have the obvious disadvantage that students cannot be given hands-on experience using library resources or practicing search skills. Students may be lulled into a passive mode, especially if the room is darkened to facilitate the display of projected images. The librarian will need to plan activities and interaction into the demonstration so that students remain active participants in the teaching and learning process.

Not so immediately obvious, though, is that a demonstration classroom may be more appropriate than a hands-on classroom when a particular instruction session focuses on the relationship between print and electronic resources, or when the research tools being taught are print only but the librarian has prepared a complementary slide show using presentation software such as PowerPoint. In such cases, students will need space to work with the print materials—space not hindered by bulky computer monitors and keyboards.

Hands-On Classrooms

Hands-on classrooms have an instructor workstation equipped with electronics as well as student workstations equipped with electronics. This set-up allows students to follow along actively during a demonstration by a librarian and then to engage in independent exploration or practice to reinforce the lesson. Using the student workstations, learners can explore library resources, practice searching, and engage in other active learning activities. Students can also personalize their learning by pursuing search topics relevant to their interests or the assignments for a particular course.

While having the obvious advantages of encouraging immediate use of the instructional content and offering students the opportunity to participate actively in their learning, hands-on classrooms have a number of challenges. Students may be easily distracted by the computers and fail to attend to the directions given by the librarian. Browsing the Web, reading electronic mail, and using chat rooms can be great temptations for students, particularly if their attendance at the instruction session is not voluntary. Malfunctioning equipment may derail a session, as could a student who insists on asking technical questions. Finally, electronic equipment requires a great deal of space and may limit the feasibility of integrating print and electronic resource instruction.

Each type of classroom has strengths and weaknesses. Selecting the appropriate type for a particular library requires careful attention to the instructional needs and institutional environment of that library. Analysis of instructional needs and institutional variables is discussed in Chapter Three. Unfortunately, you may not have the option of selecting the type of classroom that you actually need for your instructional program. The type may already be dictated by campus priorities, space availability, or budgetary limitations. Even if this is the case, you can use the planning process to design the best possible classroom within the known limitations.

JUSTIFICATIONS

Perhaps some librarians have been gifted with the opportunity to build an electronic classroom without asking for it; however, most will have to spend much time and energy justifying the expenditure. Justifying the expense of constructing and maintaining an electronic classroom—or an additional classroom or more—in the library will be more or less difficult depending on institutional culture and financial exigencies. Electronic classrooms of either type are expensive, both in terms of physical space and budgetary impact, and library and campus administrators rightly want to know that such expenditures are worthwhile.

Librarians may find themselves writing multiple proposals over a number of budget cycles before the project is approved. Perseverance, backed by compelling arguments, is a must. Perseverance requires patience and tenacity, as well as sensitivity to administrative priorities and timing. Compelling arguments, on the other hand, require careful attention to your goals and objectives and student learning. Regardless of which arguments are used, in developing a justification for your classroom, you must attend to the specific needs and appropriate arguments for your institution. Following are some justifications that you may be able to adopt or adapt for your circumstances.

Improve Student Learning

As stated above, an electronic classroom is crucial to providing the information literacy instruction so vital in today's networked information environment. Students need to be taught how to find and evaluate information and to have the opportunity to practice those skills in a supportive environment. However, let's not leave it at that. Before we go any further, let's explore some of the specific ways that teaching in an electronic classroom can improve student learning and the attainment of information literacy skills.

Transference of Skills

If students are exposed to the skills and ideas in a learning environment that closely resembles the environment in which the skills and knowledge will be used, students will more likely be able to apply the information when they are doing research outside of the classroom. Though database searching can be, and unfortunately has been, taught using overhead transparencies or handouts of screen captures, demonstration and practice using the actual interface more closely approximates the experiences that students will have when they are using a database for their own research needs. With screen captures, students must first bridge the differences between the screen capture and the actual interface before they can apply the learned information to searching the database. In bridging the differences, students can introduce errors into their research process and develop inaccurate mental models of the search process. Hands-on practice not only eliminates the need for the student to bridge the differences between the screen captures and the interface but also allows the librarian to observe students' initial use of a database. Through the observation process, the librarian can correct errors before they become habitual for the student and far more difficult to correct.

Active Learning

Active learning opportunities engage students in their own learning, thereby increasing knowledge acquisition, retention, and transferability. Students are more likely to make cognitive links between the new information that is being presented to them and the knowledge that they already have if they are actively engaged in the teaching and learning process. Additionally, active learning enables students to practice concepts and skills, making it more likely that students will retain what they learn and be able to apply it in similar, and even not-so-similar, situations. Admittedly, active learning is easier to facilitate in a hands-on classroom than in a demonstration classroom. However, active learning techniques, such as group brainstorming for subject terms, can be used in a demonstration classroom with a live database connection to involve students in the learning experience.

Focus

A separate classroom encourages students to focus on the information they are learning without the distraction of other students walking through the area, telephones ringing, or the like. If you have ever taught even a small group of students to search a particular database in the midst of the library's reference area, you have probably noticed that the students are distracted by their environment. A friend who happens to walk by, the awkwardness of holding a book bag, the discomfort of standing for 15 minutes in one place, and poor sight lines can all distract students from the instruction that they need to be successful researchers. In an electronic classroom, the learning environment itself encourages students to focus on the task at hand.

Responsive Instruction

Live demonstrations and practice allow the possibility of exploring particular tools or search strategies that are not planned but instead result from student questions and interests. By responding to student interest, librarians can further student engagement with the instruction. Additionally, the hands-on classroom enables different students to explore different topics, try a number of search strategies, and encounter various difficulties that are relevant to their own topics. Of course, a savvy librarian can also use these varied experiences to encourage students to share successful strategies with one another and thereby facilitate peer and collaborative learning. This type of responsive instruction is far more difficult, if not impossible, to attain outside of a classroom or with a canned demonstration.

Modeling Research as an Integrative Process

If the classroom workstations are designed as scholar's workstations, the research process can be taught as an integrated, iterative process of seeking out existing information and creating new knowledge. A scholar's workstation approach in the library classroom means that the computers provide access to both library resources as well as word processing, spreadsheets, and other personal productivity software. Such workstations allow students to follow the model of professional writers and academic scholars who flow naturally from research to writing and back again multiple times during the drafting and revising processes. Students who master this way of working are well on their way to information literacy—not only gathering information but also applying that information in the creation of new knowledge. Library instruction that models this process will be perceived by students as more relevant to the work assigned in their courses.

Facilitate Training and Development

Though electronic classrooms are most commonly used for library instruction, an electronic classroom can also be used for staff development and training programs. Such sessions may be taught by library staff members or outside professionals—vendor representatives or computer trainers. In this day of information explosion, information repackaging, and ever-evolving interfaces, library employee training is of heightened importance, and an electronic classroom provides a wonderful facility for group-based training sessions. Of course, an electronic classroom will facilitate active, focused, integrative, and responsive instruction for library staff just as it will for students. Likewise, if staff are able to practice the skills being presented, they are more likely to apply them in work situations, such as, at the reference or circulation desk.

Appeal to the Larger Institution

Once the case has been made internally in the library, the justification may have to be extended further in order to be attractive to the larger institution. Most appealing should be arguments based on improved student learning; however, librarians must be prepared to make arguments based on pragmatic and political grounds as well. Your library director should be able to provide the necessary information (for example, about institutional objectives) for these justifications.

Alignment with Institutional Objectives

Librarians working on proposals for review by the campus administration or academic senate should look for opportunities to align their classroom proposal with larger institutional objectives. Possible documents to examine include the institution's mission and vision statements, stated long-range and short-term goals, past accreditation reports, the campus technology plan, and special initiatives relating to student learning or to using technology in teaching. Even if the proposal guidelines do not require that you make a connection with institutional priorities, doing so will show that you are aware of the institution's goals and that your project will assist with the attainment of those goals.

Partnership Opportunities

Depending on organizational structures and the campus building priorities, the library might also approach another campus unit, (for example, academic technologies, the campus computing center, media production, or the distance learning unit) about the possibility of cosponsoring the classroom proposal and sharing the facility once it is constructed. The best possible partner would be a campus unit that has its greatest demand for the electronic classroom during times that the library instruction program has few or no sessions. For example, perhaps the education department sponsors an intensive technology training program for primary and secondary teachers in the first part of the summer but the library has very few instruction sessions during that time. Regardless of which unit the library chooses to collaborate with, in order to avoid future misunderstandings and conflicts, details about who will manage the classroom and provide technical support and how the classroom will be shared should be established before a cosponsored proposal is put forward.

Outreach to Other Groups

If scheduling demands will allow, librarians might consider offering campus faculty the opportunity to use the electronic classroom for nonlibrary-related activities and/or opening the classroom area to students as an open computer laboratory when library instruction classes are not in session. Most institutions have faculty members who would very much appreciate the opportunity to teach at least some sessions in an electronic classroom. For example, a political science professor might want to show students how to use statistical analysis to predict election outcomes and then have the students investigate how different variables affect the predictions. Such faculty members will likely be advocates for the library's proposal if they know that such access to the classroom will be possible. Many institutions are also experiencing continued demand from students for open computing access. The student government association may be willing to support the library's classroom proposal if students will be able to use the space for general access computing when classes are not scheduled. If the institution emphasizes outreach to the community or other academic institutions, the librarians could also opt for giving these groups access to the classroom.

Librarians might also consider training faculty and staff to use technology in teaching. Unlike other units on campus, the library probably started using technology early on to accomplish core activities and participate in library networks and consortia. For example, using and teaching others to use the online public access catalog and indexes and abstracts on CD-ROM were probably day-to-day reality for librarians at the reference desk long before most faculty had their own office computers. Librarians have had many years to learn effective strategies for using technology and teaching students how to use it. As such, librarians are potentially in a unique position to serve as campus leaders in integrating technology in teaching.

Finally, librarians might choose to make the electronic classroom available to outside groups for a fee. Whether this option is feasible will depend on both institutional climate and culture as well as on administrative and legal regulations governing the library. If it is feasible and can be managed without disrupting to the library's instructional program, the potential income for the library or the larger institution may be attractive to campus administrators.

Benchmarking

Almost all colleges and universities have a list of peer institutions that they use in evaluating the institution's programs and effectiveness. Investigating whether the libraries at your peer institutions have electronic classrooms may help you bolster your argument that your library needs one. If the libraries of these other institutions have electronic classrooms and your library does not, you may be able to use this fact to leverage funds and commitment for your electronic classroom. Even if none of the libraries at the peer institutions have electronic classrooms, you may still be able to use this information by arguing that adding a classroom will raise the status of your library and the institution. You might also consider explaining how the proposed electronic classroom would be better than the classrooms at the other libraries. Though a survey of the libraries at the peer institutions is not likely to be effective for your library if it is the only evidence offered, it may help support your request, particularly if your institution relies on benchmarks in other areas of decision making.

Chapter Two

Planning

Beginning the planning process will probably be a necessary component of developing a credible proposal for an electronic classroom whether you are seeking institutional or grant funding. This process may seem a bit circular—begin to plan the project in order to get funding to do the project you are planning—but it will be almost impossible to argue the case for a new classroom without at least some specific information about why the classroom is needed and how it will be used. The good news is that no planning time is wasted time; once you have funding, you will be ready to begin construction promptly.

Beyond the political need to begin planning in order to convince others of the importance of your classroom project, careful planning is simply a must for any project to be successful. The planning stage is the time to detail needs, obstacles, issues, and so on. Once construction begins, in all likelihood, anything that was not considered during planning will not come to be. Or, if new components are now considered, they will cost a great deal of money. It is far better to spend time planning carefully and considering all of your options up front. As the trite but true saying goes—if you fail to plan, you plan to fail!

The planning process is presented here as a fairly linear activity for clarity and organization. In reality, of course, the planning process is iterative and nonlinear, with multiple efforts occuring simultaneously. At times it may feel like chaos. Do not try to force the process into a linear mode. It just won't work. On the other hand, do organize yourself to be certain that no part of the process gets left out. It is not so important that all of the steps occur in the order presented here as it is that all of the aspects are considered.

As a final note, the planning process presented here isolates planning for an electronic classroom from other planning that may be occurring in the library or institution. If there is other planning occurring, e.g., the classroom is part of a proposed new library building, you will have to align the planning for the classroom with the other planning processes as well.

PLANNERS

Deciding who to involve in the planning process is the first step of the planning process. Generally speaking, one should follow the advice of M. E. L. Jacob in selecting participants. Involve "everyone who will be affected or who may be essential to achieving the vision identified in the plan" (1990: 9). Be assured, though, that you need not involve everyone in the same way or in every discussion and decision. Some individuals might participate only or primarily in gathering information, while others serve in decision-making or advisory roles. The key is to balance interests, expertise, and efficiency.

Project Leader

To ensure that the planning process is successful, an individual should be identified as the project leader. A project leader is responsible for facilitating the planning process, coordinating efforts, and helping the planning team address issues and timelines successfully. The library instruction coordinator or the administrator charged with oversight of public services is likely the appropriate person to serve as project leader. In some circumstances, for example, if the classroom will be shared between the library and another campus unit, you may wish to have co-leaders. In such cases, the division of responsibility and authority should be clear to both the co-leaders and to others participating in planning. Regardless of who is selected, the project leader(s) must not only have sufficient expertise and interest for the project but they must also have the necessary time to commit to the project. Building an electronic classroom is a significant undertaking with respect to time, money, and expectations, and thus the project must be a high priority for the project leader if it is to be successful.

Planning Team

Instruction librarians and staff, computer and network support staff, and library administrators are key members on an electronic classroom planning team. These people will be most heavily involved in using and supporting the classroom. As the members of the planning team, they should take primary responsibility for the project, serve as liaison between the library and any campus or vendor contacts, and make recommendations and decisions with respect to the classroom. Given the network-dependent nature of an electronic classroom, it is vital that the library's network administrator or network support staff be involved in all phases of classroom design. A beautiful classroom with poor-quality equipment and poor network support will be a constant frustration for those teaching in it.

Since many library instruction sessions are developed in collaboration with faculty members teaching discipline-based courses, it may also be desirable to include on the planning team one or two faculty members from different campus departments. They must have experience with library instruction sessions for their students, but, more important, almost all faculty members have taught in a variety of classrooms. Therefore they may be able to provide insight, based on their experiences, regarding how different room designs facilitate or hinder learning. If at all possible, choose faculty members who either have experience teaching their own classes in an electronic classroom or who are interested in doing so. They are more likely to be motivated to commit their time and talent to serving on the planning team.

Finally, thinking back to the teaching and learning purpose of an electronic classroom, the importance of including students on the planning team is obvious. The teaching perspective is well represented by the library's instructional staff and the campus faculty. The learning perspective is also an important point of view. Students can bring a very different perspective about what makes a classroom a comfortable and supportive environment for learning. It is far better to have students provide this perspective than to have librarians and faculty members guessing at what the students might think. If possible, include at least one student representative from each of the groups served by the library's instructional programs (for example, an undergraduate student, a graduate student, and an international student). If you do not already know students who might be asked to serve, consider involving some of the students who work in the library or contact the student government association for recommendations.

Another option for involving students is to establish a separate student advisory committee. This advisory committee could review and react to proposed layouts and design decisions without attending all of the planning team meetings. The members of this committee could rotate attendance at the planning team meetings or elect a representative to the planning team. This approach will maximize student involvement in the planning process without overly taxing students who are probably already juggling classes, homework, employment, and personal obligations. The student advisory committee could also be responsible for seeking input from student groups on campus (for example, through a presentation to the student government association).

Other potential members of the planning team might include a librarian from a peer institution or a librarian from a local library who has already experienced the process of building an electronic classroom and who knows some of the pitfalls. A staff member from campus computing or the manager of another electronic classroom on campus might also be considered.

Though it is important to involve those who need to be involved, it is also important that the planning team be manageable in size. In general, look to the size of other library and campus committees that have been successful in completing their tasks.

Resource People

Library staff who are not members of the planning team can serve as resource people, providing information and advice based on their own experiences and expertise. Special attention should be paid to asking for input from the librarians who will teach in the classroom and the technology staff who will support it. Likewise, focus groups held with campus faculty and students can reveal helpful insights to consider in developing your classroom.

In addition, most colleges and universities have a number of offices that can provide support and assistance in the planning process. Campus policies and procedures may even require some involvement from these groups. For example, the director of space utilization may be required to review any room layouts for consistency with campus standards and guidelines. The office of disability services may require that the classroom plans be audited for compliance with laws and regulations governing accessibility for persons with disabilities. Depending on the extent of the involvement, it may be most efficient for the planning team to include a staff member from the appropriate campus unit.

Campus units that may be of assistance in planning an electronic classroom include the facilities office, the physical plant, an office of disability concerns, the campus safety and security office, a center for teaching enhancement, the classroom space committee, the department of instructional or academic technology, and the media center. These units have different names on different campuses so you will have to browse the campus phone book or online directory for the appropriate units on your own campus. In general, staff from these units will be able and willing to offer insights and expertise not necessarily available from the library staff. Also look into whether your institution has a committee similar to the Classroom Environment Committee at Binghamton University (*www.ecc.binghamton.edu/cecchrg.html*). Such a committee may be able to provide information about campus standards for classrooms that would otherwise be unknown to the librarians.

Consultant

Also consider whether you want to involve a consultant in your project. A consultant can bring additional expertise, time, energy, and perspective, and can help reconcile differences of opinion. If need be, an outside consultant can also address politically problematic issues and advocate for the library with campus and external groups.

A consultant can serve in a variety of roles—as a data gatherer, an advisor, an implementer, or a coach (Ucko, 1990: 29). You will have to decide what type of consultant will best serve your needs. In most cases, if you decide to hire a consultant, you will probably want an electronic classroom consultant who will provide advice and recommendations for your consideration.

If you decide to hire a consultant, consider the following points in making your selection:

- Expertise—What is the depth and range of a consultant's expertise? How much expertise does the consultant have with electronic classrooms and with how many classrooms and institutions?
- Experience—Does the consultant have experience with classroom design in libraries?
- Enthusiasm—Is the consultant excited by your project and the task at hand?
- Communication—Does the consultant communicate well with different groups of people?
- References—Have other libraries hired the consultant and was the consultant's work satisfactory?
- Expense—Is the consultant's fee within your budgeted range and the general range of other consultants?
- Availability—Is the consultant available to work on your project within your time frame?

If you are considering hiring a consultant, get a copy of *Selecting and Working with Consultants* (1990), by Thomas J. Ucko. Though Ucko's advice is not specific to libraries, the book is highly practical and provides detailed advice. Lee Brawner (1992) provides similar advice in his discussion of selecting a consultant to work with a library building project.

FROM GATHERING INFORMATION TO MOVING IN

Establishing goals and timelines for the planning process, as well as establishing expectations and channels for clear and timely communication, are essential in managing the planning process. Make such goals and timelines known to all participants in the planning process so that those involved can plan their work activities to meet deadlines. If possible, establish an electronic mailing list or discussion forum to facilitate information flow and decision making. Planning team members should know the current status of the project and upcoming deadlines at all times.

Chapter Three

Gathering and Analyzing Information

The planning team must begin its work by gathering and analyzing information. Gathering information involves fact-finding as well as brainstorming and creative thinking. Analyzing information requires careful consideration of facts and hypotheses, prioritizing, and decision making. The planning team must analyze the current situation as well as identify potential future scenarios and then make initial decisions about goals and objectives for the classroom. These initial decisions are not irrevocable for the most part but they set the stage for decisions made during the design process about space, infrastructure, software, and hardware. As such, these decisions must be made thoughtfully and carefully.

This chapter suggests approaches for gathering information and considering variables that affect the future. You may find that some information is already collected because of previous projects or reports. If there is an annual report on library instruction, it will likely contain a great deal of the information that the planning team will need. The library's annual report and information submitted for consideration during accreditation visits will also be useful. Some information may not be available to the planning team or it may not be available until after the optimal time in the planning process. Don't despair—just keep working away at the plan and adjust previous decisions when needed.

INSTRUCTIONAL NEEDS ASSESSMENT

Given the instructional purposes of an electronic classroom, the instructional needs of the library must be specifically and carefully investigated. Ask yourself what are the teaching and learning needs in this library?

Do not only consider needs that have already been expressed through other planning processes. Consider also what needs might arise in the future and what the library's users expect or are soon likely to expect of the library (West, Farmer, and Wolff, 1991: 230). For example, as electronic books become more readily available, library users will likely expect the library to have electronic books in its collection as well as to provide instruction on accessing and using them.

In doing the instructional needs assessment, consider the questions below and be clear on the answers for your program. With each question, give both an answer based on *current circumstances* and then an answer based on a *desired future*. (See Figure 3.1 for a reproducible worksheet to assist with your instructional needs assessment. Figure 3.2 is the same worksheet filled out for a hypothetical library as an example. The worksheet can also be downloaded from this book's Web site at *www.neal-schuman.com/eclassroom.html*.)

- Who are the *learners*? Undergraduate students? Nontraditional students? Graduate students? Community members? Librarian employees? Faculty? Campus staff? Alumni?
- What is the instruction session *format*? Orientation? Open workshop? Course-integrated? Required out-of-class experience? Credit course?
- *Where* is group instruction given?
- *When* is group instruction given? What times of day? Which days of the week? What is the cycle during the semester?
- What is the *extent* of the instruction program? How many sessions? Of what type? How many learners in an average session?
- Who are the *teachers*? Librarians? Computer trainers? Faculty? Students? Staff? Novice instructors? Master teachers? Technophiles? Technophobes?
- What instructional *methods* are used? Lecture? Discussion? Demonstration? Active, cooperative and collaborative learning? Small groups? Practice and exploration? Programmed, tutorial, or computer-based instruction?
- What is the instructional *content*? Concepts? Objectives? Skills? Dispositions?
- What types of instructional *materials* and *technologies* are used? Handouts? Overhead transparencies? Visual aids and artifacts? Audio materials? Presentation software?
- What are the *limitations* affecting the instruction program? Staffing levels? Campus culture? Attitudes? Lack of space?

- What are the *trends* in the instruction program? Expansion? Contraction? More emphasis? Less emphasis?

SITUATIONAL AUDIT

Because an electronic classroom is an instructional space, the instructional needs assessment is of primary importance in considering what type of classroom you need. However, realistically, other factors must enter into the decision. These factors include financial issues, general library issues, institutional issues, and perhaps even issues that are being raised in education generally. These factors also include any known parameters and limitations, such as, location of the classroom. In determining your electronic classroom needs, the planning team must consider these factors. The process of identifying and analyzing the variables that affect instruction is a situational audit (West, Farmer, and Wolff, 1991: 213, 221–222).

Financial Variables

Electronic classrooms, demonstration or hands-on, are expensive. Identifying financial variables that will affect the classroom is very important since, without funding, there will be no electronic classroom. Financial considerations include whether a budget has been established within which the planning team must work, the sources of funding—library, institutional, state/federal, capital campaign, gift, bequest, and/or grant—considerations of initial and ongoing expenditures, and the general financial standing of the library and the larger institution. The first question to answer is whether a budget has been imposed on the project or whether the planning team is required to create and defend a budget. If the budget is imposed, then the planning team must work within the established parameters in designing the classroom. This task may be relatively easy or relatively difficult, depending on the extent to which the allocated funds are realistic for the project to be undertaken. If the planning team must create a budget, consideration of the sources of funding becomes very important.

Because of the size of the expenditures required to build and support an electronic classroom, a thorough understanding of library and campus budget processes and facilities improvements is of utmost importance. Is the library able to transfer funds from various accounts into a building fund? Can funds from one year be saved and spent in the following year? Is the library's materials budget keeping pace with inflation? Can salary savings due to retirements be applied to equipment

Figure 3.1: Instructional Needs Assessment Worksheet

Consideration	Present	Future
Learners		
Instruction Session Format		
Where		
When		
Extent		

(Figure 3.1: *continued*)

Consideration	Present	Future
Teachers		
Instructional Methods		
Instructional Content		
Instructional Materials and Technologies		
Limitations		
Trends		

Figure 3.2: Example Instructional Needs Assessment Worksheet

Consideration	Present	Future
Learners	*First and second year students – traditional and nontraditional. community members.*	*Same plus campus faculty and staff.*
Instruction Session Format	*Orientation tours. Course-integrated.*	*Same plus open workshops.*
Where	*In the reference and periodicals areas of the library.*	*In an electronic classroom.*
When	*Mondays-Fridays, 8:00 a.m.– 10:00 pm, primarily 9:00 a.m. – 2:00 p.m. Occasional Saturday mornings.*	*Same*
Extent	*About 125 sessions/semester in fall and spring. About 25 sessions in summer. 25 students/session.*	*Increase to 150-175 sessions/semester in fall and spring. Same number of students/session.*

(Figure 3.2: *continued*)

Consideration	Present	Future
Teachers	*Librarians comfortable with technology but little teaching experience.*	*Librarians comfortable with technology and trained to teach in the electronic classroom.*
Instructional Methods	*Lecture, demonstration, and some limited discussion.*	*Lecture, demonstration, discussion, active/collaborative learning, small groups, hands-on practice.*
Instructional Content	*Identifying reference materials and basics of using online catalog and CD-ROM databases.*	*Same plus more advanced searching techniques, information evaluation, and the research process.*
Instructional Materials and Technologies	*Handouts.*	*Handouts, computer-based slide show presentations, and Web pages.*
Limitations	*No classroom. No dedicated instructional space.*	*Lack of time to train librarians and prepare computer-based slide show presentations and Web pages.*
Trends	*Program expanding in two ways: reaching more sections of same course and reaching new courses.*	*Continued expansion. Increasingly important library service.*

purchases? What opportunities exist for reallocating funds or receiving monetary infusions for special projects? Is there a budget for facilities improvements that focus on improved student learning or technological enhancements? What ongoing funds are available for classroom support and maintenance as well as equipment recapitalization? The library's financial officer may be able to provide insight or suggestions into these matters. In the end, the financial standing of the library and the institution will likely affect whether external funding must be sought.

To whatever extent the planning team is required to take a leadership role in defining and defending the budget or acquiring grant funding for the classroom, the timeline for design and construction is likely to be lengthened. If your planning team is required to establish initial and/or ongoing budgets and identify funding sources up front, see Chapter Eight and the section "Ongoing and Ancillary Expenditures" in Chapter Ten for additional useful information.

Library Variables

Primary among the library variables to consider is the building that will house the electronic classroom. The most fundamental consideration is whether the classroom is being designed for a new building or whether the classroom will occupy renovated space within an existing structure. Both situations provide challenges; however, remodeled space is more likely to include infrastructure limitations related to wiring for electricity and power, load-bearing walls, and the like. More classrooms than one might suspect have a pillar somewhere in the room blocking sight lines because during renovation a particular pillar could not be removed without threatening the structural integrity of the building! In addition, if you are remodeling existing space, be certain to check into whether asbestos abatement will be required; as if it is, the cost is likely to be considerable.

Even a new building can present challenges depending on the architectural design. A classroom is a large space requiring good sight lines, sound control, and light control. A library with an open, minimal-walls architectural design featuring vaulted ceilings and large picture windows, for example, may necessitate special provision for classroom needs in some section of the building. On the other hand, newly constructed space is less likely to be hampered by a lack of electricity and network connectivity.

If any characteristic of the classroom (the location, the general layout, its use for joint instruction or as an open computer laboratory) has already been determined, include that in your list of library variables.

You may decide to attempt to change an established characteristic or you may not, but acknowledging these known parameters makes clearer what might have to be negotiated.

Issues related to organizational culture and politics are also important to consider. Does the instruction program enjoy support from the library administration and other library departments? Are other departments interested in using the proposed classroom space for the classroom for their own projects? Has information about the needs of the instruction program been communicated regularly to other units in the library? Issues related to staff readiness and skills should also be explored. Some librarians may resist teaching in an electronic classroom because of a philosophical opposition to technology. Others may be reluctant due to lack of knowledge and training on the topic. Will the staff at your library use the electronic classroom? Are they willing to attend training and practice new skills? How much support will they require? Though not directly related to the nuts-and-bolts of classroom design, these organizational variables are likely to affect greatly the success of any classroom proposal.

Institutional Variables

Of course, the library exists within a larger institutional context. Knowledge of campus issues and trends is also important. Are class sizes increasing or decreasing? How are specific programs and curricula changing? Has the curriculum committee approved new programs or curricula, especially any related to technology? Are the institutional mission and goals clear—are they changing? Are revenues increasing or decreasing? Are there initiatives to integrate technology into classroom teaching? Did the last accreditation report raise any issues related to student research skills or library services? In sum, what is happening on campus and what is likely to happen in the future? Understanding issues affecting the larger institution will help you craft a proposal that responds to current concerns and areas of emphasis.

Institutional politics can also be powerful forces. One person who is in a powerful administrative position or who is respected as a campus leader can do a great deal of good or harm to a project depending on his or her stance toward it. Is the campus administration generally supportive of the library? Specifically consider whether the chief administrative officer to whom the library reports views the library and the electronic classroom project favorably. What about the deans of the colleges and/or the chairs of academic departments; how do they perceive the library? If there are individuals who might not be supportive of the electronic classroom project and who may be able to derail the project, you will have to consider ways to minimize their influence or to convince them of the importance of your project. Just recognizing that such individuals exist in your institution, or maybe even in your library (though hopefully not!), will prepare you better to respond to their objections to your proposal.

Education Variables

An academic institution also exists within the education sector of the society. Though the effects may be indirect, issues in education may nonetheless significantly affect the library's efforts to construct an electronic classroom. Awareness of current trends in education (such as beliefs about student learning and pedagogy or emphasis on distance education) will enable you to relate your proposals to the topics likely to receive the most attention by your institution.

Your efforts to build an electronic classroom may be effected not only by general issues in education but also by state or local jurisdiction trends and ideas about education and technology in education. For example, if the belief exists that too much money has been spent on technology relative to other concerns, administrators may be reticent or unwilling to allocate funding for what may be perceived as throwing money into the black hole of technology. Awareness of such beliefs will help you draft a proposal that addresses administrators' concerns and focuses on positive issues.

TAKE A TOUR

Having thought through your instructional needs and the situational factors at your institution—both somewhat abstract activities—you are probably ready for a more concrete activity. Take some time to tour the classroom buildings at your institution to see how they are designed and what characteristics you like. If one or two faculty members are willing to have you attend some classes, sit in and observe how they use the room. In addition to examining the electronic classrooms on your campus, take time to tour a few of the traditional classrooms. Though some design considerations are unique to electronic classrooms (such as equipment selection) others (such as writing surfaces and aesthetics) are common to all classrooms, whether they are electronic or traditional. If you have the opportunity, tour the facilities at other academic institutions and, if you can, at a corporate facility as well. In all cases, be certain to secure advance permission to tour the facilities. Not only will you maintain the good will of the institution but you may also be given the opportunity for a guided tour during which you can ask questions and possibly see behind-the-scenes operations.

Searching the keyword phrase "library electronic classroom" in an Internet search engine will retrieve hundreds of Web pages describing electronic classrooms at a great variety of institutions. Unfortunately, however, there is not a list of the "top ten" electronic classrooms in libraries. As such, your planning team will need to select institutions to visit. Your selections may be influenced by the travel funds available and by how many planning team members participate in the classroom visits. The least expensive options are to travel to institutions within driving distance of your campus, or to go to a metropolitan area with multiple schools that you can visit in one trip. Alternatively, you might consider visiting peer institutions. These college and universities have usually been selected because they are similar to your own institution in size and mission. If they have library instruction programs similar to the one at your library, decisions they made in developing their electronic classrooms and their evaluations of the effectiveness of their classrooms may be very helpful to your planning team. Of course, the absolute least expensive touring option is to take a virtual tour on the Web. Though obviously not the same as visiting in person, you can still learn a great deal from the descriptions and pictures posted on the Web. Appendix D provides a sampling of what library Web sites can offer; however, your favorite search engine will turn up many more as well.

With respect to locating corporate training facilities to visit, again, the least expensive option will be to visit local companies. However, if travel budgets allow, you might consider visiting some of the facilities highlighted in "Best Presentation Rooms," published annually in the April issue of *Presentations* magazine (*www.presentations.com/deliver/room*). These facilities are usually impressive, both with respect to the high-quality design and materials that are used and with respect to the funds expended for construction. Even if you do not have an equivalent budget, seeing such state-of-the-art facilities can inspire you to think creatively about design elements. It may be possible to incorporate a feature that you like even without an extensive budget.

The immersion experience of touring and experiencing other classrooms will give you ideas for design features that you may want to build in—or avoid!—in your own classroom. As the planning team considers a given classroom, ask basic questions about what people like and dislike and make certain to write down their responses for comparison and discussion during a planning team debriefing session. In addition, take

Figure 3.3: Classroom Tour Comments Worksheet

Classroom:	
Purpose:	
Equipment:	
Software:	
Room Layout:	

(Figure 3.3: *continued*)

Likes:	Dislikes:
Other Comments:	
Observer:	

Figure 3:4: Example Classroom Tour Comments Worksheet

Classroom:	*Collaboratory Primo at State University Library.*
Purpose:	*Hands-on library instruction sessions. Also functions as the classroom for Information Literacy 100 (credit course for first-year students).*
Equipment:	*Instructor workstation (computer, monitor, keyboard, mouse, document camera, videocassette player), sound system with speakers mounted at front of room, ceiling-mounted projector, front screen projector, whiteboards on front and back walls, printer station, 15 student workstations (computer, monitor, keyboard, mouse). Floor lamps and electrical fans.*
Software:	*Microsoft Office, Netscape, SPSS, and MapInfo. Norton AntiVirus. Games left on computers for students to use during break. No control/collaboration software but student monitors are all connected to a master power switch, which can shut off the power to the monitors if needed to gain student attention.*
Room Layout:	*U-Shaped (Out) with center tables for print materials and discussion. Instructor workstation and entrance at front of room.*

(Figure 3.4: *continued*)

Likes:	**Dislikes:**
Room layout conducive to active/collaborative learning and makes it easy to incorporate printed reference materials and periodical volumes into an instruction session. *Selection of software customized to the content of the instructional sessions taught in the room. SPSS and MapInfo primarily used in library instruction sessions for upper-level geography classes and in Information Literacy 100.*	*Lighting is not zoned or dimmable. One light in the middle of the room cannot be shut off – it is always on.* *Air does not circulate well. If a full class of 25 students is in the room and all of the computers are turned on, the temperature becomes uncomfortably elevated.* *Much of the whiteboard surface in the front of the room is covered by the projection screen.*
Other Comments: *Color scheme is unique (mauve and blue) compared to other parts of the library (brown and cream); however, the classroom is set apart from most other public areas of the library so the color is not jarring.*	
Observer: *Lisa Janicke Hinchliffe*	

a camera on the tours to photograph classroom elements that are of particular interest or difficult to describe. Finally, write down specific models and manufacturers for any equipment, furniture, and the like that is of interest, so that it can be easily located in a catalog or through a vendor. In developing your plan for classroom visits, you may find "The Tour" Web site developed by Classrooms 2000 Project Team at Carthage College helpful (*http://ulysses.carthage.edu/classroom/tour.html*). The Web site provides details of the classrooms that the team visited, including descriptions and pictures, as well as a summary of their findings.

Figure 3.3 provides a reproducible worksheet for recording classroom tour reactions and Figure 3.4 is the same worksheet filled in for a hypothetical classroom as an example. The worksheet can also be downloaded from this book's Web site at *www.neal-schuman.com/eclassroom.html.*

ASSUMPTIONS

Finally, in completing the situational analysis, the planning team needs to articulate any assumptions that may influence decision making. A brainstorming session driven by the question "what do you want the classroom to be?" should help identify the assumptions that people have. Consider assumptions about teaching and learning as well as about classroom design. In some cases, assumptions are about the future and so they are necessarily speculative, e.g., even if budget cuts are necessary, the basic writing course will continue to enroll a maximum of 20 students per class. Other assumptions may be more reflective of belief systems or teaching philosophies, e.g., students should have simultaneous access to both personal productivity software such as word processing as well as library resources in the classroom so that they learn research writing as an integrated process. Regardless, spend some time identifying those unspoken assumptions that everyone is using (though perhaps unconsciously) to guide their own thinking.

Assumptions are not necessarily to be avoided (do examine them for truth and accuracy though, and reject them if need be); however, a shared understanding is vital for avoiding miscommunication and unnecessary conflict. Planning team members need not all have common assumptions. If they do not, the process of identifying the assumptions will highlight those conflicts that would eventually manifest themselves during the design phase. By identifying conflicting assumptions and working through any necessary compromises before starting to consider classroom layouts or equipment, unnecessary disagreements can be avoided during the design phase.

PRIORITIZE THE ISSUES

The information gathered during the instructional needs assessment and your situational audit will help you determine the type and size of electronic classroom you need. Admittedly, in most cases, politics or budgetary constraints may limit your options, particularly with respect to the design details that will be addressed later in this book. You may have already been told the type, size, location, and/or other factors. Fortunately, even in those circumstances, the instructional needs assessment and situational audit will help you to identify and prioritize the most important classroom elements and to advocate for the resources needed to construct the best classroom for your library.

An unfortunate fact of classroom design and construction is that your needs and desires will surpass the available resources—if not immediately, then within weeks after beginning to use the classroom when you discover a new technology or option not thought of during the design! New technologies may become available during the design process. If so, the planning team might choose to redesign some aspect of the electronic classroom to better meet the prioritized instructional needs. In some cases, you will have to build a classroom that is purposively less than what you want because the funds are not available. Making good choices based on established priorities will enable you to maximize the available resources while establishing a foundation upon which to build in future years.

In fact, before moving on to the nitty-gritty of design, take some time to identify the priorities and/or nonnegotiable issues affecting your design decisions. Ask yourself basic questions such as these:

- What are the pieces of information that should serve as touchpoints throughout the remainder of the planning process?
- What are the nonnegotiable issues that affect our decisions?
- What are the top priorities for the classroom?
- What must be avoided if the classroom is to be successful?

Possible answers include the pragmatic (for example, the classroom must accommodate at least 30 students) to the more philosophical (for example, the instruction program employs a collaborative pedagogy). Other specific examples of answers include a statement that campus standards must be followed; that furniture must allow the room to be reconfigured for different classes; that the hardware must be readily accessible for repairs, upgrades, and replacements; that library instructors

Figure 3.5: Design Priorities Worksheet

Priorities	
1.	
2.	
3.	
4.	
5.	
6.	
7.	
8.	
9.	
10.	

Figure 3.6: Example Design Priorities Worksheet

Priorities	
1.	*Locate on main floor of library building.*
2.	*Classroom must accommodate classes. Average class size is 35 students. The range is 18-45 students.*
3.	*Tables that recess the computer monitors will NOT be selected.*
4.	*Classroom computers will have all software for which the institution has a site license.*
5.	*All aisles must be at least 42 inches.*
6.	*The door will be in the rear of the classroom.*
7.	*The classroom must have a print station with the card-swipe payment system used elsewhere in the library.*
8.	*The classroom must have a telephone.*
9.	*Artwork purchased at the Art Department's Spring Student Sale will be hung in the classroom.*
10.	*No nonlibrary classes will be scheduled in the classroom, excepting fall computer training sessions.*

do not want to have to turn their back to the students to operate the instructor workstation; that the library's electronic classroom must provide access to the software available in all other campus electronic classrooms; or that all classroom furniture on campus must be acquired through a particular vendor.

The circumstances at each institution are different, so your planning team will have to determine the important issues for your library. If you have to make hard decisions about what elements of your design are most important or make compromises among competing preferences, these priority issues will help guide the planning team's decision making.

See Figure 3.5 for a reproducible worksheet for recording your priorities, Figure 3.6 as an example worksheet filled out for a hypothetical library. The worksheet can also be downloaded from this book's Web site at *www.neal-schuman.com/eclassroom.html.*

TIMELINE

Finally, lay out a timeline for completing the design and construction phases of building your electronic classroom. Of course, this timeline will be subject to change—in many cases due to influences completely outside of the library's control. You may be given little warning that end-of-the-year funds have been allocated to the classroom project, for example, and that you have just four days, or three weeks, to choose a classroom layout and select furnishings and equipment. Or, as if often the case, construction may take an extra month due to delays in shipping of materials or a labor shortage in the community. However, having a timeline, even one you have to adjust, will help you track the progress of your classroom more easily. Just be as prepared as possible and then do your best if and when you have to move more quickly, or more slowly, than the planned timeline indicates.

Figure 3.7 is a reproducible worksheet for detailing your timeline. Figure 3.8 is an example timeline based on experiences with a variety of classroom projects. The worksheet can also be downloaded from this book's Web site at *www.neal-schuman.com/eclassroom.html.* If you have access to project management software such as Microsoft Project (Microsoft), that software can be used both to develop a timeline and to track the progress of the classroom.

Figure 3.7: Timeline

Timeline		
Time Period	**Phase/Stage and Events**	**Notes**

Figure 3.8: Example Timeline

Timeline		
Time Period	**Phase/Stage and Events**	**Notes**
Month One	*Pre-Design Activities*	*Needs Assessment, Situational Analysis*
Month Two	*Tours*	*Web Sites, Travel to Area Libraries to Visit*
Months Three–Four	*Design*	*Space, Infrastructure*
Months Five–Six	*Design*	*Software, Equipment and Furnishings*
Month Seven	*Construction Drawings*	*Done by campus facilities management office.*
Month Eight	*Bidding*	*Managed by campus facilities office.*
Months Nine–Thirteen	*Construction*	*Local contractor. Project manager from facilities.*
Month Fourteen	*Occupancy*	*Punch-list. Cleaning. Move-In.*
Month Fifteen	*Training for Teaching*	*Presented by User Education Coordinator.*

Part Two

Designing and Construction

There is nothing nicer than a kitchen really made for a cook. Things that are designed to be used always have an innate beauty.
Julia Child

Choices, choices, choices. The design and construction phases of building an electronic classroom are full of choices. Making the right choices given the known parameters and the information gathered in the instructional needs assessment and situational audit is what the design phase is all about. In making your choices, design the classroom to be used for teaching and learning—not to be displayed in a brochure or highlighted on building tours. This part of the book details design considerations related to space, infrastructure, software, and equipment and furnishings, and it ends with discussions of budgets and expenditures and construction. Be forewarned though, there is no one perfect design. Your planning team must decide what options are best for your library—best for *teaching and learning*.

As you consider your options and make your choices, keep the following in mind:

> Students have a fundamental right to a classroom learning environment that allows them to see anything presented visually, to hear any audible presentation free from noises and distortions, and to be physically comfortable...regardless of the method of instruction used. (Allen et al., 1996: 1)

Likewise, teachers in an electronic classroom also have a fundamental right to see, hear, and be comfortable, as well as to have to have convenient control of technology and access to technical support (Miller, 1999).

To see, to hear, to be comfortable—these factors may seem so obvious that it appears strange to mention them. Unfortunately, though they may be obvious, they are not always respected in classroom design. A quick tour through a few classrooms at your institution will probably demonstrate this reality. These factors are even more important in the library classroom since most students will probably only be in the classroom once or twice a year for 50–75 minutes. It is important that librarians not waste valuable instruction time overcoming classroom design limitations.

Chapter Four

Space

The first consideration in classroom design is the space—the location, size, and layout of the classroom. Designed well, the classroom space will be a highly functional and efficient environment for instruction. Designed well, the space will accommodate changes in technology and pedagogy over time. Designed well, the classroom space will afford the teaching and learning opportunities that are so desired.

At the same time, the classroom space defines the limits of what is possible. Lacking appropriate and adequate space, all other design decisions will be constrained, and teaching and learning will be impaired. Unfortunately, the classroom space is, more often than not, dictated by other space concerns in the library, particularly if the classroom is the result of renovating existing space. If you are designing the classroom for remodeled space, acquire a copy of the original and current architectural drawings for the existing space. These drawings will help identify any structural or infrastructure limitations that already exist with the space.

If you are fortunate enough to be designing a classroom for a new building, work to get the best space you can in the location and size needed. Compromise on other design elements if you must. Those other elements can be changed and modified over time. The effort required to effect those changes will not nearly approximate the effort that would be required to change the location or size of a classroom!

LOCATION

In most cases, the location of the classroom will have already been determined before the planning team is constituted. Such a decision is likely to have been made by the library's architect and administrators,

Figure 4.1: Electronic Classroom Interaction Matrix

Fill in the two remaining column/row headings with adjacencies important to your library. Then, in the white cells, indicate the desirability of close proximity using the following:

V = Very Desirable

D = Desirable

N = Neutral

U = Undesirable

X = Extremely Undesirable

In the gray cells, indicate the reason(s) for the desirability/Undesirability of the proxmimity using the following:

1. Noise
2. Convenience
3. Technical Requirements
4. Pedagogical Concerns
5. Other (________________)

The black cells indicate the overlap of a particular issue with itself.

(Figure 4.1: *continued*)

	Classroom	Instruction Staff	Building Entrance	Reference Area		
Classroom						
Instruction Staff						
Building Entrance						
Reference Area						

Figure 4.2: Example Electronic Classroom Interaction Matrix

	Classroom	Instruction Staff	Building Entrance	Reference Area	*Media Center*	*Technical Support*
Classroom		*D*	*U*	*V*	*N*	*V*
Instruction Staff	2		*U*	*V*	*N*	*N*
Building Entrance	*1*	*1*		*D*	*N*	*N*
Reference Area	2, 4	2, 4	2		*D*	*D*
Media Center	1, 2	1, 2	2	2		*D*
Technical Support	2, 3, 4	1, 2	1, 2, 5 *(Theft)*	2, 3	2, 3	

V = Very Desirable D = Desirable N = Neutral
U = Undesirable X = Extremely Undesirable

in the case of a new building, or by the limits of current configurations, in the case of remodeling. If you decide to protest the location, first seek to understand why the location was selected. Then, once you understand why the location was chosen, determine whether you still want to try for a different space. If you do, craft your argument carefully, attempting to show how the proposed location is not the best for either the instruction program or the library as a whole.

If, however, you have the opportunity to select the classroom location or to choose between options, there are a number of factors to consider. Primary among these factors are adjacencies. The consideration of adjacencies addresses both what other things the classroom should be close to and what it should be far away from! Marvin Wiggins encourages placing the classroom near the library's entrance, the audiovisual center, library instruction personnel, and technical support (1996: 146, 150). Valerie Feinman recommends that the classroom be located in the library and near the reference area (1994: 33). The location preferred by the planning team will probably depend somewhat on local practice and preference. You might consider whether the classroom should be located just inside the library's front door for the convenience of students coming to instruction sessions or whether the classroom should be located away from the hustle and bustle of people entering and exiting the building. Or, perhaps, in order to allow the classroom to be available for open computing when the library is not open, you will want the classroom to have an entrance outside of the library's entrance. This of course will then require particular attention to security issues. An interaction matrix is a useful way of determining the relationships (Konya, 1986: 172) that are important for your classroom. Figure 4.1 is an example of a matrix that could be used and Figure 4.2 is the same matrix filled in to illustrate how the matrix can be applied. The matrix can also be downloaded from this book's Web site at *www.nealschuman.com/eclassroom.html*.

In addition to considering adjacencies, the planning team should think about traffic flow. During busy time periods, for example, between class sessions, what paths will learners take to and from the classroom? Will those paths become overly-congested and create stress and anxiety for library users? Will the traffic pattern disturb others who are studying, researching, or using library materials? Also consider traffic flow and noise relative to library staff offices and administration. If possible, map out the likely pathways between the library entrance, the reference desk, study spaces, and other areas popular with students, and then walk along them at different points in the day to locate any potential trouble spots.

Finally, remember that "where we teach shows how much we value the learning process" (Feinman, 1994: 33). If the classroom is hidden away in the recesses of the building, students are likely to think that the instruction sessions held there are not very important. Plus, they are also more likely to get lost and never find their way to the sessions!

SIZE

If the classroom location was already determined for the planning team, in all likelihood the size of the classroom was also. However, while one can fairly easily make do with an inconvenient location through clear signage and library maps, an undersized classroom will be a constant irritation for the instructors as well as the learners. Crowding and the resulting restlessness will not be conducive to learning or teaching. Lack of sufficient space can also lead to violations of accessibility guidelines and fire codes when instructors attempt to "squeeze in" a few more people. Finally, an undersized classroom may be wasted space and expenditure since, if the classroom is not big enough to accommodate the attendees at an instruction session, that session will be held elsewhere, or—even worse—maybe not at all.

The primary driving factor in determining the size of your electronic classroom is the size of the classes taught in the instruction program. Using the data that you gathered through your instructional needs assessment, determine the average, largest, and smallest class sizes that the instruction program serves, particularly those classes that the electronic classroom is intended to house. If some classes will not fit into the classroom, note them and determine how they will be served. For example, it may never be reasonable to expect to accommodate the largest classes at a large university in a library classroom; instead the librarian may have to "guest lecture" in a campus hall seating 300 to 400 people.

In general, to accommodate the same number of people, demonstration classrooms require less space than hands-on classrooms because of the difference in the size of the student workstation. In the demonstration classroom, each student requires about 15 to 25 square feet, whereas in the hands-on classroom, a student workstation requires 35 to 45 square feet. The total number of student workstations that can be placed in any particular hands-on classroom will also depend on the layout selected.

Regardless of classroom type, the front eight feet or so of the classroom will be used solely as instructor workspace in order to accommodate the instructor workstation and equipment, as well as to create sufficient distance from the students to the projection screen. All aisles must be a minimum of three feet wide, but they should actually be wide enough to accommodate the items that students commonly have with them (such as, backpacks, art portfolios, and outerwear—especially in cold climates!) and to allow the instructor to walk behind students when they are seated. In general, aisles that are four feet wide allow for sufficient space for students and their belongings as well as for instructor passage. The amount of space devoted to aisles varies greatly depending on the classroom layout that is selected.

In addition to the overall size of the classroom, attention must be paid to the proportional dimensions of the room. Kory Terlaga recommends a square room but states that a rectangular room is acceptable if "the length of a room should not exceed its width by more than 50 percent" (1990: 113). For example, a classroom that is 30 feet wide should be no more than 45 feet in length. If your classroom length exceeds the recommended proportion, establishing acceptable student sight lines will be difficult and acoustics may be problematic.

LAYOUT

Room arrangement affects not only the total number of students who can be accommodated in the classroom but also communicates messages about the relationship between the instructor and the learners and about expected classroom activities. If the classroom layout looks like a lecture setup, instructors will tend to lecture and students will tend to see themselves as the listeners. Alternatively, if the classroom layout is nontraditional, students and instructors may be more willing to experiment with teaching and learning approaches, though admittedly some will not welcome such an opportunity. With the availability of increasingly modular desks, classroom layouts are not as fixed as they once were (that is, when chairs bolted to the floor were the norm in campus classrooms). However, the degree of flexibility that instructors have is also dictated by the time available to rearrange the room, the network and electrical infrastructures, and the overall size of the room.

Figure 4.3 is a preconstruction drawing of one of the electronic classrooms in the Charles J. Keffer Library at the University of St. Thomas, Minneapolis. The classroom is approximately 21 by 38 feet. One interesting challenge in designing this classroom was that the floor could not be used for wiring because of circumstances stemming from the floor below; all power and network connectivity had to come through the walls or be dropped from the ceiling.

In selecting your classroom arrangement, think back to the findings of the instructional needs assessment while considering these factors suggested by Terlaga (1990: 11–12):

- What are the advantages/disadvantages of a particular arrangement for the instructor?
- What are the advantages/disadvantages of a particular arrangement for the learners?
- What are the trades-offs between the instructor and the learners when comparing arrangement options?
- How conducive is the layout to class discussion?
- How conducive is the layout to lecture/demonstration?
- How conducive is the layout to active or collaborative learning activities?
- How easy is it to have students work in small groups or pairs?
- What is the general "feel" of the arrangement?

The following sections include are line diagrams of common electronic classroom layouts and a short discussion relating the strengths and weaknesses of each type. The arrangements can all be used in either demonstration or hands-on classrooms, though some are more appropriate for one than the other. Also note that the number of additional student workstations that can be accommodated by increasing the room size depends on the layout selected. The discussion is based on comments from a number of sources (Allen et al., 1996; Terlaga, 1990; How to Design, 1989). All diagrams represent rooms 25 feet by 35 feet with aisles 3 to 4 feet wide and with the door and the instructor workstation at the front of the room. The scale of all diagrams in this chapter is the same ($^1/_2$ inch = 5 feet).

Boardroom/Seminar

The Boardroom/Seminar arrangement (Figure 4.4) consists of one large table, or multiple smaller tables pushed together, in the center of the room. Learners sit around the table and look toward each other across the table. As an electronic classroom layout, it is best suited for demonstration because sight lines will be hampered if there are monitors on the table, unless monitors are recessed or laptops are used.

This layout allows for close interaction between the instructor and the learners and facilitates discussion among participants. As such, it is best for 20 people or fewer. If the group becomes too large, participants at the end of a long, narrow table are not likely to participate fully in the session.

Figure 4.3: Example Preconstruction Drawing

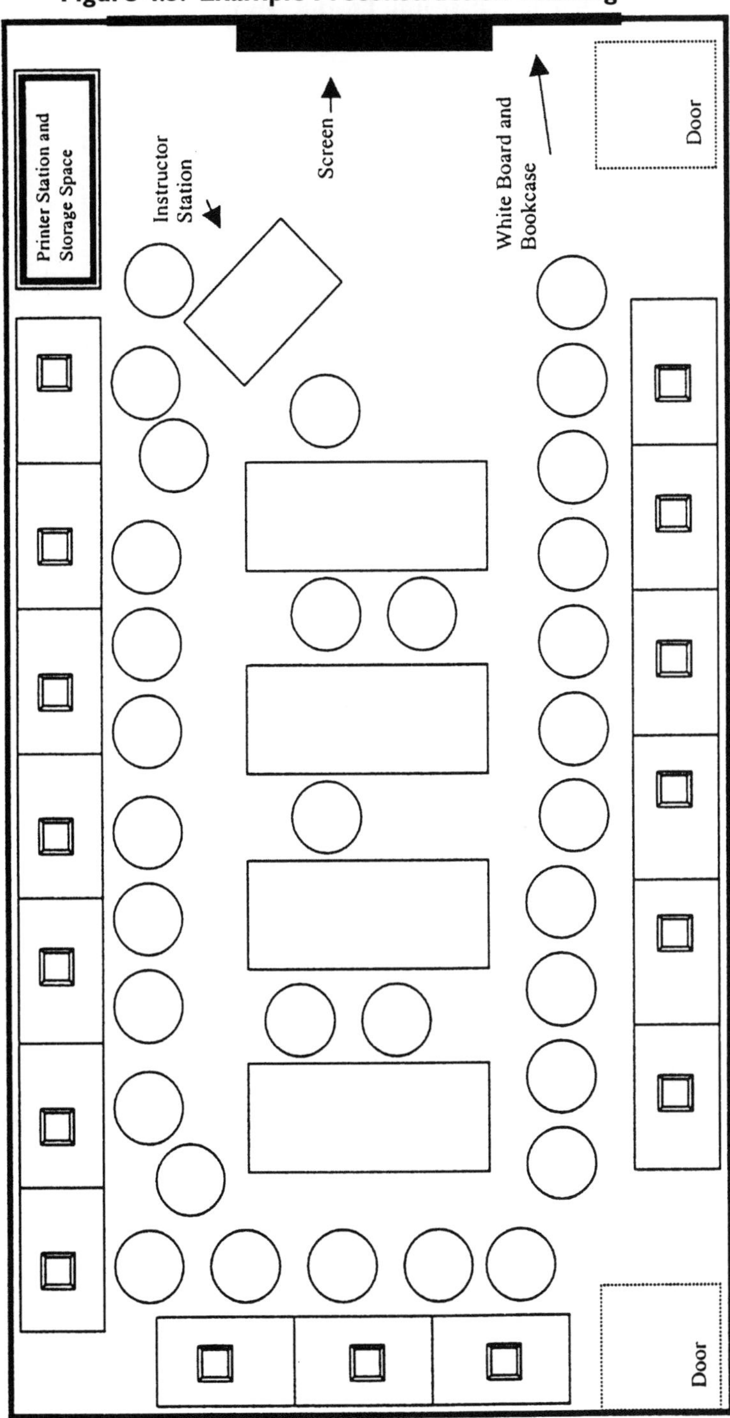

Figure 4.4: Classroom Layout—Boardroom/Seminar

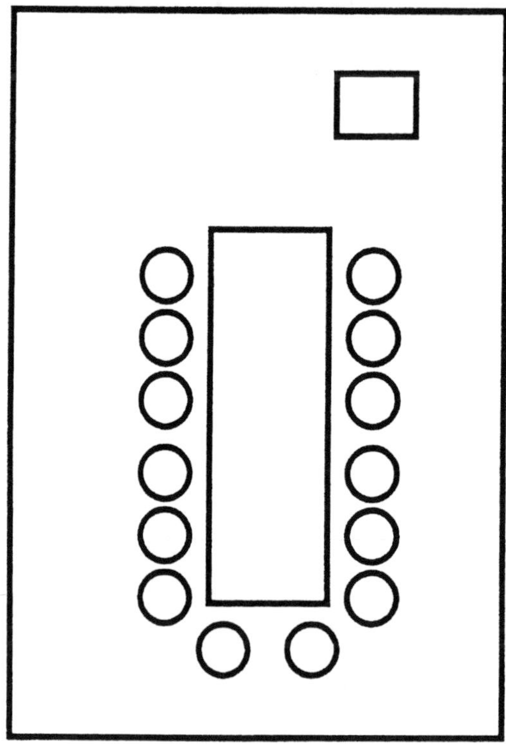

Rows, Parallel (Middle Aisle)

The Rows, Parallel (Middle Aisle) arrangement (Figure 4.5) consists of a series of tables placed in rows parallel to the front of the room with one middle aisle. Learners face the front of the room and generally have good sight lines to view the instructor and any projected images. Depending on the space allocated to each student workstation and the placement and height of the projection screen, sight lines may be hampered if there are monitors on the tables

This layout communicates a lecture/demonstration focus because of its resemblance to a traditional classroom layout, even if students have hands-on capabilities. The focus is on the front of the room and the instructor workstation. This layout makes poor use of the best viewing location—the space devoted to the middle aisle, and it may also discourage students in the back row from participating. However, this is also one of the most compact arrangements possible, maximizing the number of students who can be accommodated in the space.

Figure 4.5: Classroom Layout—Rows Parallel (Middle Aisle)

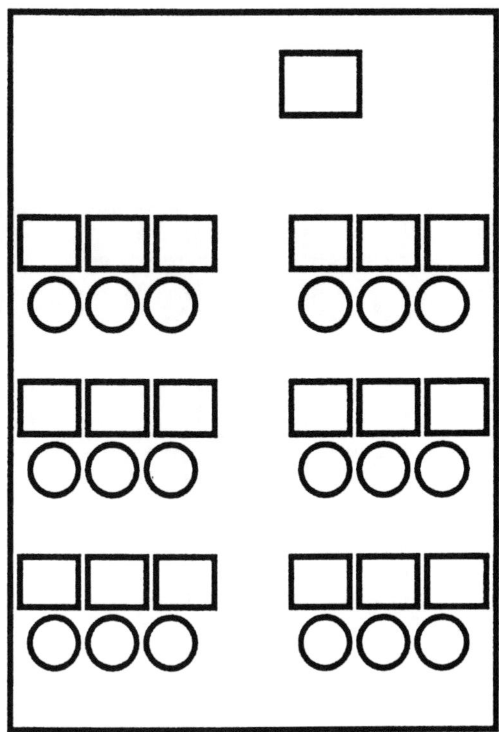

Rows, Parallel (Side Aisles)

The Rows, Parallel (Side Aisles) arrangement (Figure 4.6) consists of a series of tables placed in rows parallel to the front of the room, with two side aisles. Learners face the front of the room and generally have good sight lines (especially from where a middle aisle might otherwise be) to view the instructor and any projected images. Depending on the amount of space allocated to each student workstation and the placement and height of the projection screen, sight lines may be hampered if there are monitors on the tables.

This layout also communicates a lecture/demonstration focused session, perhaps even more so that the Rows, Parallel (Middle Aisle) arrangement. This layout can also make it very difficult for the instructor to assist students seated in the middle of the rows during hands-on practice time and may discourage students in the back row from participating. Even with two aisles, this is still a very compact arrangement.

Figure 4.6: Classroom Layout—Rows Parallel (Side Aisles)

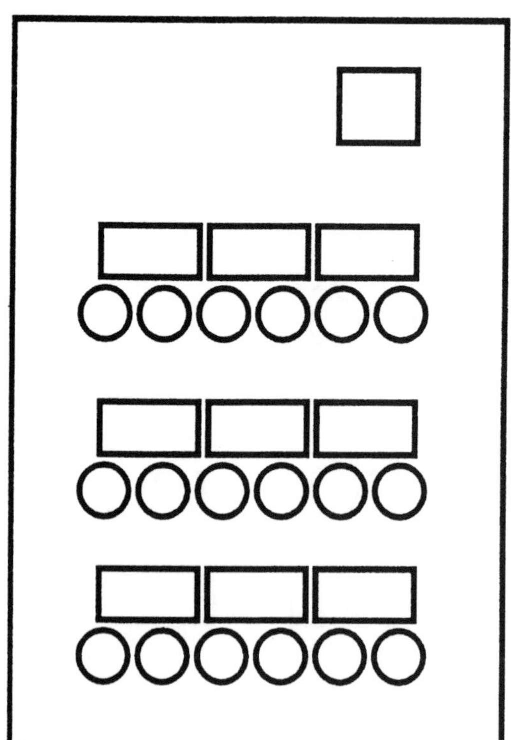

Rows, Perpendicular

The Rows, Perpendicular arrangement (Figure 4.7) consists of a series of tables placed in rows perpendicular to the front of the room, with two aisles. Learners face each other or the side walls of the classrooms and then look to their right or left to see the front of the room. The sight lines are generally good and are not usually obstructed even if there are monitors on the tables; however, students farthest from the front of the room may have their sight lines blocked by students sitting in front of them.

This layout takes advantage of traditional row seating, maximizing the number of students who can be accommodated, but in a nontraditional way that does not place the focus of the room on the instructor. As such, though a lecture/demonstration teaching approach can be easily used, the room also communicates a focus on active, hands-on learning. With sufficient aisle space, instructors will be able to move easily from assisting one student to another.

Figure 4.7: Classroom Layout—Rows Perpendicular

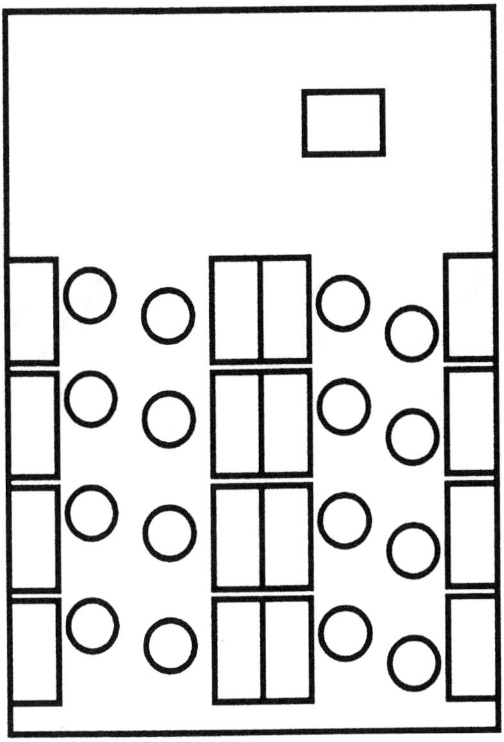

Clusters

The Clusters arrangement (Figure 4.8) consists of groupings of modular table pieces or specially designed tables placed throughout the room. Students may face the front, side, or back of the room depending on where they sit. They may or may not have to turn their heads to see the instructor and may or may not have clear sight lines. This layout communicates a focus on active and collaborative learning, and does not easily support a traditional lecture presentation. Small-group work is easily facilitated with this arrangement. Instructors will likely be frustrated if they attempt a lecture/demonstration session.

Access to electrical power and network connections can be complicated in this layout and may require that power and data poles come from the ceiling or floor to each table. The layout communicates a collaborative teaching and learning approach in which both the instructor and the students will actively participate. Preferred by instructors who want a learning-oriented classroom, this layout does require a large amount of space because of the amount of room required between tables.

Figure 4.8: Classroom Layout—Clusters

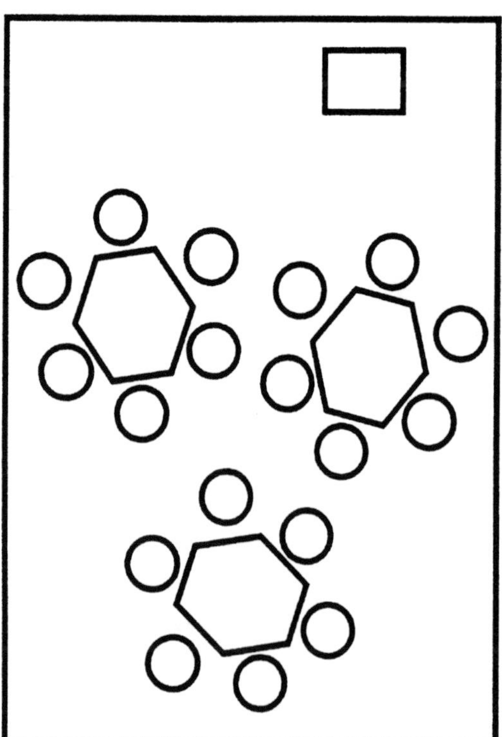

U-Shaped (In)

In many ways, the U-Shape (In) arrangement is similar to the Boardroom/Seminar layout. The U-Shaped (In) arrangement (Figure 4.9) consists of a series of tables placed in a horseshoe shape in the center of the room. Learners face each other across the horseshoe. The instructor can use the central space to walk close to all of the students. As such, this layout allows for close interaction between the instructor and the learners, and facilitates discussion among participants.

This layout makes poor use of the best viewing location—the space in the middle of the horseshoe. As an electronic classroom layout, it is best suited for demonstration and discussion because sight lines will be hampered if there are monitors on the tables.

U-Shaped (Out)

The U-Shaped (Out) arrangement (Figure 4.10) consists of a series of tables placed around the perimeter of the room. Learners face the perimeter of the room when seated at their workstations and thus this lay-

Figure 4.9: Classroom Layout—U shaped (In)

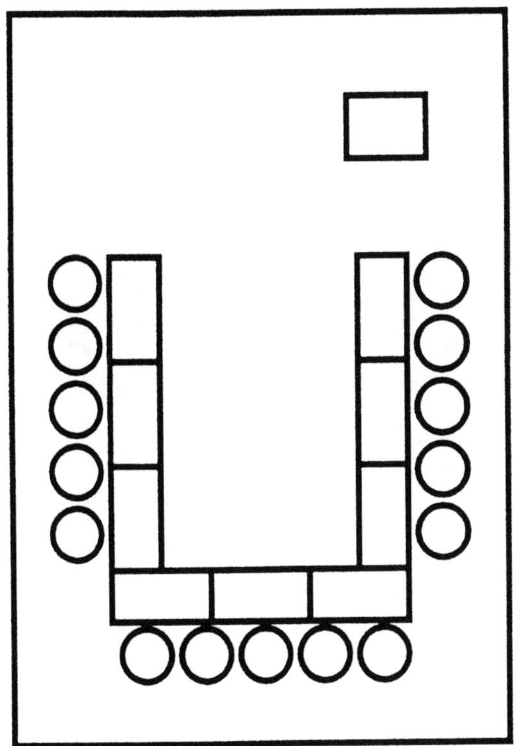

out is best suited to a hands-on classroom because the student workstations face away from the instructors when at their workstations. The instructors can easily view the monitors on all of the student workstations from the front of the room. The center of the room can be left empty to allow the instructor to easily move from one student to another or, alternatively, a table for print materials and noncomputer work can be acquired. Though lecture/demonstration can be easily used in this layout, the room communicates a focus on active, hands-on learning.

This layout allows for close interaction between the instructor and the learners, and facilitates small group work and collaboration. Because the computers are located on the perimeter of the room, sightlines are good, access to electricity and network connectivity is simplified, and wire management is easier. If the middle of the room is left empty, this layout most easily accommodates the needs of learners with physical disabilities.

Appendix A contains reproducible figures that your planning team can duplicate, cut out, and then use to actively explore layout options for

Figure 4.10: Classroom Layout—U-Shaped (Out)

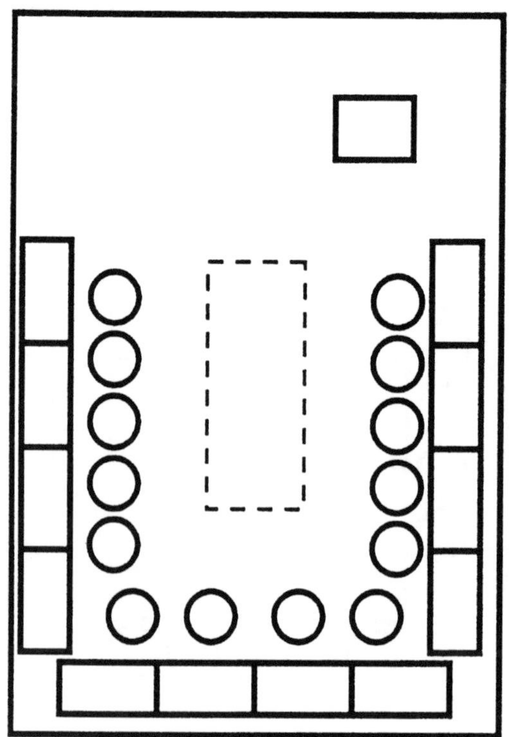

your classroom. To develop more sophisticated layouts for your space, you may wish to use a relatively inexpensive software package such as FloorPlan (IMSI).

As a final word on room layout, SMARTdesks provides a myriad of room plans on its Web site (*www.smartdesks.com*). Though obviously designed to showcase the company's products, the options presented are numerous and do not necessarily require furniture from SMARTdesks to be implemented.

ENTRANCES/DOORWAYS

The placement of the classroom door is a matter of preference in most cases. Placing the door at the rear of the room is said to help minimize disruptions from latecomers, though students may also use it to slip out quietly during a presentation. Placing the door at the front of the room leaves more room for student seating and workspace. Fire codes may require that a classroom have more than one entrance or require that the entrance be placed in a particular location.

Classroom entrances should be at least three feet wide. The area around the entrance must also be free of clutter and equipment so that people can enter and exit the room easily and safely. If possible, include a vision panel in the door so that someone can check if the room is occupied without opening the door. Finally, outside of the entrance there should be a place to hang the classroom schedule, announcements, policies, and other signs.

WINDOWS

Windows can be problematic in electronic classrooms because they allow light into the room; however, many instructors and students like that same natural light. If blackout curtains or other opaque window coverings are installed, the light can be blocked when necessary, while allowing natural light in when it does not disrupt class activities. The window coverings must fit tightly to the windows and cover the entire space of glass to be effective in blocking out all natural light.

If the windows can be opened, then they must have secure locks installed which can only be unlocked by authorized personnel. This precaution is particularly important if the classroom is on the ground floor and the windows are large enough for equipment to pass through. In some cases, if the library's ventilation and air conditioning system is not sufficient to cool the electronic classroom outfitted with heat-generating equipment, it may also be necessary to plan for window-unit air conditioners.

Installing interior windows in classroom walls may help with room monitoring and equipment security, especially if the classroom is also used as an open lab. For example, if a classroom were located next to the reference area in a library, installing windows in the wall separating the classroom from the reference room would allow the reference librarians to monitor room use from the reference desk. Though more expensive, a wall constructed of privacy glass panels which can be set to transparent or opaque depending on room use, such as the one in the University of Iowa Library's Information Arcade, allows staff to monitor use even more easily during open lab times. Privacy glass is also called switchable glass and is available from Wearing Williams Limited. A less expensive option would be to install regular windows with curtains that can be opened or closed depending on the activities in the classroom.

WALLS AND CEILINGS

The walls and ceilings in the classroom should be painted in a basic color that is compatible with the color scheme of the classroom, which is hopefully compatible with the color scheme of the library. Frederick Knirk recommends that to encourage students "to reflect or integrate information, [classrooms should] use dull shades or quieting colors such as blues, greens, gray, or beige" (1987: 25). If the classroom is crowded, as most electronic classrooms tend to be, a light tone of paint will create a sense of spaciousness (Knirk, 1992a: 28). The paint should be washable so that scuffs and stray marks can be cleaned away without causing damage. If acoustical tiles are installed on the ceiling (see "Sound System and Acoustics" in Chapter Seven), the tiles should be the same color as the painted surfaces.

As much wall surface as possible should serve as a writing surface for instruction (see specific recommendations in "Writing Surfaces" in Chapter Seven). A place to post announcements, policies, and schedules, such as a cork board strip or bulletin board, should be provided to discourage people from posting items directly on the walls and damaging them. If the classroom will also be used for open computing, a bulletin board for hanging diskettes and printouts that students have left in the room may also be useful.

With respect to hanging artwork in the classroom, librarians should weigh the aesthetic advantages against the potential for student distraction. The degree to which distraction is a concern may depend both on the type of artwork as well as the learner population. Aesthetically, wall hangings can brighten a room and decrease the sense of "institutionalism" that can be discomforting to learners.

FLOORING

Flooring in an electronic classroom involves consideration of two components—the floor itself and the floor covering. In many cases, a library's floor is poured concrete and the only option is to install a flooring covering over the concrete. In other cases, particularly in a new building, it may be possible to have conduit laid in the concrete or to have the floor "trenched" so that wiring can be laid in grooves in the floor. Alternatively, a raised floor could be installed over a regular floor for the same purpose, though attention to accessibility and safety must be given if the floor is raised. If computers or other equipment connect to wiring laid in the floor, the connection boxes should be flush to the floor and not stick up where they will be a safety hazard and vulnerable to damage.

Most library classrooms will not be large enough to accommodate a sloped or tiered floor design. If the floor is already sloped or if the classroom is auditorium-sized, a sloped or tiered floor may be desirable to improve sight lines. In such cases, careful attention must be paid to safety and accessibility issues. Having the plans carefully reviewed by an accessibility expert is recommended before details are finalized.

Floor coverings include hard flooring such as tile, resilient flooring such as vinyl, and soft flooring such as carpet (DePaoli, 1995: 57). All can be aesthetically acceptable. Only carpet, however, will also assist with sound control in the classroom. Carpet in an electronic classroom must be antistatic and easy to clean so that static electricity and dust do not build up. Carpet tiles may be preferable if cabling is in the floor and carpet removal is occasionally necessitated or if one anticipates areas of heavy wear, (such as, the entryway) where it may be desirable to replace the carpet tiles sooner than those in the rest of the room.

STORAGE AND SECURITY

Both the classroom itself and the people who use it should be safe and secure. Appropriate locks and security devices should be installed to prevent theft and vandalism. Depending on institutional practice and patterns of theft, you may wish to lock down computers, monitors, keyboards, mouses, headphones, and the extra equipment at the instructor workstation. The extent to which lock-down devices are needed will also depend on the degree to which the classroom is monitored, where the classroom is located, and whether it is also used for open computing. It may be that you choose to lock down the computers, monitors, and the extra equipment at the instructor workstation, but decide that it is less expensive to replace keyboards and mouses than to purchase and spend staff time installing lock-down devices for them. In selecting lock-down devices, check that they do not impede use of the equipment and, preferably, that they will not impose difficulties for staff who are repairing or upgrading equipment.

Though hopefully rare, disruptive students displaying inappropriate or even dangerous behaviors, natural disasters, and other crisis situations may arise in an electronic classroom or during an instruction session. Emergency telephone numbers, an easily accessible telephone, and a flashlight are the minimum for negotiating any situations that may arise during an instruction session in the classroom.

An electronic classroom must also have an area for storage. Pens, whiteboard markers, remote controls, telephone books, dictionaries, handouts, and so on all need a place that is easily accessible but that does not interfere with use of the instructor workstation. If this storage area is locked, be certain that it can be accessed by anyone who needs the materials and not just the room coordinator. One option is to install a combination lock on the storage area and distribute the combination to everyone who is authorized to access the storage area. The combination could be changed once a semester or year. If a combination lock is also installed on the instructor workstation or any other area in the classroom that needs to be secured, all locks could be set to the same combination. If regular locks are used, the same key should open all locks in the room.

AESTHETICS

An electronic classroom should be aesthetically pleasing and the aesthetic design should be consistent with the rest of the library. Attention to and careful selection of desk, chair, paint, and equipment colors will help create a room that appears visually coordinated and consistent. Artwork or other wall hangings can help make the room more pleasing aesthetically and therefore more comfortable for students. Posters from the American Library Association READ series are a popular choice for adding color and a positive message to the classroom. You may also be able to work with your fine arts department to acquire artwork produced by students studying painting or drawing. Avoid options that are trendy unless you are certain that budgets will allow for redecorating once the design becomes dated. Similarly, avoid a monotonous color scheme which will be aesthetically unappealing. The goal is a timeless and attractive color scheme that facilitates learning without being a distraction.

Chapter Five

Infrastructure

Though behind the scenes, the classroom infrastructure is vital to a successful electronic classroom. Most people do not think a great deal about the infrastructure that supports their personal offices. Likewise, you may not initially realize how many infrastructure considerations affect your classroom. Without adequate electricity, network connectivity, lighting, and environmental controls, an electronic classroom will not serve teaching and learning very well. Because these issues are highly technical in nature, librarians should consult professionals with appropriate expertise. A baseline knowledge of the components will help you determine which issues need attention as you design your electronic classroom and will assist you in understanding what the experts are recommending and why. In addition to consulting the library's network administrator, the planning team should call on the expertise of the library's building manager if you are fortunate enough to have one.

DATA NETWORK

Access to information resources through network connectivity is crucial in the library electronic classroom. Indeed, in some ways, if network connectivity had not radically altered the world of information and library resources, you may not have needed an electronic classroom. Consider both those resources available through the library's local area network and those delivered via the Internet. Your library's technology plan should provide you with sufficient information to determine what type of network the library has, who is responsible for installing and maintaining it, and what issues must be considered. Because the network in your electronic classroom must be compatible with the rest of the library's network, the details of networking the classroom must be negotiated with the library's network administrators. It may also be necessary to consult with the institution's network administrators.

Daniel Niemeyer recommends that electronic classrooms be wired with three types of data connectivity—telephone (twisted pair), television distribution (coax), data (category 5)—and that sufficient conduit for the wiring be installed during remodeling or construction (Niemeyer, 2000: Online). Surface-mounted conduit is not very attractive and so, if at all possible, conduit should be placed inside the classroom walls. If you are building a demonstration classroom and have a long-term plan to convert it to a hands-on classroom, install sufficient conduit to accommodate the additional wiring that you will eventually need.

The total number of network ports needed in an electronic classroom is dictated by the number of devices needed to connect to the network. Minimally, each computer and networked printer will need a network port. However, if learners will be invited to bring their own laptop computers to instructional sessions, additional network ports will be required. These details will need to be discussed with your network administrator. If there is a per port charge for activating and maintaining network ports, your network administrator may prefer to phase in the activation of network ports and monitor whether all active ports are being utilized.

While it is not necessary to be a network specialist to design an electronic classroom, it is necessary to have a basic vocabulary and understanding of the issues involved. If you need to develop some additional background knowledge, "Chapter 1: What Does a Manager Need to Know About Technology?" in Donald Barclay's *Managing Public Access Computers* (2000) provides a valuable introduction.

Disk Space on the Network

If users will be downloading files or saving search results, they will need a place to store their data. Options for saving files include diskettes, a computer hard drive, Zip disks, recordable compact discs, and disk space on the network. The planning team, in close consultation with the library's network administrator, should determine which of these options will be available in the electronic classroom. Diskettes are convenient for smaller files, provided that the user has brought a diskette to the classroom. Some libraries sell diskettes and other supplies, either at the circulation desk or from a vending machine, for the convenience of users in such circumstances. Users should be discouraged from saving files to the hard drive of a computer. In general it is wise to discourage users from accessing the hard drive, especially to prevent problems of accidentally erased files. Furthermore, users often forget which computer they were using when they saved their data.

For larger files, diskettes will not have sufficient space to store the needed data. Zip disks and recordable compact disks can both hold files that are quite large; however, both also require that additional equipment be available in the electronic classroom—a Zip drive and a compact disk recorder respectively. If the campus computing center provides students, faculty, and staff with drive space on the campus network, the most convenient approach will probably be to set up the classroom computers so that users can access their campus network accounts. If the campus computing center does not provide this service, it may be possible to set up a public drive on the library's network; users can save files on the public drive until they can be downloaded to diskette or attached to an electronic mail message addressed to the user.

A Word About Wireless

The promise of reliable wireless network access has been realized at some institutions; however, for most institutions, wireless is still a bit too expensive. Having said that, in some circumstances wireless technology may be preferable, even if more expensive. The flexibility of wireless computing is pedagogically attractive for some instructional programs. If modular furniture is selected for the classroom, a wireless network will allow instructors to use one classroom layout with one class and another arrangement with a different class, depending on the goals and objectives of each class and the students attending. If the instructional needs assessment revealed that your library's instructional programs are diverse and varied in their approaches, a wireless network and laptop computers may accommodate the needs of many instructors. Additionally, if your institution is looking to experiment with wireless technology, offering the library's electronic classroom as a pilot installation may leverage additional funds from the campus administration.

Whether you choose a wireless classroom will depend primarily on budget, the need for flexibility as reflected in your instructional needs assessment, and the ability of the library's network administrators to install and support wireless connections. In a wireless classroom, in addition to the data network and laptop computers, each computer must also have an additional device through which it communicates with an access point. Access points interface the wireless network with the data network and require both electrical and network connectivity. A given access point can usually communicate up to approximately 300 feet but it provides connectivity for only a specified number of wireless devices (Wireless Infrastructure, 2000: 22). Multiple access points may be needed in a classroom to accommodate the total number of wireless devices in use. Finally, even with wireless network connectivity, access to electricity or a plan for recharging laptop batteries will be needed.

ELECTRICITY

An electronic classroom, particularly a hands-on classroom, requires a great deal of electricity. Philip Leighton and David Weber recommend that each workstation have four outlets (2000: 597). Unfortunately, in libraries built before library automation was on the scene, the electrical power and circuits are rarely adquate to accommodate the demands of computers, unless there has been an electrical retrofit project. Careful attention to electrical load and overloading of circuits is required if you are remodeling space for an electronic classroom. In addition to having enough electrical power, it also needs to be accessible. Extension cords should be avoided whenever possible in the electronic classroom as people can trip over them and injure themselves or damage the equipment. As a general rule, put in more electrical power than you think you could ever need, and then include the possibility for more. Allen et al. recommend that plans include provisions for 20 to 40 percent future expansion in the power needs of classrooms (1996: 19). You will never regret installing too many electrical drops.

The instructor workstation will need even more power than the student workstations because of the additional equipment that it houses. As a rule of thumb, for each piece of equipment that needs electricity, plan for a minimum of two electrical outlets. The instructor workstation should also include sufficient electrical power to accommodate additional equipment that is not permanently installed in the classroom. For example, for an instruction session for an art history class, a portable projector might be brought in so that the instructor can simultaneously display slides of paintings and demonstrate how to search a database for information about a painting and artist.

Finally, if you are building a demonstration classroom with the long-term plan of converting it to a hands-on classroom, be certain to install sufficient electricity when the classroom is built to accommodate the equipment planned for the hands-on environment. And, remember, even if computers connect to a wireless network, they still need electrical power.

LIGHTING

Different classroom activities require different amounts of lighting. Watching a projected image requires no more than 5 to 20 foot candles of light, while viewing a computer monitor requires 60 to 70 foot candles and reading a flipchart requires 70 to 100 foot candles (Gayeski, 1995:

159). In many cases, simultaneous activities may require a variety of lighting. For example, students might be viewing a projected image and completing a worksheet while the instructor is consulting his or her notes and typing on the keyboard. To accommodate these varying needs, lighting must be dimmable and zoned. Pay particular attention to accommodating the lighting needs for situations in which the students are watching a demonstration by the instructor while also working on their own computer terminals, consulting handouts, or completing a worksheet.

Lights should be zoned in banks parallel to the front of the room. In addition, it may be useful to have multiple zones in the very front of the room—whiteboard, projected image, and instructor station. At a minimum, it should be possible to shut off the lights around the projection screen without darkening the entire room. The need to keep the projection screen dark while lighting other areas of the room also precludes the use of indirect lighting which will reflect onto the projection screen and wash out the image (Niemeyer, 2000: Online). Light fixtures should be carefully positioned so that they do not create glare on computer screens or printed materials (Loomis, 1995a: 71).

Light switches should be located at the entrance to the classroom as well as near the instructor workstation. For safety reasons, avoid having all of the light switches at the entrance and none near the instructor station. An instructor should never have to be concerned that someone could enter the room, close the door, and shut off all the lights—thereby leaving the instructor and/or students vulnerable to theft or attack. If the zoned lighting plan is complex, preset lighting levels for various activities (such as a computer demonstration with students taking notes) should be programmed through a control device (see "Source Switching/Control Panels" in Chapter Seven). All switches should be clearly labeled so that instructors do not waste class time figuring out which switch controls which lights. Finally, in addition to having separate switches for each zone, there should be one master switch to turn off all of the lights simultaneously.

If zoned and/or dimmable lighting is not possible or is prohibitively expensive, and this is often the case in renovated space, consider purchasing floor lamps. When the overhead lights must be turned off so that learners can see the projected image, strategically placed floor lamps can provide students with enough light to take notes or operate their own keyboards. While not ideal, this arrangement is better than having the room completely dark. A small light for the instructor's workstation, preferably dimmable, will allow the instructor to see notes, the keyboard, and the control panel with greater ease.

HVAC

Heating, ventilating, and air conditioning (HVAC) systems create and regulate comfortable environmental conditions in the electronic classroom. In considering the HVAC requirements for your classroom, focus on the classroom with all of the equipment on and people in it—HVAC needs are quite different when a room is in use than when it is empty. For example, C. William Day points out that cooling needs can double if 20 computers are in use (1997). Generally speaking, the temperature should be about 68 to 75 degrees Fahrenheit and the relative humidity about 50 percent (Allen et al., 1996: 18). People will be comfortable and the equipment protected from extreme heat and cold.

In all likelihood, the classroom will share an HVAC system and thermostat with the entire library or a large zone within the library; however, if possible, a separate set of HVAC controls in the classroom is desirable (Heaton, 1995: 50). Additionally, there should be a separate control for the fan so that, even if the heating/cooling system is not needed, the air will still circulate (How to Design, 1989: 5). If separate controls are not possible, a low-cost solution to addressing some human comfort needs is to purchase a few quiet floor fans to turn on and off as needed. Another option, since people could trip over floor fans, is to install ceiling fans if the classroom ceiling is high enough.

Chapter Six

Software

It may seem odd to address software before discussing hardware; however, the purpose of hardware is to support the activities people want to do with software. It is software, not hardware, that is most closely related to the learning activities in the electronic classroom. As such, it is vital to know the system requirements for the desired software before selecting hardware.

TYPES

The software in an electronic classroom can be categorized into several types—operating systems, library resources, personal productivity, data analysis, accessories, and control/collaboration systems. For each category, it must be decided whether to include such software in the classroom and, if so, which specific program or programs to purchase and install. Library and campus standards and site licenses will both have to be considered in making these decisions as well.

In general, any software accessible on a public workstation in the library should be installed on the classroom computers. Any additional software installed in the classroom should be selected based on the findings of the instructional needs assessment. In cases where a hands-on classroom will also serve as an open computing lab, additional software may be needed for open computing that would otherwise be unnecessary in the electronic classroom.

Operating Systems

The operating systems run a computer and/or network. Operating systems include DOS (Microsoft), MacOS (Apple Computer), OS/2 (IBM), Windows (Microsoft), Windows NT (Microsoft), Windows 2000

(Microsoft), UNIX, Linux, and NetWare (Novell). Most computers will already have an installed operating system when they are purchased. The operating system used in your electronic classroom should be the same as that used in the rest of the library unless the library's network administrator specifically recommends otherwise. Supporting the operating systems is primarily the responsibility of the library's network administrator and so it is best to install the operating system that the network administrator recommends.

Library Resources

Library resources software is the least likely category to cause debate among members of the planning team. This category includes the online catalog, electronic databases, and locally developed software products. In the past, this category would have included a great number of specialized software packages; however, with the advent of Web-based interfaces for library resources, access to library resources may really require no more than a Web browser and maybe a telnet client.

If the library has specialized software packages to access specific information resources, it is best to install the software on all computers in the classroom; however, licensing agreements may restrict the library to a limited number of simultaneous users or may only allow one login at a time. In such cases, it may be preferable to install the software only on the instructor workstation, even in a hands-on classroom.

Personal Productivity

Personal productivity software is comprised of the software packages commonly found on personal computers. Word processors, spreadsheets, presentations, and database management packages are examples of personal productivity software. Microsoft Office (Microsoft) and AppleWorks (Apple Computer) are both common personal productivity software bundles. Deciding whether to install such software is often the most contentious decision in selecting software for an electronic classroom. The usual objections are that such software is not directly related to library research, that students will spend time exploring it during instruction sessions and not pay attention to the presented information, and that librarians should not be required to assist students who want to use it. The other view is that providing such software creates an integrated research environment that allows learners to experience the relationship between gathering information and creating new knowledge. Additionally, it is becoming more and more common for databases and Web sites to present information in various file formats for downloading, including word processing and spreadsheets formats. Users may need such personal productivity software to access library information. In making the decision at your library, it will be necessary for the planning team to consider the elements identified through the instructional needs assessment, as well as whether the classroom will also be used as an open computer laboratory.

Web browsers such as Netscape Communicator (Netscape) and Internet Explorer (Microsoft) are also a type of personal productivity software, as are helper applications such as Adobe Acrobat Reader (Adobe Systems), Quick Time Player (Apple Computer), and Real Player (Real Networks). Given the Web-based nature of so many library research databases and the development of Web interfaces for library online catalogs, a web browser has become a necessity for computers in a networked electronic classroom. The selection of helper applications may be less straightforward, especially when you consider those that enable a learner to access sound and video files. Many helper applications do have the advantage, however, of being available for use without charge. If your instruction program includes teaching Web and/or graphics development, such software as Dreamweaver (Macromedia), FrontPage (Microsoft), and Photoshop (Adobe Systems) may also be needed. Again, the planning team should look to the instructional needs assessment and the identified priorities for a framework for making these decisions.

A specialized type of personal productivity software to consider for the electronic classroom is bibliographic management software. Such packages store bibliographic information about research materials and then generate bibliographies as needed in any of a great variety of formats. Many work in an integrated manner with word processing programs. After being trained to use the software, learners could create a personal database of research materials, storing the data files on a network drive, personal computer hard drive, or diskette, and adding citations found during each subsequent research project. Examples of bibliographic management software include the following:

- Bookends Web (Westing Software)
- EndNote (ISI ResearchSoft)
- ProCite (ISI ResearchSoft)
- QuickBib! (InfoWorks Technology Company)
- TakeNote! (Prentice Hall)
- Reference Manager (ISI ResearchSoft)

Data Analysis

While text and document files are easily accessed via library resource and personal productivity software packages, networked information access allows library users to locate and manipulate statistical data and mapping files. The planning team should examine topics covered in your instructional program and consider whether the classroom will also function as an open computing laboratory. This process will help them to determine if data analysis software is needed in the classroom.

Excel (Microsoft) or a similar spreadsheet program may be sufficient for basic statistical manipulations. However, if learners will be accessing large data sets, such as those available from ICPSR: Inter-University Consortium for Political and Social Research (*www.icpsr.umich.edu*) or the Lijphart Elections Archive (*dodgson.ucsd.edu/lij*), a more advanced statistical package may be needed. SPSS (SPSS Inc.), SAS (SAS Institute), and Stata (Stata Corporation) are all examples of statistical analysis software. A statistical file conversion software package such as Stat/Transfer (Circle Systems) that converts, for example, an SPSS file to a Stata file, will also be useful.

Mapping software may also be needed, particularly if the library provides access to a geographic information system for researchers. Geographic information files from the Census Bureau, the National Weather Service, and the Environmental Protection Agency are just some of the mapping files that might be used in the classroom. Such software as MapInfo (MapInfo Corporation) and ARCView (Environmental Systems Research Institute) could be considered by the planning team, depending on the findings of the instructional needs assessment.

Accessories

The catch all category of accessories may be the most challenging category for the planning team to discuss and manage. These programs can be very useful but they can also be very distracting for students. Many computers come with a number of preinstalled software programs—games (such as, Solitaire) and/or single-purpose programs (such as, Calculator). A simple text editor, (such as Microsoft's WordPad) is usually included and can be very useful for taking notes, copying selected paragraphs of text from longer documents, and, in cases where a complete word processing package is not available, for beginning to draft the text of a paper. Depending on the configuration of the computer, your network administrator may allow you to select which accessory programs you want to keep, if any, or you may be required to have all or none of what is available. You might, for example, decide to delete all games, except Solitaire which is used in an Introduction to the Web workshop to help new computer users become comfortable with using the mouse.

In addition to the preinstalled software programs, other accessory programs may be made available on your campus. For example, such software as ConversionsPlus (DataViz), which assists users accessing files in unexpected formats downloaded from Web sites or received via electronic mail, may be commonly installed in all computer laboratories on campus. Other accessory programs might assist with very basic graphics development or playing audiovisual files.

Control/Collaboration Systems

In the hands-on classroom, instructors are often concerned that students are not attending to the demonstration and are instead using the computers for other activities, such as electronic mail and chat. Some instructors also wish to use the technology to foster collaborative learning. Control/collaboration systems is the category for software programs that address these two issues and allow the instructor to monitor and guide the flow of classroom activities and blend demonstration and hands-on instruction.

Classroom control systems have been defined as systems that "provide various software and hardware that allow instructors in networked classrooms to monitor and control students' work stations" (Teaching Methods Committee, 2000). Some of the control systems also offer collaboration modes. Using control/collaboration software, instructors can broadcast displays from instructor to students, student to student, and student to instructor; blank out student monitor displays and disable mouses and keyboards; control an individual workstation; oversee and monitor student practice; create collaborative groups; and send/receive messages (Peterson, 1999). Some systems also allow the instructor and students to establish chat sessions and to send and receive files from one another.

Some control/collaboration systems are more appropriate for semester-length courses because of the student training required to make full use of the interactive features. Others only allow the instructor to manipulate the system, and thus they can be used for a single classroom period without any student training. Most products are software solutions; however, a few require hardware as well. Features vary from product to product. If your planning team is interested in purchasing control/collaboration software, you will need to identify the features important for your instructional setting and then compare your requirements with the capabilities of the available products. Control/collaboration systems include the following:

- Apple Network Assistant (Apple Computer)
- Altiris Vision (Altiris)
- ClassNet Control Systems (Minicom Advanced Systems Inc.)
- CommonSpace (sixth floor media)
- Daedalus Integrated Writing Environment (Daedalus Group)
- Electronic Classroom (TechSight Engineering Services)
- InSight (Tech Electronics, Inc.)
- KnowledgeWEB (COMWEB Technology Group)
- LanSchool (Intel)
- LINK Systems (Company Applied Computer Systems, Inc.)
- NetMeeting (Microsoft)
- NetOp School (CrossTech Corporation)
- NetSupport Manager 5.0 (NetSupport, Inc.)
- Remotely Possible (Raxco, Inc.)
- Screen to Screen (PowerOn Software)
- SmartClass (Robotel Electronique, Inc.)
- SynchronEyes (SMART Technologies)
- V-Net (Inline, Inc.)
- TIMBUKTU (Netopia)

SECURITY

With respect to computer security, you may wish to install software that requires students to log in with a password in order to access the library network. Depending on your campus network infrastructure, it may be possible to use the same login system that is used in the open computer laboratories on campus. If the planning team determines that a login system is desirable or if it is required by library or institutional policy, you will have to work with the library's network administrator, and possibly the campus network administrator, to determine your options and to select an approach.

Logins and passwords may also be required for access to a given database or document archive. It may be possible to create a script that automatically logs the user into a given resource or to use Internet Protocol number-based authentication. But, if not, you will need to establish a system for distributing the logins and passwords efficiently during an instruction session and for ensuring that they are not disseminated to unauthorized users.

Virus detection software should be installed on all computers in the classroom, particularly if the classroom will also be used for open computing. Users sharing files and exchanging electronic mail can easily and unknowingly introduce a virus into the network or a given computer's hard drive. Without proper virus detection programs, the virus could easily spread throughout the library's network or disable some of the classroom's computers. Virus detection software should be set to scan all downloaded files, including electronic mail messages, as well as files accessed from the diskette drive. Virus detection programs include McAfee VirusScan (McAfee) and Norton AntiVirus (Symantec). Such software programs must be updated regularly so that newer viruses can be detected. If possible, for the convenience of the technicians who must update the software, install the same virus detection software in the electronic classroom that is used in the rest of the library. Some virus detection software packages can also be configured for automatic updating on a regular basis through access to the company's Web site or a designated campus server. The library's network administrator will be able to determine whether manual or automatic updates are preferable for your classroom setup.

In some circumstances, it may also be desirable to install a software package such as Fortres 101 (Fortres Grand Corporation), Storm Windows (Cetus Software), or NetFortress (Fortress Technologies) on the student workstations in the classroom. These software programs can be set to prevent students from altering the settings on the computer; accessing specified network or local drives; running particular software programs; and/or downloading and installing software from the Internet. In some cases, the software can also be set to allow a student to make changes to the computer settings or install software while using a given computer but, when the computer is turned off or the user logs off, all of the settings are returned to their default values and any newly installed programs are removed. Before investing in such software, check with your network administrator—some operating systems include some or all of these security features (for example, the system policy editor in Microsoft's Windows NT).

Finally, so that you are prepared in case a user deletes important system files or changes a computer's settings, or in case a virus corrupts the hard drives of the computers, you may wish to create an electronic image of the computer hard drives in the classroom and store it elsewhere. In doing so, you will have saved the configuration you want, with everything installed and working correctly. If something happens to change the configuration of a classroom computer or all of the computers, you can restore the original configuration with less effort than if you had to start all over again. If all of the classroom computers have exactly the same hardware and software, as recommended, you can set up the configuration once and then clone it throughout the classroom. Ghost (Symantec) is an example of a drive-image software program which will allow you to save and then propagate the desired configuration.

LICENSING AGREEMENTS

Because software licenses are contracts, they are legal agreements. If you are responsible for designing an electronic classroom, you need to be familiar with and, in some cases you will be responsible for, negotiating the terms and conditions of the licenses. In particular, be aware of limits on the number of simultaneous users for a particular resource. If your instruction classes tend to be a great deal larger than the maximum number of users, try to negotiate for additional access during training sessions. Many vendors are willing to set up training logins and passwords which are solely intended for use during classroom instruction but which allow groups of students to practice searching, even if your license only allows a small number of simultaneous users outside of the classroom. If you need help with licensing issues, Michael D. Cramer (1994) and Arlene Bielefield and Lawrence Cheeseman (1999) provide straight forward advice to save you worry and hassle when negotiating for the access you need.

REMOTE ACCESS

If remote access to library resources is different from access in the library building, and it most likely is, then the electronic classroom should be configured so that both situations can be demonstrated at the instructor workstation. For example, if off-campus access requires that library users configure their Web browser for a proxy server or that they authenticate their access through a login and password process, then, minimally, the instructor should be able to demonstrate these processes. Setting up the instructor workstation to mimic off-campus access may be challenging; however, if most students access library resources remotely, it is important to be able to teach them how to do so in your classroom.

One way to mimic off-campus access at the instructor workstation would be by having an account with an outside Internet Service Provider (ISP). If there is an ISP that is popular with students, choose that one. The instructor workstation will also need a modem and a telephone line for the modem. During an instruction session, the instructor can then initiate a modem connection with the Internet Service Provider and go through the steps of authenticating access to library resources. As an added advantage, this process will offer librarians a better understanding of student experiences with library resources. It may be that certain library databases function differently when accessed via a patron identification number than when accessed through a computer in the library.

It would be best if students could also practice the remote access process in the electronic classroom; however, the costs of doing so are likely to be prohibitive. A handout with screen captures will allow students to follow along during the instructor's demonstration. This handout can also function as an instruction manual when students are connecting remotely to library resources.

Chapter Seven

Equipment and Furnishings

Having decided on the software to be installed in your electronic classroom, you should determine hardware specifications based on the requirements of the software programs. Such resources as the annual "Buyers Guide" in *Training* and *Presentations* magazines and ZDNet's *ComputerShopper.com* (*www.zdnet.com/computershopper/*) are helpful in making equipment decisions. In the past, concerns about compatibility among products acquired from different manufacturers were very important to consider when selecting equipment. Computability is much less of an issue now because of standardization; however, it is still good to be aware of and question any potential incompatibilities.

Finally, then, it is also time to select the best furniture to accommodate human needs and equipment demands. In selecting furniture, the planning team should consider safety, comfort, flexibility, utility, aesthetics, durability, ease of operation, and maintenance issues (Terlaga, 1990: 48). WorkspaceResources (*www.workspace–resources.com*) is a useful Web site for investigating and making furnishing decisions.

STUDENT WORKSTATIONS

As mentioned in the discussion of classroom space in Chapter Four, the requirements for student workstations differ greatly between a demonstration classroom and a hands-on classroom. In summary, student workstations in a demonstration classroom are more compact and more flexible because no accommodations for computing technology are necessary and rearranging the tables and chairs does not involve any wiring considerations. Students workstations in the hands-on classroom require more space for both the equipment and the furniture necessary to accommodate the equipment. Regardless of classroom type, tables that can be pushed together to make a continuous surface will provide more workspace than individual tablet-arm chairs or separate desks.

Equipment

The equipment for a typical student workstation in a hands-on classroom includes a computer, monitor, keyboard, and mouse. Left-handed users will appreciate being able to move the mouse to the left side of the keyboard. A mouse pad and wrist rest will also add to the usability of the workstation. If learners will be accessing audiovisual materials on the computers, headphones will also be needed. In some specialized classrooms, students might also have access to a document scanner, slide scanner, printer, or other electronic device. To the extent possible, all student workstations should have identical equipment. This consistancy will assist with both teaching and technical support issues. If identical equipment is not available, try to limit the number of types that are installed, for example, half of the computers might be of one brand and half of another brand.

Computers

Though it may be tempting to use the classroom as a "last stop" for computers that are no longer desirable in other areas of the library, absolutely resist this. At a minimum, the computers selected for the classroom should be equivalent to those in the public areas of the library. Even better, though, is to have classroom computers that are more powerful and that process data more quickly than the public computers, so that instruction can proceed without interruption or delay. Any time spent waiting, and waiting, for a computer to respond in an electronic classroom represents lost instructional time. During such waiting periods, student attention may wander to other topics and the flow of instruction is interrupted, potentially distracting the instructor from the objectives of the class as well. This means that the classroom is not serving its purpose of teaching and learning.

Desktop computers are less expensive than notebook computers and are also less at risk of theft or damage because of mishandling; however, they are also bulky and the monitors can occupy a large proportion of the available work surface. The monitors can also interfere with student sight lines. Installing flat-screen monitors will decrease the amount of space required for the monitor; however, the increase in cost may be prohibitive and sight lines remain a concern. If a hands-on classroom is going to serve as an open computing laboratory when not scheduled for a class, desktop computers are preferable to notebook computers because of theft and damage concerns. In general, if the computers will to be installed and stay in place, desktop models are less expensive, less at risk of theft or damage, and easier to monitor during student practice time.

Notebook computers do offer greater flexibility than desktop computers. They take up less space than desktop machines and are less likely to block student sight lines than traditional monitors. If wireless networking is available, notebook computers can also allow the instructor to arrange the classroom into different configurations depending on the objectives of particular instructional sessions. Additionally, when not in use for a class, notebook computers can also be made available for patron use, either in the library or elsewhere, depending on the library's circulation policies. The challenge with such an approach is ensuring that the notebook computers are available when needed for a class session—and not checked out or in need of reconfiguring or recharging due to the nonclassroom use. Depending on the technological literacy of the learners, notebook computers can also present additional challenges if students are not familiar with the compact keyboard arrangement and the alternative mouse devices of notebook computers. Finally, setup for a class session will require approximately one to three minutes per laptop, depending on the complexity of the setup and the proximity of the laptop storage to the classroom. If your classroom has more than eight to ten laptops, the time required to set up the room for an instruction session may be problematic.

Regardless of whether desktop or notebook computers are selected, if at all possible, have available a back-up student computer that is already configured like the classroom computers. This back-up computer can be swapped with a malfunctioning computer in the classroom when necessary. In this way, computer technicians will not have to compete with instruction sessions scheduled in the classroom in order to repair and troubleshoot equipment.

Monitors

The size of the computer monitor is also an important consideration. Currently, most computers come with a 17-inch monitor, which is probably adequate for most library instruction offerings; however, larger and smaller monitors are available. Smaller monitors can cause eyestrain problems. Larger monitors tend to be more expensive but they also reduce eyestrain and allow more information to be displayed at one time. Larger monitors may also take up a great deal of the available workspace or create sight line problems if students cannot see the instructor or a projected image without peering around the sides of the monitors. The extent to which sight lines are a concern depends on the classroom layout selected by the planning team. Monitor size is less of an issue with notebook computers; to minimize eyestrain with notebook computers, it is probably best to get the largest screen size possible.

Furniture

The furniture in an electronic classroom must be selected with consideration to usability, comfort, durability, aesthetics, and expense. The key is to find a balance among these factors. Highly durable furniture that is affordable but aesthetically displeasing will not create an environment conducive to learning. Likewise, however, furniture that is aesthetically pleasing at installation but shows signs of wear after one month of use will also not create the learning environment that you want. Be certain to investigate whether the furniture you are considering is intended for public use or if it was designed for use in private offices. The perfect office desk may not withstand heavy use in an electronic classroom that is also used for open computing. Ask vendors for references from other libraries that have installed their furniture and contact those libraries to find out whether they would recommend the furniture to you and whether they have encountered any problems with it.

Tables and Desks

A great variety of student tables and desks are available for purchase. For the demonstration classroom, the emphasis is likely to be on providing students with sufficient workspace to take notes and handle printed library materials. A table that is 24 inches deep may be sufficient and will allow you to maximize the number of students that can be accommodated in a demonstration classroom. However, if you are building a demonstration classroom with the long-term plan of converting it to a hands-on classroom, install the tables needed for the hands-on at the outset so that the conversion does not require new furniture. Avoid built-in tables that are incorporated into the construction of the room, they limit long-term flexibility, since any change in classroom layout will require remodeling.

For the hands-on classroom, many types of tables are designed to accommodate desktop computers. Most are a minimum of 30 inches deep. Some are very similar to a traditional table but then include wire management features to channel and/or hide wiring so that it is not damaged, disconnected, or a safety hazard. Such tables generally provide for easy access to the equipment should technical repairs be needed. Placing the monitors on the top of the desks allows the instructor to scan the monitors easily during hands-on practice and identify any students who are in need of assistance; however, the monitors may also partially obscure sight lines during demonstrations and make it difficult for the instructor to make eye contact with students. Some manufacturers offer computer tables that are less traditional in shape, (for example, Techline's Learning Curve) in order to overcome some challenges of desktop monitors and sight lines; however, these tables require more space than a traditional table.

Alternatively, some tables recess the monitor into the table in part or completely, thereby improving student-teacher sight lines. Some tables that recess the monitors completely allow one to "cover up" the computers during instruction sessions that do not require hands-on capabilities. Recessed monitors present challenges, however. First, the design of the desks can make it difficult to troubleshoot or repair the equipment. Second, during an instruction session, it may be difficult for the instructor to see what is displayed on a student's monitor and thus to provide assistance. Likewise, it may be difficult for another student, especially during collaborative hands-on work, to see the monitor. With completely recessed monitors, it is unlikely that two or more students could easily share one computer. Finally, if the recessed monitors are under a glass surface, glare from lights can make it difficult for the user to view the monitor. Additionally, the glass surface will pick up fingerprints and require regular cleaning.

Computer workstations designed for an individual student using a single computer should be at least three feet wide. Computer workstations for two students sharing one computer should be at least five to six feet wide. In addition to ensuring that students have sufficient workspace, consider also the ease with which technical support for the equipment is facilitated by the design of the tables or desks. Furniture manufacturers and vendors include KI, Grafco, Nova Solutions, Blackwelder's Industries, Computer Furniture Direct, SMARTdesks, Spectrum, and Vertiflex.

Chairs

When selecting chairs for the student workstations, regardless of the classroom type, follow the advice of John Vasi and Cheryl LaGuardia and select "a secretarial chair, ergonomically designed and easily adjusted, with appropriate casters on a five leg base." (1992: 45). With this type of chair, there is almost no end to the options made available by vendors; they come in a great variety of colors and patterns, fabrics, and design styles. Because these chairs will be used heavily and by different people each day, maybe each hour, be certain to select chairs with high-quality construction and adjustment mechanisms as well as stain-resistant upholstery. Some chair manufacturers (such as, Herman Miller) have also developed comfortable and attractive chairs that are not upholstered. The adjustment mechanisms on chairs in an electronic classroom will be used far more often than the mechanisms on chairs in private offices, so it is crucial that they be sufficiently durable to withstand multiple adjustments by a variety of people. To test the comfort of a chair, borrow one from the vendor and sit in it while working for an hour or two (Duggan, 1994: 24). Or, if you are trying to decide among different chairs, acquire multiple samples, place them in a public area of the library, and then observe which ones patrons use more often.

Keep in mind that the leg base and/or the seat pan determines how much floor space a chair will occupy. Use whichever is larger in determining how many chairs will fit into a classroom. If the chairs are too close together, their legs can become entangled. If the seat pans are larger than the leg bases, be careful that students will not be required to sit uncomfortably close together. This last concern is especially important if two students will be sharing one computer. Be certain that the table they will share is sufficiently wide to allow both students to pull their chairs up to the table. Both students should also be able to reach the keyboard and to comfortably view the information displayed on the monitor.

In addition to workstation chairs, additional chairs may be needed to accommodate classes with more students than the classroom has workstations. These additional chairs should be stored in the classroom or in close proximity so that they are readily available. As such, the chairs should be stackable and, if they are not stored in the classroom, on a rolling chair rack so that they can be easily brought into the classroom.

INSTRUCTOR WORKSTATION

An instructor workstation is essentially the same in both demonstration and hands-on classrooms. The installed equipment is not dependent on the type of classroom but on the needs of the library's instructional program. In general, the instructor workstation should accommodate multiple teaching styles but avoid looking like a teaching "bunker" set up to protect the instructor from the students (Niemeyer, 2000). Additionally, the instructor workstation should not be placed on a platform unless the classroom is a very large lecture hall and provisions have been made for an instructor with a mobility disability. The instructor workstation should be designed to facilitate instruction and not be a hindrance to it.

Most classroom layouts place the instructor workstation at the front of the room, either to the right or left of the centered projection screen. If the projection screen is on the left or right side, the instructor workstation is commonly placed on the opposite side. Rarely is the instructor workstation placed in the front center of the room. Many instructors are uncomfortable in the front center. Additionally, front center is the location with the best sight lines in classroom, so it is best used for written or projected information. The instructor workstation might also be placed in the rear or middle of the room; however, such arrangements take away from the total space available for student workstations. Student workstations cannot be placed in the very front of the room because of sight line issues, so the front of the room is a good place for the instructor workstation, as well as the printer workstation and storage cabinets or bookshelves. Avoid a built-in instructor workstation that is incorporated into the construction of the classroom since any change will then require remodeling.

Equipment

The basic equipment for an instructor workstation includes a computer, monitor, keyboard, and mouse. To increase the options for presentation, and depending on the materials used in the library's instructional offerings, the instructor workstation might also include equipment to display various media, such as, a document camera or visualizer, overhead transparency projector, digital video disk (DVD) or videocassette player, and slide projector. The equipment at the instructor workstation must be connected to the projection and sound systems in the classroom; these systems are discussed later in this chapter. The instructor workstation might also include a printer if the workstation's computer is not attached to a networked printer in or conveniently near the classroom.

The computer, monitor, keyboard, and mouse at the instructor station should be identical to the student equipment so that the instructor and students use the same procedures to manipulate their computers. Of particular concern is the keyboard layout, especially with notebook computers, and the mouse functionality (for example, whether the mouse includes scrolling capabilities). If the workstations are not identical, the instructor teaching a class must be aware of the differences between the systems and be able to instruct students in the procedures appropriate for their computers while simultaneously executing different procedures at the instructor workstation. The exception to the general rule of having identical instructor and student equipment is in cases where the instructor will be demonstrating a particular resource (such as, a CD-ROM database) that requires additional computing resources or peripherals, that the students will not use at their workstations. In such cases, the instructor workstation will need computing power or peripherals beyond that of the student workstations; however, to the extent possible, it is still desirable to have identical keyboards, mouses, and monitors.

Media Display

Having a document camera or visualizer, overhead transparency projector, slide projector, and a DVD or videocassette player at the instructor workstation allows the instructor to display information that is available in a variety of formats. A slide projector, DVD player, or videocassette player will be most useful for displaying typical library materials. For example, an instructor teaching students how to research an artist might include in the demonstration examples of the artist's work from the library's slide collection. Or, an instructor might show a videocassette-based overview of the library and its services to introduce students to the library and provide them with a general orientation before hands-on instruction begins.

In a similar way, a document camera, also called a visualizer, allows an instructor to display a book, periodical, or other printed text so that it can be seen simultaneously by all students in the classroom. Three dimensional objects, such as the contents of a curriculum kit or educational game, can also be displayed using a document camera. Because no advance work is needed to prepare the materials for display, a document camera allows instructors to adapt their demonstrations to student interests and to respond to questions posed during the instruction session. Though an overhead transparency projector can also be used to display portions of text, the instructor must create the transparencies before the class session, limiting flexibility and the ability to be responsive to the learners. However, if budgetary concerns prohibit the purchase of a document camera immediately, an overhead transparency projector can provide at least some of the functionality of a document camera until sufficient funds are available.

Accessories

The instructor workstation should also include a number of accessories that facilitate teaching. These items include a clock, a desk lamp, a laser pointer, and, depending on the size of the classroom and the strength of the instructors' voices, a wireless microphone.

The instructor workstation should include a telephone for contacting technical support, the reference desk, and appropriate emergency personnel. A cordless telephone will allow the instructor to take the telephone to malfunctioning equipment while discussing the problem with technical personnel. If you do have a cordless telephone, however, special care will be required to ensure that the telephone remains in the classroom and does not get lost.

Though not equipment strictly speaking, the instructor workstation should also include office supplies (paper, pencils, pens, and stapler), classroom supplies (whiteboard markers, erasers, and cleaner, and projector bulbs), a telephone directory, a wastebasket, and a recycling bin. A pencil sharpener and a flashlight may also be desirable. A written instruction manual for using all of the equipment in the classroom will also be useful.

Figure 7.1 contains a checklist of the instructor workstation equipment discussed above.

Furniture

As mentioned previously, the instructor workstation should not resemble a teaching bunker—a hulking cabinet filled with mysterious electronic devices that an instructor must monitor constantly. To the extent possible, the instructor workstation furniture should match the student workstation furniture in order to create a coordinated classroom look. Fortunately, many furniture vendors that sell computer desks for students also sell instructor workstations. In selecting the instructor workstation, keep in mind the accessibility of the equipment for troubleshooting and repair.

To provide a sufficient and preferably generous amount of instructor workspace, it may be useful to acquire both a teaching workstation for the equipment and an ordinary table for the instructor to use for print resources and handouts. Depending on the extent to which library print materials will be used and/or stored in the classroom, a bookcase near the instructor workstation may also be useful. Likewise, if handouts and worksheets will be stored in the classroom, a filing or storage cabinet for the instructor will be needed.

In selecting a chair or stool for the instructor workstation, coordinate with the student chairs. In many cases, it may be possible to use the same chair. In other cases, the instructor workstation will require a stool so that the instructor can be seen by the students even when he or she is seated. Once again, test the instructor chair or stool by borrowing one from the vendor and sitting in it for an hour or so. Because the instruc-

Figure 7.1: Instructor Workstation Equipment Checklist

INSTRUCTOR WORKSTATION EQUIPMENT CHECKLIST

- ❒ Computer
- ❒ Monitor
- ❒ Keyboard
- ❒ Mouse
- ❒ Document Camera/Visualizer
- ❒ Overhead Transparency Projector
- ❒ Digital Video Disk or Videocassette Player
- ❒ Slide Projector
- ❒ Printer
- ❒ Clock
- ❒ Laser Pointer
- ❒ Microphone
- ❒ Telephone
- ❒ Telephone Directory
- ❒ Office Supplies (e.g., Paper, Pencils, Pens, and Stapler)
- ❒ Classroom Supplies (e.g., Whiteboard Markers, Erasers, Cleaner)
- ❒ Pencil Sharpener
- ❒ Flashlight
- ❒ Wastebasket
- ❒ Recycling Bin
- ❒ Equipment Instruction Manuals

tor is likely to stand up and walk around the room during an instruction session and then return to a seated position, also test how easily one can move from seated to standing positions and back again.

WRITING SURFACES

Chalkboards should be avoided in an electronic classroom because of the potential damage to electronic equipment, from chalk dust. Whiteboards are the preferred alternative and they offer the added advantage of multiple marker colors for writing. Whiteboards can be relatively inexpensive; however, those that are most inexpensive can become stained with color over time, especially if they are not regularly erased and cleaned. A ceramic whiteboard, though more expensive, will be more durable and more resistant to stains. Mount whiteboards on all easily accessible wall surfaces. Having a generous amount of whiteboard space encourages creativity and brainstorming, particularly during active learning exercises.

A high-end alternative is an electronic whiteboard. The functions of these systems range from simple electronic whiteboard (which will save a copy of the writing on the board) to combination whiteboard/projection systems (with which the instructor "writes" onto the projected image using specialized devices instead of traditional markers). Electronic whiteboards range in price from under $1,000 to more than $5,000, depending on the features. SMART Boards (SMART Technologies), Interactive White Board (Numonics), Ibid Electronic Whiteboard (MicroTouch Systems, Inc.), and Electronic Whiteboards (SoftBoard) are some of the available electronic whiteboard products. A recently introduced and relatively inexpensive product, Mimio (Mimio), occupies a middle ground between the traditional whiteboard and a full-fledged whiteboard/projection system. The Mimio attaches to a regular whiteboard and captures what is written on the whiteboard and then transmits it to a computer file (which can then be printed, saved to a diskette, and/or mounted on a Web site).

Finally, depending on the instructional content and teaching methods employed in the classroom, a flip chart with appropriate markers might also be provided. Instructors must take care that the flip chart markers are not used on the whiteboards or the whiteboards may sustain irreversible damage.

PROJECTION SYSTEM

The video/data projector is a key piece of equipment in an electronic classroom as it is through the projector that the learners observe the materials and information resources that the instructor is demonstrating on the computer, with a document camera, and similiar equipment. Without a high-quality display of a clear, crisp image with true colors, even the most engaging demonstration will seem drawn out and tedious. With respect to brightness, 600 ANSI lumens, the measure of display brightness, is the minimum for a classroom setting (Niemeyer, 2000: Online). Web sites such as ProjectorCentral (*www.projectorcentral.com*) and Presentations.com (*presentations.gearworks.com*) provide detailed advice for selecting the projection system that will work best in your classroom.

A projection screen is the surface onto which an image is projected and both front and rear projection screens are available. For use with a front projection screen (meaning that the image is projected onto the front side of the screen) a video/data projector can be mounted in the ceiling, on the back wall, or placed on a table in the classroom. A ceiling-mount is generally preferable, if electrical power and network connectivity are available in the ceiling, so that the projector is not accidentally bumped and put out of focus. A front projection screen for video/data projector display is similar to the traditional overhead transparency projector screen and it has a white matte finish. Some classrooms are designed so that the image is projected directly onto a white wall or onto a traditional whiteboard. These options, though low-cost, do not provide a high-quality image for viewing. The front projection screen should be motorized so that the instructor need not struggle to pull it down or put it up. This requirement will also protect the screen from damage.

Rear projection screens have the image projected onto the back side of the screen. Using a rear projection screen requires that space be available behind the screen for the video/data projector. Such space is usually not available in a library electronic classroom. In general, rear projection systems also cost more than front projection systems. However, if space and funding is available, rear projection does provide a higher quality image than front projection and does not require the room to be as dark.

Sight lines are a top concern in the electronic classroom. Projection screens can be installed in the front of the room either in the center of or offset to one side, as long as sight lines are maintained. Most projection screens allow a viewing angle up to 45 to 60 degrees from the center axis of the screen. To determine the width of the projection screen needed in a particular classroom, divide the distance of the farthest viewer from the screen by 4 (Allen et al., 1996: 23). For example, if the back row of students is 28 feet from the screen, the projection screen should be 7 feet wide. Most projection screens are currently sized in a ratio of 3 units high to 4 units wide. Niemeyer (2000: Online) predicts that screen proportions will soon change to that of high definition television—9 units by 16—and thus recommends that any new projection screen be installed in such a way that it is easily replaceable with one that is wider. Also, be certain to mount the screen high enough for individuals in the back of the room to see the bottom of the image. Finally, check that the instructor can use the projection system and the whiteboard simultaneously. The projection screen should not cover the entire writing surface.

Under certain circumstances, the planning team might consider other display output options. In a very small room, a large display monitor (for example, at least 36 inches) attached to the instructor workstation might be an acceptable alternative to a projection system, particularly for a demonstration classroom where sight lines are less complicated. In larger classrooms, multiple monitors could be located in various places, especially if structural components, (such as, pillars in the center of the room) block student sight lines; however, it may then be difficult for the instructor to maintain eye contact with students and observe their nonverbal signs of confusion.

Another alternative for the planning team to consider in a hands-on classroom is to not have a projection system. Instead, the planning team might choose to install a control/collaboration software system and have the instructor broadcast the instructor workstation output directly to the student workstation monitors. This setup may make it even more difficult for the instructor to monitor student understanding, and it can create in the students a sense of isolation and disconnectedness from the instructor; however, such an approach overcomes the sight line challenges of even the most cumbersome classroom layout challenges, (such as, an L-shaped classroom with multiple pillars or a classroom 15 feet wide and 40 feet long).

SOUND SYSTEM AND ACOUSTICS

Amplifying desired sounds and minimizing undesirable sounds can be a difficult task, particularly in a hands-on classroom with its large amount of equipment. Depending on the classroom, amplifying and projecting desired sounds requires a microphone (with a sufficient supply of batteries if it is a wireless microphone), appropriate acoustical design, and an audio system integrated with the projection system. High-quality speakers positioned appropriately in the classroom are also a must.

If amplification of desired sounds is required, acoustical design to control unwanted sound is probably also required. Acoustical design has three goals: "to keep out exterior noise, limit extraneous noise, and control echoes between walls, floors, and ceilings" (Price, 1991: 15). Controlling sound involves absorbing sound inside the classroom as well as containing sound so it does not "bleed" into adjacent areas. Likewise, it may be necessary to prevent sound from surrounding areas from "bleeding" into the classroom. Carpeting, acoustical ceiling tiles, sound-absorption panels, and fabric will all help minimize noise, as will mounting speakers on the ceiling rather than on the walls (Niemeyer). For example, acoustical tiles can be added around the perimeter of the ceiling to improve classroom acoustics. Robert Allen et al. recommend that, if the ceiling height is between 10 and 12 feet, 50 to 60 percent of the ceiling should be covered with acoustical tile (1996: 14).

Though librarians involved in designing electronic classrooms should have a general understanding of the issues involved with sound control, classrooms with complex acoustical circumstances require the services of an acoustical engineer. Bruce Ledford and John Brown (1992) provide a readable technical overview of the issues involved in acoustical design which will help you understand the technical recommendations of an acoustical engineer.

SOURCE SWITCHING/CONTROL PANELS

The instructor in the electronic classroom is managing multiple data feeds into the projection system—computer, document camera, video, slides, and so on. Though this can be done manually through the use of multiple remote controls and settings, source switching through a control panel automates the process and makes it easier for the instructor to manage the instructional session. Crestron and Panja both provide products to automate switching between different information sources at the instructor workstation and, in some cases, to provide for preset controls for lighting and other classroom elements. Clearly written instructions and advance training will be required to ensure that instructors are able to use the control panel effectively.

PRINTER STATION

A printer might be included as a component of the instructor workstation so that the instructor can demonstrate printing, for example, a selected set of citations from a database. If, however, students will also be able to print jobs, it will be desirable to establish a separate printer station so that students retrieving printouts do not disturb the other equipment at the instructor station. Because sight lines are not a concern for the printer station, it can be located in an area is not suitable for student workstations, usually at the front of the room or behind a pillar.

In selecting a printer, consider the kinds of documents that users will be printing and the kinds of printers used elsewhere in the library and on campus. In all likelihood a high-quality, black-and-white laser printer will be sufficient for an electronic classroom. However, if users need access to color printing, you must consider the additional expense of purchasing and maintaining a color laser printer.

If students are not charged for printing in the rest of the library, they should not be charged for printing in the classroom. If they are charged in the rest of the library, they should be charged in the classroom, unless collecting money is done manually and would disrupt the flow of instruction. In such cases, the library should either make alternative provisions for the money to be collected outside of the classroom or consider offering free printing during instruction sessions.

ASSISTIVE TECHNOLOGIES

Assistive technology concerns relate to both the student and the instructor workstations since both students and instructors with disabilities could potentially use an electronic classroom. Disabilities can be either temporary or permanent (McNulty, 1999: 5). Both temporary and permanent disabilities can be accommodated through advance planning and careful attention to accessibility guidelines.

In an electronic classroom, the challenges of negotiating the classroom layout, manipulating a personal computer, and viewing displayed, projected, and written images are likely to be the most common difficulties encountered by persons with disabilities. Hearing impairments can also create difficulties. Assistive technologies can assist in overcoming all of these problems. In selecting assistive technologies, get advice from your institution's disability concerns office. If possible, select assistive technologies for the library's classrooms that are used elsewhere on campus so that users more likely will already be familiar with operating the equipment.

The mobility difficulties related to navigating the classroom layout are best addressed by designing wide aisles and entranceways, installing non-skid flooring, and selecting adjustable furnishings. Additionally, some furniture vendors sell specialty desks designed to meet the needs of persons in wheelchairs. Mobility difficulties related to manipulating a personal computer are quite varied. Keyboards and other input devices can be difficult to manipulate. Alternative input devices include modified keyboards, miniature keyboards, alternative layout keyboards, touch screens, ability switches, headpointers, mouthsticks, trackballs, joysticks, and braille writers (Wilson, 1996; Bragman, 1987; Applin, 1999), many of which are available from IntelliTools, Inc.

Visual and hearing difficulties also vary. For some individuals, magnification of the display is sufficient accommodation for a visual disability. A number of software packages magnify the display on an individual computer monitor, including ZoomText (Ai Squared) and MAGic (Henter-Joyce). Alternatively, an oversized monitor may be sufficient. For other individuals, alternative output is required. Alternative output options include braille writers and speech synthesizers (Wilson, 1996), such as the JAWS screen reader (Henter-Joyce). Individuals with hearing impairments may find a portable assistive listening system such as the Easy Listener FM Wireless Hearing Assistance System (Phonic Ear) helpful. Which assistive technology or set of assistive technologies is appropriate in a given situation will depend greatly on the extent of the visual or hearing disability and the individual's skills in using the alternative output device.

Because the needed accommodations for disabilities can vary greatly from one individual to another, sensitivity to the individual needs of instructors and learners with disabilities is paramount. Library staff should receive training on the needs of individuals with disabilities so that they are comfortable working with the individuals (Applin, 1999: 140). In addition, staff should receive training in using the assistive technologies, preparing instructional content, and understanding legal obligations (Deines-Jones, 1999: 147).

If you have difficulty locating the assistive technology needed for your classroom, use the ABLEDATA Web site (*www.abledata.com*). ABLEDATA is a national clearinghouse and through the Web site you can search a database of more than 18,000 currently available assistive technology products. Information about disabilities and accessibility is also available from the National Rehabilitation Information Center (*www.naric.com*) and the Disability and Business Technical Assistance Center (*www.adata.org*).

ERGONOMICS

Ergonomics are somewhat tricky to address in an electronic classroom. Ergonomic guidelines are usually written for individual workstations used repeatedly by the same person; however, in the electronic classroom, the instructor and student workstations will be used by multiple people during any given day. As such, the best approach to considering ergonomics in an electronic classroom is to offer flexibility in workspace configuration. In particular, students and instructors should be able to adjust the height of their chairs comfortably and have sufficient space to use the keyboard, mouse, and resource materials comfortably.

High-quality furnishing vendors should be able to provide information about which ergonomic guidelines their products are designed to meet. Some furnishings are designed according to the principle of "enforced ergonomics"—in other words, the design of the furniture encourages people to use them in an ergonomically sound manner. Ask your vendor to discuss what ergonomic testing was done in developing the furnishings you are considering.

Michael Weisberg addresses group learning environments in "Ergonomic Guidelines for Designing Effective and Healthy Learning Environments for Interactive Technologies" (1993). Many of Weisberg's recommendations are discussed elsewhere in this chapter (for example, power supply, wire management, air conditioning, and projection systems). He raises one particularly troublesome concern in group learning environments, however the radiation emitted from traditional computer monitors, particularly from the backs and sides of the monitors. Like Wiseberg, Carol Wright and Linda Friend recommend that library staff "arrange group workstations so that users are at least four feet from the sides or back of adjacent monitors" (1992: 18). A U-Shaped (Out) classroom layout with a generous amount of space between each student workstation can meet this criterion as well as respond to Weisberg's recommendation that the learning environment include other types of furniture for noncomputing activities.

Librarians who use the instructor workstation in a particular classroom on a regular basis may be able to identify particular ergonomic issues that effect their teaching. If your institution has a safety or wellness office, the staff in that office may be willing to talk with the library instructors about ways to quickly adjust the instructor workstation between instruction sessions. *Zap! How Your Computer Can Hurt You—And What You Can Do About It* (Sellers, 1994) provides a very readable and balanced explanation of health issues and options to consider in using computer workstations.

AUDIENCE RESPONSE SYSTEM

For classrooms spaces that are too small to accommodate a hands-on design, audience response systems can provide a mechanism for engaging students in active learning, even without hands-on computing capabilities. Through small keypads, response systems allow each individual to respond in real time to yes/no, multiple choice, and other questions. The individual responses are tallied immediately so that the instructor can determine the extent to which students understand the presented information and can decide if any concepts need further emphasis. Response systems are available from One Touch Systems, Innovision, Fleetwood, and Audience Response Systems.

MOBILE CLASSROOMS

As computing technologies become increasingly mobile and networking connectivity more stable, mobile classrooms, or classrooms on wheels, are being developed by some libraries. A descendant of the nonnetworked mobile presentation station (MacDonald, 1998), new mobile classrooms take advantage of wireless network connections to provide real-time demonstrations of information resources and library tools. The mobile demonstration classroom consists of a portable instructor workstation and a wireless network transmitter. A hands-on portable classroom consists of multiple notebook computers, network transmitters, and a specially designed cart for recharging and storing the computers (such carts are available from Spectrum or Bretford Manufacturing).

While these mobile classrooms allow librarians greater flexibility with respect to where an instruction session is presented, they also present a number of challenges. Wireless network connections or access to a network port in every classroom on campus are not yet common on most campuses and, without connectivity, instruction is limited to "canned" demonstrations. Such demonstrations are necessarily carefully scripted and do not allow the instructor to ask students for search topics that are of interest to them. Notebook computers must be carefully stowed into the portable carts so that their batteries are recharged. This requirement, as well as the time required to unpack and set up a portable hands-on classroom, may be very time-consuming. Finally, it may be physically difficult to move the carts from one building to another, especially during inclement weather. Though these challenges admittedly exist, the portable electronic classroom holds much promise for the future as networking and notebook computers develop.

DISTANCE LEARNING TECHNOLOGIES

Incorporating distance learning technologies into the library electronic classroom can be relatively simple, involving the mere addition of a Web camera to the instructor workstation, but will most likely be exceedingly complex, involving an understanding of two-way television broadcast through a variety of telecommunications systems and the installation of large pieces of equipment that require much classroom space. Webcasting, streaming audio, and streaming video add further complexity to the mix. Challenges include compatibility of equipment and broadcast systems, having sufficient technical expertise, and the expense of purchasing and upgrading equipment. Librarians who need to incorporate distance learning technologies will find the works by Philip D. Leighton and David C. Weber (2000), Denny Gilbertson and Jamie Poindexter (2000), the Video Development Initiative (2000), Randall C. Porter (1999), Lynnette R. Porter (1997), Russ A. Hart and Roger Parker (1996), and Ann Pederson (1995) helpful in beginning to understand the issues involved before consulting with the distance education professionals at their institutions.

ACCOMMODATING PRINT MATERIALS

Before leaving the design phase, a word about print materials is in order. In addition to accommodating the demands of electronic equipment, the electronic classroom must enable instructors and students to work with printed materials. For the foreseeable future, research is a process that requires integrating both print and electronic resources. Minimally, students need a place to put handouts, textbooks, and notes. In selecting computer furniture and developing a classroom arrangement, remember to include sufficient allowance of space for these print materials.

WRAP-UP

As you wrap–up the design phase and prepare for construction, take at least a few minutes to examine the final design document and "walk through" some sample scenarios involving common activities during instruction (helping a student individually, turning lights on/off, presenting information in lecture, students walking into the room and settling in). Are they how you imagined them? Double-check details—especially those related to space and infrastructure. New equipment and software can usually be acquired in the future but most institutions will be loathe to remodel recently built space because of a lack of conduit, insufficient electricity, or inadequate soundproofing.

Chapter Eight

Budgets and Expenditures

Electronic classrooms, hands-on and demonstration, are expensive to build and support. Expenditures for construction, software, equipment, furnishings, technical support, and professional development for library instructors quickly mount up. The bottom line is that the classroom will cost a great deal of money. The other bottom line is that not having a classroom, and not teaching information literacy skills, is also very expensive in terms of student and librarian frustration, wasted research time, and ineffective use of technological resources. The planning team must carefully consider the budget for the electronic classroom but should also be prepared to explain the value of the expenditures.

WHAT WILL THIS COST?

Most electronic classrooms seem to require an initial budget of approximately $50,000 to $100,000, though this figure will increase significantly if extensive space remodeling or equipment expenditures are required. Initial budgets for electronic classrooms are reported in a number of publications. For example, Keith Arlitsch reports expenditures of $110,483 to remodel and equip two library classrooms with a combined total of 27 student workstations (1998: 208). Dorothy A. Warner, John Buschman, and Robert J. Lackie were fortunate to receive grant funding for over 85 percent of the $56,100 spent on their classroom (1999: 540). The equipment and furniture for a 30–workstation classroom totaled $28,502 according to Donna Lehman and Charlene Loope (1998: 129). Stuart Glogoff details the costs of equipment, furniture, and accessories for two classrooms as $44,758 and $44,758, with each classroom having 12 computers and 28 chairs (1995: 9–10). John Vasi and Cheryl LaGuardia total the major costs for their classroom at $106,700, which included room rehabilitation, network installation, equipment, and furniture (1994: 84). Though these amounts are wide ranging because of the specific circumstances at each institution, they do demonstrate that electronic classrooms require a significant initial budget.

Much depends though on the equipment, software, and furnishings that you select and the extent of the remodeling that is required. Daniel Niemeyer (2000: Online) estimates that a "plug and show computer presentation classroom"—akin to a demonstration classroom but requiring the instructor to bring in a laptop computer—requires $15,000 in capital expenditures and $13,000 for renovation. He also estimates that a hands-on computer classroom to accommodate 24 students requires $110,000 in capital expenditures and $40,000 for renovation. You may even find that the statement "the average e-classroom installation costs $175K to $300K" (Coppola and Thomas, 2000: 31) is more accurate for your design.

Beyond the initial budget, it is worth remembering that the electronic classroom will require an ongoing budget. The ongoing expenses, discussed in detail in Chapter Ten, include the costs of repairing and replacing equipment, refurbishing, and staff time.

PREPARE YOUR BUDGET

In most circumstances, the planning team will have some notion of how much money is available for the electronic classroom project. Either consciously or unconsciously, that notion will have guided members of the team during the design process. In some cases, a specific budget and a maximum level of expenditure will already be imposed on the project. However, in some cases, the planning team will be tasked with determining the budget based on the preferred design and defending that budget to library and campus administrators.

Regardless of whether a budget has been set, but particularly if the planning team is to establish the costs of the preferred design, it is important to prepare a detailed initial budget after making your design decisions. You may be surprised by how expensive or inexpensive some component of the classroom design is. Return to the design decisions that the planning team made with respect to classroom space, infrastructure, software, equipment, and furnishings, and determine the estimated costs. The hope is that sufficient resources exist to construct the classroom according to the preferred design. Even better, of course, will be a situation in which the allocated funds exceed the basic design and the planning team can upgrade some of the classroom elements. Unfortu-

Figure 8.1: Example Initial Planning Budget

ITEM AND DESCRIPTION	ITEM COST	QUANTITY	TOTAL
Equipment			
Instructor Station (Manual Screen, Ceiling-Mounted Projector, VCR, Overhead Projector and Computer)	$15,000.00	1	$15,000.00
Student Workstation – Desktop	$2,000.00	12	$24,000.00
Student Workstation – Laptop	$2,700.00	4	$10,800.00
Laser Printer	$1,400.00	1	$1,400.00
Telephone	Included in the Telecommunications Budget.		
Software			
Software for Library Databases and CD-ROM Products	Included in Library's license agreements.		
Standard St. Thomas Productivity Suite and Internet Software	Provided by Computing and Communication Services.		
Control/Collaboration Software	Purchase postponed until a need is established.		
Furnishings			
Desk – Instructor Station	$1,800.00	1	$1,800.00
Desk – Computer Tables (2 ½' x 4')	$294.95	16	$4,719.20
Desk – Center Worktables (3' x 7') – *Designed by Spectrum*	$194.45	4	$777.80
Chair – Student	$200.00	32	$6,400.00
Chair – Instructor	$200.00	1	$200.00
Whiteboard	$464.95	1	$464.95
Storage Cabinet	$499.95	1	$499.95
Bookcases	$129.95	2	$259.90
		TOTAL	$66,321.80

nately, in many cases, the available resources will not be sufficient. If the resources are not sufficient, then additional funds must be acquired or the design revised.

Figure 8.1 is an example of an initial planning budget. The budget is the one created for the classroom represented in Figure 4.3. Because the classroom was part of a new building, expenditures for construction and infrastructure were not budgeted separately.

GRANTS AND EXTERNAL FUNDING

If the library's budget is not sufficient to fund the development of an electronic classroom, grants and external funding sources may be available. While you may be able to locate a grant source sufficient to fund the entire project, consider dividing the project into parts and writing targeted grants. For example, perhaps the funding for equipment can be acquired through a federal grant, the furniture through a local interior design company, and construction through the library's budget.

According to David G. Bauer, "the best strategy is to approach the federal grants area first" (1999: 71) because the United States government is the largest grantor in the world. Grants relevant to electronic classrooms are offered by state library systems under the *Library Services and Technology Act* (20 U.S.C. §§ 9121–9123), as well as by the Institute for Museum and Library Services (*www.imls.gov*), the National Science Foundation (*www.nsf.gov*), and the United States Department of Education (*www.ed.gov*). In addition to looking at the Web sites for the specific agencies, you should also check the "Catalog of Federal Domestic Assistance" (*www.cfda.gov*) for grant opportunities.

Private foundations, such as the W. M. Keck Foundation (*www.wmkeck.org*), your college/university foundation, and local companies may also have grant programs that could fund an electronic classroom project. The Bill and Melinda Gates Foundation (*www.gatesfoundation.org*) has provided grants to a number of libraries and educational institutions to design and equip computer classrooms, particularly in the Pacific Northwest. To identify local companies that might fund an electronic classroom, investigate which companies are the area's largest employers, have their headquarters in the community, or might take a particular interest in teaching, learning, and technology. These companies are most likely to be interested in investing grant funds in your library. Remember too that not all gifts need be monetary. For example, perhaps your community has an office supplies distribution center that would donate the whiteboards for the classroom.

If the planning team will be seeking grant funding for an electronic classroom, be sure to consult with your campus grants office and refers to *The "How To" Grants Manual* (Bauer, 1999), which includes directions for creating a proposal development workbook. The institutional grants office can provide you with basic institutional information to include in an application and may already know which local agencies or companies might be approached to fund your project.

IMPACT OF BUDGET LIMITATIONS

If the total proposed budget is beyond the scope of allowed expenditures and if grant funds are not available, the planning team must revisit the design decisions and consider alternatives. After making alternative selections, the planning team should do an impact analysis to determine the effect of the alternative design on the eventual effectiveness and efficiency of the classroom. G. Kent Stewart states that:

> Consensus of opinion among many design professionals and education executives suggests that budget inadequacies often adversely affect interior space, finishes, and furnishings. This includes size of instructional rooms and environmental components—acoustics, lighting, color, temperature (including humidity) and moveable and built-in equipment and furnishings (1993: 19).

Though Stewart is referring to elementary and secondary settings, the potential impacts are the same in other settings as well. The purpose of an impact analysis is two-fold: to advocate for additional funding and to minimize the negative impacts of budget limitations through planned deferrals. If you must defer some expenditures, select items that can be easily added at a later date—equipment, software, furnishings, and artwork. Do not compromise location, size, or infrastructure systems, such as the data network, electricity, lighting, or heating, ventilation, and air conditioning—these elements are not easy to alter and are also very expensive to address at a later date. It is much easier to overcome the limitations of equipment and furnishings, for example, during an instruction session than to work around the physical confines of a classroom that is too small, too hot, or without adequate electricity.

PHASED IMPLEMENTATION

You might also consider establishing a plan for phased implementation. With a demonstration classroom, this might mean setting up a minimal instructor workstation, adding equipment each budget cycle for a number of years until the workstation is complete, and then beginning the process of replacing pieces of equipment on a regular basis so the workstation is upgraded regularly. For a hands-on classroom, phased implementation might entail designing and furnishing the classroom for a hands-on arrangement but then only installing an instructor workstation for the first year, and maybe a limited number of student workstations. During the budget cycles that follow, student workstations could be added until the desired number is attained. Regardless of the approach selected, the planning team should carefully weigh the impact of the decisions on the success of the classroom.

Chapter Nine

Construction and Occupancy

As design decisions get set in concrete (perhaps very literally!), it is both inspiring and perhaps a little nerve-wracking to see the space develop. The construction and occupancy phase of building an electronic classroom is perhaps the most exciting as well as the most stressful. Exciting as the design manifests itself in the physical materials and the ideas that were just lines on paper come to life. Stressful, though, as one discovers mistakes that were made during planning and design, thinks of ways that a particular need could have been better met, or finds out that construction delays meant that the projected completion date is only days before the planned open house for the campus! Enjoy the excitement—celebrate the progress and development of the construction. As for the stress, recognize that it will be there, handle any problem situations promptly and professionally, and know that you are not alone in experiencing construction-related stress and worry. In the end, it will be worth it!

AN ARCHITECT AND/OR A PROJECT MANAGER

A series of architectural drawings and other documents are necessary to provide the data that a contractor will need to construct your classroom. Producing such documents requires a high level of technical and architectural understanding as well as knowledge about how physical structures, electrical systems, data networks, and heating, ventilation, and air conditioning systems interact with and affect one another. This knowledge is not something that a layperson can muddle through easily without the potential for grave error. It is best to employ the services of a competent professional.

Hopefully your institution has a staff member in facilities planning or a similar administrative office who has the skills and knowledge necessary to produce the construction documents for you, particularly since building an electronic classroom is usually a fairly small construction project. Additionally, if you are able to work with an architect from your institution, the library may not have to pay for the services. If your institution does not have a staff member who can develop these plans for you, you will need to find out how the campus acquires architectural drawings for projects; you will probably end up hiring an architect. If you need to hire an architect, Richard McCarthy provides excellent advice and guidance in "Chapter 12: Finding, Selecting and Hiring an Architect" in his book *Designing Better Libraries* (1999).

Whether you have an architect from your institution or an architectural consultant, you will also need a project manager from your institution to oversee the construction project. The project manager is responsible for tracking the progress of construction, investigating concerns, and managing communication flow between the planning team, the library, and the contractor. The project manager may or may not be the professional who produces the construction documents.

DRAWINGS AND SCHEDULES

Constructing a classroom requires numerous drawings and other documents. Depending on how early in the design process an architect is involved, you may or may not have professional schematic drawings. Schematic drawings show proposed floor layouts and other general design elements (for example, the classroom layouts in Chapter Four) but they do not include specific details and may not even be drawn to scale. Schematic drawings give a sense of what the space might be like and allow you to try out various approaches without being concerned with the specifics of design and layout. In most projects, the planning team will have created multiple schematic drawings in the process of discussing various room layout options and will have already selected a specific layout before beginning to work with an architect.

Construction Drawings

The drawings to be created by the architect for most classroom projects are the construction drawings. These drawings cover architectural, structural, mechanical, and electrical components (McCarthy, 1999: 48). In addition to general plans, section plans are also needed. Section plans detail any "architectural feature that needs such careful illustration in order to ensure that the required soundness and appearance will be incorporated into the building" (Leighton and Weber, 2000: 609). In an electronic classroom, the instructor workstation is likely to require such a section drawing because of its complexity, particularly if a control panel is used to manage the interconnectedness of media display equipment, lighting, and projection. Other examples of potentially useful section plans include the details of conduit and wiring plans or any custom fixtures to be fabricated for the room.

Members of the planning team should carefully review the construction drawings, particularly if multiple drafts are produced. It may be helpful to ask for a key to the architectural symbols used in the drawings. Even though the drawings are highly technical in nature, patience, experience, and a little bit of training will go a long way in helping you develop your ability to read such drawings. Be certain to ask questions if you do not understand the relationship between the construction drawings and the decisions made by the planning team during the design phase. Even with the most careful architect, details may be mistakenly omitted or a design specification changed accidentally during the process of drafting the documents.

Clarification and Shop Drawings

During construction the architect may also provide clarification drawings, which "enlarge and clarify sections of the original drawings so that the parts in question may be manufactured and installed" (Leighton and Weber, 2000: 615) as intended. Clarification drawings are provided to the contractor. In comparison, shop drawings are provided by the contractor to the project manager. Shop drawings are prepared by manufacturers or equipment suppliers and detail the features of special equipment or furnishings to be fabricated for the classroom. The project manager and/or architect should approve shop drawings before the equipment or furnishings are fabricated and installed (Leighton and Weber, 2000: 844). Members of the planning team are not likely to have the opportunity to review clarification and shop drawings unless they specifically ask to do so since these drawings are produced during construction. If you wish to see these drawings, ask the project manager if it is possible.

Schedules

In addition to providing drawings, the architect will also likely produce a series of schedules. Schedules are detailed written directions that annotate and further explain elements of the construction drawings. Of primary concern in the electronic classroom will be schedules related to hardware, furniture, finishes, painting, mechanical systems, and wiring. Taken together, "the drawings and the schedules explain and illustrate the size, shape, finish, and relationship of all the spaces, walls, and materials" (Leighton and Weber, 2000: 611). Though schedules can include a great deal of technical information, they are worth reviewing to double-check, for example, that all woodwork in the room will be stained the same color.

BIDDING

The bidding process will greatly affect the outcome of your classroom construction project but it is, for the most part, likely to be outside of the library's control. Bidding is affected by laws and regulations, union rules, and institutional guidelines. The process of bidding involves soliciting contractors to submit bids on the project, receiving bids, analyzing the submissions, and selecting a bid.

The packet that is sent out to contractors usually includes an invitation to bid, a description of the work to be done—a "scope of work" statement, instructions to bidders, copies of construction drawings and schedules, specifications of the quality of materials and workmanship, timelines, the process for submitting questions, and procedures for selecting a winning bid. Many of the bid packet components can be developed using standard forms available from the American Institute of Architects Contract Documents Program (*www.aiaaccess.com*). In all likelihood, the facilities management office or budgets and contracts office at your institution has a standard procedure for preparing and managing the bidding process.

Pre–bid Meeting

In most cases, contractors will have an opportunity to attend a pre–bid meeting about the construction project a few weeks before the deadline for bid submissions. At the pre–bid meeting, the project is explained and contractors have the opportunity to ask questions. The project manager/architect should take minutes and record attendance. Minutes as well as any changes to the construction documents should be distributed to all potential bidders (McCarthy, 1999: 55).

Reviewing Proposals and Awarding the Bid

When the bids have been received and opened, they must be examined for completeness and accuracy. In general, the lowest bidder will be awarded the contract, provided that the bid is accurate, complete, and within the general range of the project budget. If no bids are within the project budget, then either additional budget funds must be obtained or the construction drawings and specifications must be reworked and the project re–bid. In such a case, expect approximately a one or two month delay in your projected project timeline.

In awarding the contract, some negotiations may occur; however, a contractor may be willing to begin construction if a letter of intent is issued. A letter of intent indicates the conditions under which the institution intends to award the contract (Leighton and Weber, 2000: 621). If the contractor will be using subcontractors to complete some of the construction work, negotiations may be particularly important to ensure that the subcontractors are acceptable to the project manager/architect.

BUILDING

The first step in the actual construction is the preconstruction meeting. At the preconstruction meeting, all of the people involved should be introduced and their responsibilities outlined. The contractor should also receive a formal notice to commence work. Conditions of the contract, payments provisions, and the project schedule should be discussed, as well as a schedule for project construction meetings. In addition, any topics of particular concern to the library (such as, dust and noise abatement) and other miscellaneous topics (for example, an invitation to construction staff to use the library's staff lounge) should also be discussed (McCarthy, 1999: 61–62).

As building or remodeling begins, the projected date of completion will likely be at the forefront of concerns expressed by the librarians. The project timeline finalized during the preconstruction meeting is a relatively good indicator of the time frame involved; however, unforeseen difficulties can arise. In general, it is best to assume that construction will take at least 15 percent longer than planned (Rohlf, 1986: 103) and best not to count on using the classroom the day after its predicted completion. If you are planning an open house or tours, schedule them far enough beyond the projected completion date so that, if delays occur, the events will not have to be rescheduled.

Change Orders

At some point it is likely that an element of the original design will need to be changed—perhaps to accommodate standards or guidelines, as a result of a mistake in the construction drawings, or because of a misunderstanding in the negotiating process. To deviate from the established contract, a change order must be negotiated and agreed upon. For example, if, after the contract was awarded, the project manager discovered that the networked print station did not have a data network connection, a change order could be negotiated to add the necessary conduit and cabling to accommodate the needed network port. Likewise, if the wrong color stain had been specified for the baseboard, a change order could be negotiated. Change orders may be used not only to correct errors but also to reinstate components omitted because of budget constraints. For example, perhaps the original plans only included conduit for student workstations but not wiring, because funds were not available to purchase the computers. If the library were to receive a grant for the computers, a change order to install wiring could be negotiated.

Because a change order usually results in some additional cost to the library, it must be very clear who has the authority to negotiate a change order and whether budgetary limitations will allow such additional expenses. Clearly designating who has authority in this area will limit confusion on the part of both the contractor and the planning team. If changes are necessary, it is better to fund the needed change orders, since it will be more costly to remodel the affected area after construction is complete. However, if the changes are outside the scope of the current budget, note the needed items or alterations so that they can be attended to at a later date. (Leighton and Weber, 2000: 627–629).

Inspections

The project manager should regularly inspect both the drawings that are being used to construct the classroom and the construction itself. If there have been multiple drafts of the construction drawings, it could be all too easy for a superceded version to make its way into the construction area and a worker to follow its directions accidentally. Inspections are also likely to reveal whether change orders are needed.

Walking around, observing, taking notes, and asking others to share things that they notice are low-key ways to keep abreast of construction developments and potentially head off egregious errors in the construction process. However, if lines of communication are not clearly established and followed, confusion can occur. Members of the planning team should ask questions or make suggestions through the project manager rather than discussing them with the contractor directly.

Once the classroom is declared ready to occupy, a punch list will be prepared. The punch list is compiled by the project manager/architect and identifies incomplete or otherwise unacceptable items (McCarthy, 1999: 67). Members of the planning team and other library staff should submit any items for the punch list to the project manager/architect for consideration. Items on a punch list might include the following: remove paint from stereo speakers, repair scratch on west wall, install lock on front door, install blinds on north windows, stain chair railing, and secure carpeting to floor near print station. Be certain to check that the items on the punch list are completed before final payment is made to the contractor.

A final set of inspections by local building officials and/or campus inspectors may also be required before the classroom can be used.

MOVING IN

Even after the construction is completed, an electronic classroom may require a substantial move-in period. Furniture must be put together and arranged. Computer technicians and network administrators will have to install and test electronic equipment and software. Keys must be duplicated and distributed. Finally, the classroom manager will need to be trained in using and troubleshooting the equipment, as will the librarians who will teach in the room.

If possible, save any extra paint, carpet tiles, or fabric that remains, particularly if the materials were custom-produced for the classroom. These items can be very useful if any materials in the classroom are damaged and need to be replaced. Also acquire a copy of the as-built drawings for your classroom. These drawings represent the actual construction of the classroom rather than the planned construction and will be important for any future renovations, either of the classroom itself or adjacent spaces.

Part Three

Day-To-Day Operations

A building is not something you finish.
A building is something you start.
Stewart Brand (1994: 188)

The day-to-day operations of classroom administration, teaching, and evaluation will in large part determine the ongoing success of your electronic classroom. A well-supported and well-managed classroom can be an oasis for teaching and learning, a joy to teach in, and a comfortable environment in which to learn. The goal is an atmosphere that is conducive to good teaching and to student skill development, knowledge acquisition, and reflection.

Library instructors should be able to predict with confidence that the resources and equipment they need will be available and fully functioning, and know that any problems will be attended to promptly. The classroom should be clean and neat. Instructors should receive adequate training in the technology and in how to teach with technology, as well as opportunities for continued learning and development.

Learners should perceive the classroom as inviting and comfortable, but the atmosphere should also communicate the importance of the instruction they will receive.

The challenge for the classroom administrator is to organize day-to-day operations in such a way that the desired classroom environment is created. Many details must be considered but the classroom administrator must also be able to look beyond the specifics of any particular issue or problem and plan for long-term maintenance and upgrading.

Chapter Ten

Classroom Administration

Managing an electronic classroom in a library is a complex assignment. Personnel, policies, procedures, scheduling, reporting, finances, and ongoing maintenance and upgrading must all be addressed. At the same time the classroom must be available for its main purpose—teaching and learning—to the greatest extent possible.

PERSONNEL

An electronic classroom involves a great number of people. First, there are the instructors and the learners. Librarians who teach in the classroom will have views about how best to manage the space and accommodate their teaching needs. These librarians are also likely to effect changes in room design and layout over time through use. For example, if there is not sufficient space to accommodate instructional materials, someone is likely to bring an extra table into the classroom and place it near the instructor workstation. Students will likely also have views on classroom accessibility and use. These views may or may not be consistent with the views of the library staff.

Next, there are the professionals who support and maintain the classroom, including network administrators, computer technicians, telecommunication experts, and facilities operations workers. Primarily charged with ensuring the continued operation of the equipment and facility, these professionals may suggest actions that seem incompatible with the overall teaching and learning purpose of the room but are necessary to provide for the ongoing operation of the classroom. For example, if a virus is propogating through the library's network, the technical support staff may require that all computers in the classroom be shut off so that they are not affected, even though an instruction session is about to begin. In reality, the teaching and learning purpose of the classroom is being protected—it would be far more disruptive to have all of the classroom computers incapacitated for a week—but in the short term the library instructor will likely feel frustrated.

If the classroom is also to be used as an open computing laboratory, consider who will supervise the classroom at those times. If the classroom is in close proximity to the reference or circulation desk, the desk staff may be able to monitor use; however, this arrangement may not be desirable even if it is possible. In all likelihood, students using the classroom for open computing will have a number of questions related to word processing, printing, saving and deleting files, and the like. If the reference or circulation staff are answering these questions, service at the reference or circulation desk may suffer, depending on patron demands. Additional staffing at the reference or circulation desk may then be needed. As such, perhaps a better approach is to hire additional staff. At an academic institution, the least expensive option is to hire student assistants to check people in and out of the room and provide general assistance. However, even in this scenario, a library staff member will have to hire, train, and supervise the student workers, as well as answer questions that are beyond the expertise and training of the student assistants.

Finally, then, there is the classroom administrator. In most cases, this will either be the instruction coordinator, the library administrator over public services, or a classroom committee. If a committee is charged with this oversight, the chair or a member of the committee will likely become the de facto classroom administrator, as it will be difficult to have committee meetings each time a decision must be made about some aspect of the classroom; the committee will focus instead on long-term planning. The classroom administrator is charged with balancing requests of the individuals involved, while attending to the instructional purposes of the room as well as the technical support requirements for ongoing operations. The classroom administrator will likely make a number of decisions every week related to the classroom—mostly about small issues and details but sometimes about larger and more consequential items—and some of these decisions may even involve considerations of library politics and culture.

ONGOING AND ANCILLARY EXPENDITURES

Electronic classrooms are expensive, period. A classroom is likely to be one of the largest budget items for an instruction program. In addition to the initial expense, which is considerable, an electronic classroom requires an ongoing budget. If an electronic classroom is not maintained and upgraded, its usability and effectiveness as a teaching and learning environment will decrease over time. Software upgrades, equipment replacement, supplies, and maintenance can add up to a significant expenditure on an annual basis. Glogoff recommends that libraries budget at least $2,000 each year for room supplies as well as allowing for the potential expense of computer maintenance (1995: 12). In addition to $4,000 annually for parts, supplies, and staffing for a "plug and show" classroom, and $19,000 annually for a computer classroom, Niemeyer (2000: Online) states that a "fund of approximately 10% of the value of the classroom hardware is needed each year for equipment renewal and replacement." Though $19,000 seems a bit high as an annual estimate, there is no doubt that ongoing expenses can be significant. In addition to upgrades and maintenance, on average, you should expect to replace the computers in the classroom every three years.

Once the classroom is built and equipped, additional library materials will be required to support teaching and learning in the electronic classroom. For example, each library classroom at Illinois State University contains at least two sets of the *Library of Congress Subject Headings*, copies of the *Statistical Abstract of the United States*, and multiple examples of popular, trade, and scholarly periodicals. The particular items that you need will depend on the content of your instruction programs. A budget for duplicating handouts, worksheets, and other instructional materials will also be required. If the classroom is used for open computing, some basic computer and software manuals, as well as a dictionary and copies of the citation style manuals, may also be useful to have on hand. Though a relatively small expenditure compared to the expense of constructing a classroom, funds must be found to provide these materials if instruction is to be effective.

Finally, training and support for the staff members who teach in and maintain the classroom may also require additional funds. The specific expenditures will depend heavily on whether staff members with appropriate skills and knowledge are already employed by the library or institution, or whether additional staff or outside consultants will need to be hired to provide the necessary training. However, even if the current staff members who will have the added responsibilities of teaching in or supporting the classroom have appropriate baseline skills, professional development opportunities should be made available so that their existing skills can be upgraded and new skills acquired. Again, the expense of doing so will vary depending on whether staff are already available to provide this training and development or whether it will require new staff or payment to outside agencies.

MAINTAINING, REFURBISHING, AND UPGRADING

The task of coordinating the maintenance, refurbishing, and upgrading of electronic classrooms encompasses a wide variety of components, from the minor and mundane to the extraordinary. The classroom administrator must be vigilant about monitoring the state of the classroom and specifing needed funds in annual budget requests.

At a basic level, classroom maintenance involves regular cleaning (such as, vacuuming, cleaning the whiteboards, and wiping fingerprints off the monitors) as well as occasional deep cleaning (such as, washing the carpets, blowing dust out of the electronic equipment, and cleaning the keyboards and mouses). Basic maintenance will preserve the aesthetic qualities of the classroom as well as help prevent a need for early refurbishing. However, even with careful maintenance, an electronic classroom will need refurbishing after a few years. Minimally, window coverings will need to be replaced, broken chairs and tables repaired, and walls repainted. In other instances, the wear and tear on the room because of high use will necessitate new carpet and furnishings.

Technical problems will also necessitate unscheduled classroom maintenance. Instructors should be encouraged to report any technical difficulties immediately so that they can be addressed in a timely manner. If technical problems persist, be certain to let instructors who are scheduled to use the classroom know what the problems are and when they might be resolved. Leave a note with this information in the classroom at the instructor workstation as well. Though unscheduled downtime and equipment malfunctions are to be expected in any electronic classroom, clear communication will ease instructor frustration with such situations.

Upgrading an electronic classroom is a more expansive and expensive undertaking. Software programs must be regularly updated. The demands of the software are likely eventually to require upgrading the operating systems and processing capabilities of the equipment. In general, one can expect to have to replace a computer every three to five years. The best approach to managing this issue is to establish a systematic plan for upgrades and replacements. This plan should be integrated with the library's overall technology plan and indicate how often software and equipment will be upgraded, when, and by whom.

An inventory of classroom furnishings, equipment, and software is necessary to manage electronic classroom upgrading. The inventory

Figure 10.1: Classroom Inventory Chart

Control Number	Item	Date Purchased

should itemize all components of the classroom and, for each component, include relevant details, including any institutional property control numbers. For example, a classroom may have two printers, purchased in 1999, under warranty through 2002, and assigned property control numbers 1999–100–76 and 1999–100–132. The inventory should be updated regularly to reflect any changes in the classroom.

Figure 10.1 is a reproducible Classroom Inventory Chart that can be used to track the furnishings, equipment, and software in your electronic classroom. The chart can also be downloaded from this book's Web site at *www.neal-schuman.com/eclassroom.html.*

POLICIES AND PROCEDURES

Classroom policies and procedures are needed to determine who can use the classroom for what purposes, when, and under what conditions. In some cases, the conditions will be determined by the source of the funding for the room. For example, a library classroom funded by student technology fees may have to be open for general computing when it is not being used for a class. In other cases, the library will be free to determine the policies and procedures that it prefers. In addition to policies that cover room use, many libraries also have acceptable use policies that cover computer use anywhere in the library. Brittney Chenault's "Electronic Classroom Policies" (*www.moorhead.msus.edu/chenault/epolicies.htm*) Web page is a useful resource for locating policies to use as models for drafting your own.

One of the primary issues to settle in an electronic classroom policy is whether the classroom can only be used for library-related instruction or whether any groups needing access to an electronic classroom facility are welcome. Though it will no doubt engender goodwill if the library offers use of its classroom to others, a clear statement of priorities will be required so that the library has access to the room for its instructional sessions. It may be that you allow others to use the classroom but that they can reserve it no more than one week in advance, allowing the librarians the opportunity to schedule their classes first. Related to the issue of nonlibrary use is the issue of whether the classroom will be available for general open computing when not in use for a class. Once again, the potential for goodwill is quite large; however, clear statements of priorities and procedures will be required so that general users understand the need to vacate the room when it is reserved for library instruction sessions.

Figure 10.2 is the policy and procedures document for Electronic

Figure 10.2: Example Electronic Classroom Policy and Procedures

Electronic Classroom 213c
Milner Library, Illinois State University

Principles:

1. Library instruction sessions have priority over any other uses of the classroom. The only exception to this will be the weekend prior to the beginning of Fall semesters when Passages technology training is scheduled.
2. When the Computer Study Area is experiencing overflow demand, the classroom will function as an overflow computer lab with limited software availability.
3. A list of available software will be posted at the entrance to the room.

Scheduling:

1. Library faculty and staff should schedule library instruction sessions using the networked Room Scheduler. If possible, entries should be made at least two hours in advance.
2. Any other requests for room use should be referred to the Library Instruction Coordinator for consideration and resolution. The Library Instruction Coordinator will work closely with the Library Administrative Office in responding to such requests.
3. A schedule of library instruction sessions will be posted daily by the Training Team.

Overflow Procedures:

1. Overflow demand for the Computer Study Area will be determined by the Computer Study Area (CSA) Manager (or a member of the Systems Department when the CSA Manager is not available) during the day. From 4 p.m. to 11:45 p.m. the student supervisor will determine overflow demand and from 11:45 p.m. to 7:45 a.m. the overnight Graduate Assistant (or student on duty) will determine overflow demand.
2. When the CSA is experiencing overflow demand, the CSA Manager, the student supervisor, or the overnight Graduate Assistant (GA) will examine the library instruction schedule and determine if 213c would be available to function as an overflow lab for at least one hour. If no, 213c will not be opened as an overflow lab. If yes, the CSA Manager, the student supervisor, or the overnight GA will determine if a student worker is available to monitor 213c. If yes , 213c will be opened as an overflow lab. If no, 213c will not be opened as an overflow lab.
3. To open 213c as an overflow lab, the CSA Manager, the

(Figure 10.2 continued on following page)

(Figure 10.2: *continued*)

student supervisor, or the overnight GA will unlock the door to 213c, open the blinds on the windows facing the CSA, and post the sign alerting users that they must check-in at the CSA before entering 213c. The overnight GA will secure the key to unlock 213c from the student at the Circulation Desk.

4. Once opened as an overflow lab, 213c will remain open as an overflow lab for a minimum to one hour.
5. Lab Assistants will monitor the use of 213c whenever the room is opened as an overflow lab.

Procedures for Closing the Room or Vacating the Room for Instruction:

1. One hour before the start of any library instruction session, another scheduled event, or shutting down the room as overflow, the CSA Manager, the student supervisor, or the overnight GA will alert users in 213c that they will need to vacate the room in one hour.
2. The CSA Manager, the student supervisor, or the overnight GA will make similar announcements at 30 minutes prior and 15 minutes prior.
3. Any computer users in 213c who refuse to vacate the room when requested will be dealt with according to Milner Library's problem patron behavior policies and procedures.
4. At the end of the last instruction session of the day, all of the computer terminals should be shut down. Terminals will be turned on as needed for overflow.

Approved: Library Instruction Committee, Leadership Council, and Milner Library Faculty, April 1999
Revised: Milner Library Faculty, November 1999

Classroom 213c in Milner Library, Illinois State University. Electronic Classroom 213c is a hands-on classroom with 34 student workstations, a networked printer station with a swipe-card payment system, and a lockable instructor workstation with computer, document camera, video-cassette player, and access to the campus cable system. When not in use for an instructional session, the classroom can be used for open computing if the computing lab across the hall is full. During such times, the computing lab staff also monitor users in 213c. The other hands-on electronic classroom in the library is not located in a staffed area and so is not available for open computing.

Figure 10.3 is an agreement for shared use of an electronic classroom at Purdue University. The agreement clearly spells out the roles, responsibilities, and obligations of each unit, and can be found on the library's Web site at *http://thorplus.lib.purdue.edu/library_info/departments/ugrl/lec/g959.html*.

MARKETING AND PROMOTION

At many institutions, electronic classrooms are evidence of the old adage "build it and they will come." Faculty who were previously uninterested in scheduling a library instruction session for their classes will now ask for sessions. Faculty who previously scheduled one class each semester now want two or three. Groups of students (for example, the sociology club) seek out opportunities to develop their skills further. In many cases, this interest is due to the technological tools and not because of a sudden interest in enhancing conceptual understanding or developing information literacy competence. Regardless, though, such interest provides librarians with the opportunity to reach students who were previously underserved by the library's instructional programs.

Recognizing that electronic classrooms generate student and faculty interest, librarians can use a new electronic classroom as a way to market and promote the library's instructional programs. For example, when the University of Arizona Library built two Electronic Library Education Centers, staff held a dedication and ribbon cutting ceremony during parent's weekend. Parents and university officials visited the classroom and were given assistance in using the computers (Glogoff, 1995: 9).

Hosting a grand opening of the classroom facility to which campus faculty and staff are invited, including the classroom on library tours for new students, and providing information about the classroom on the library's Web site and in library publications are just a few strategies for alerting people not only to the existence of the classroom but also to the instructional sessions that take place in it. In a very short time, you could find that due to instructional demand, you need to start planning for the library's next electronic classroom.

Figure 10.4 is a copy of the Frequently Asked Questions Web page (*http://nursing.cua.edu/resources/donl-faq.cfm*) for the Conley Center computer classroom at Catholic University of America's School of Nursing. This Web page is an example of a relatively easy way to promote an electronic classroom while also providing important information to users. In addition to posting this information on the Web, the same information can be provided in a handout.

Figure 10.3: Example Shared Use Agreement

The Libraries' Electronic Classroom UGRL, HIKS G959

Agreement for Use
Purdue University Libraries/Management Information

mission I design I scheduling I maintenance I use

The Libraries Electronic Classroom (LEC), G-959, is located in the Undergraduate Library (UGRL, HIKS) and provides a location for teaching both students and staff. The classroom is equipped for demonstration of, and hands-on experience with many electronic systems. This agreement covers the exclusive use of G959 by the Libraries, and Management Information and will be in effect for three years.

Mission/Policy
This agreement outlines how the Libraries and Management Information will use the Libraries Electronic Classroom, UGRL G-959 for instruction of students and staff.

The final policy has been developed jointly by the Libraries and Management Information to provide a working agreement appropriate for the needs of both organizations.

Facilities Design
It is understood that Management Information will provide 22 PC computers for students and instructors, a server to be used exclusively for support of this room and housed in G64 STEW, a printer, and all related software as specified in The Equipment Proposal for the Hicks Undergraduate Library Training Room. The Libraries will provide and maintain the furniture and chairs, Sharp projector, video visualizer, VCR, and flip chart. Any future changes in the facilities design will be discussed jointly during the life of this agreement.

All equipment will remain in the room.

Scheduling
The Libraries Electronic Classroom will be available for classes during the hours of operation of the Undergraduate Library. Scheduling will be handled by Undergraduate Library Reference (46734) between 8 a.m. - 5 p.m. Monday-Friday. A minimum of 8 hours a week during the semester will be available for Management

(Figure 10.3: *continued*)

Information to schedule classes. During summer, vacations, and breaks the proportion of time available to MI will be increased. The Libraries will allocate specific times for credit courses (ex. GS 175) taught by librarians, and then identify specific hours for Management Information classes a semester in advance (by July 1 for Fall semester, by November 1 for Spring semester, and by April 1 for Summer session). Management Information will provide a list of individuals authorized to schedule this facility. All equipment and software to be used for a class must be identified at the time the classroom is reserved. An UGRL Reference Assistant will forward information about any needed software changes to the Information Technology Department (ITD).

The Libraries Electronic Classroom can be made available for additional training during times outside of the normal 8:00 a. m. and 5:00 p.m. employee work schedule and on weekends. This additional time is made available, provided the scheduled times are during the normal operating hours of the Hicks Undergraduate Library. Prior arrangements for the use of these times must be made at least three weeks in advance of the use of the Libraries Electronic Classroom.

It is understood that support (ITD and UGRL Library) staff is only available Monday-Friday from 8 a.m. - 5 p.m. However, by scheduling in advance and by communicating specific software and support needs at that time, accommodations to have needed services or support available at other times may be possible.

To accommodate maximum use of the facility, cancellations should be communicated to UGRL Reference as soon as possible. This released time will then be available for scheduling on a first come, first served basis by either organization.

Maintenance
The Libraries Information Technology Department (ITD) will keep an accurate log of all installations, set-up changes, and software removals on the classroom equipment. Each organization will define what their standard software configuration in the classroom needs to be. This mutually agreed upon list of standard software including specific versions will be maintained along with a copy of this agreement.

Any configurations, and/or software changes including installation and removal of software on even a temporary basis on either instructor or student stations must be approved and done by ITD

(Figure 10.3 continued on following page)

(Figure 10.3: *continued*)

staff. Management Information will designate a computer specialist to assist ITD in first time installation and testing of any software used exclusively by Management Information. Each organization supplying software (either standard software for the classroom or specially installed for an individual instructor) w ill be responsible for maintaining proper licensing.

A minimum of 72 hour advance notice (3 working days) to UGRL Reference (49-46734) for installation of any nonstandard software or setup will be required. If needs change, instructors must notify UGRL in time that this much notice can be given to ITD. ITD will make a reasonable effort to load any nonstandard software for one time use, but cannot guarantee successful installation.

Routine maintenance and service for all equipment will be handled and paid for by the Libraries. Should specific equipment need to be replaced before the end of this agreement, responsibility will be mutually agreed upon through discussion between the Libraries and Management Information at that time.

Use of the Room
The room will be locked when not scheduled for a class. Library staff members are available to unlock the room for scheduled classes.

It is recommended that all instructors have an orientation session given by UGRL staff before using the classroom for the first time.

Due to the specialized equipment, both parties agree that this room will not be used as a general meeting or conference room.

Food and Drink / Smoking
No food or drink will be permitted in the room. There is no smoking in the Undergraduate Library building (HIKS).

Opening, Closing and Emergency Procedures

Management Information staff will be expected to follow the opening and closing procedures of the Undergraduate Library in regards to staff entering the building before opening, unlocking doors for the public, lights out, and locking door procedures at closing time. A manual is available for these procedures and for emergencies.

REQUESTING INSTRUCTION

The addition of an electronic classroom will likely herald the beginning of an increase in the number of requests librarians receive for course-related and course-integrated instruction sessions. Students may also request that class sessions be spent in "working sessions"—research time scheduled in the electronic classroom during which students work on research projects with the support and coaching of both their course instructor and a librarian. Librarians may wish to design an instruction request intake form to track and schedule requested sessions more easily. Such an intake form may be made available as a paper form and/or on the library's Web site.

See Figure 10.5 for a sample intake form designed for use in a library where one librarian receives all instruction requests and then assigns sessions to other librarians.

SCHEDULING

As an electronic classroom becomes popular, a convenient and easy-to-use scheduling system is needed. Some libraries use a printed calendar kept either by the instruction coordinator who does all of the scheduling or at the reference desk so that individual librarians can enter their own sessions. Though easy-to-use, a printed calendar located in one centralized location may not be convenient, particularly if a librarian's office is located some distance from the reference desk.

Electronic scheduling options are quite varied. A number of libraries use Microsoft Outlook Calendar (Microsoft) to create a public calendar for the classroom, and all librarians who schedule instruction sessions are given read/write privileges. Instruction sessions can be easily copied from the classroom calendar to a given librarian's personal calendar, they can also export onto a sign to be posted daily or weekly indicating when the room is scheduled and for what classes. Other software options for creating calendars include meetingmaker (Meeting Maker) and the Web site *When.com* (*www.when.com*). Some online catalog systems also include a scheduling module.

If a hands-on electronic classroom is also used as an open computing laboratory, additional signs may be needed to indicate when a class is in session, when the classroom is available for open computing, and when the classroom is closed. Depending on the procedures for computer and network maintenance, signs may be needed for when the classroom is unavailable due to upgrades or repairs. Careful placement of these signs

Figure 10.4: Example Promotional Web Site

Frequently Asked Questions about the Donley Center

When is the Donley Center open?
Fall 2000 hours are as follows:

Monday	9:00 a.m. - 9:00 p.m.
Tuesday	10:00 a.m. - 9:00 p.m.
Wednesday	9:00 a.m. - 7:00 p.m.
Thursday	9:00 a.m. - 5:30 p.m.
Friday	9:00 a.m. - 5:00 p.m.
Saturday	Closed
Sunday	1:00 - 9:00 p.m.

Changes to the schedule will be posted on the door.

When is the lab reserved for classes?
A list is posted on the door of the Donley Center.

I'm not a School of Nursing student. May I use the lab?
No. You'll need to go to the Users' Area in Leahy.

Why do I need to log on to the computers?
This is required by CUA's contract with our Internet access provider. Due to the way Windows 95 is set up, you need to log on even if you aren't going to use any Internet applications.

Why do I need a separate username and password for Windows 95? I already have an e-mail account.
Your VAX account (which is the one you use for e-mail) is not part of the campus Windows 95 network. In order to use Windows 95, you need to use your Windows 95 password.

I changed my password on the VAX. Why won't it work for Windows 95?
Your VAX password and your Windows password are verified by two different computers, and when you change your password on the VAX, it doesn't affect your Windows password. To log on to Windows 95, use your old password, then change it to match your new VAX password.

I've never used Windows at CUA before. How do I get in to the system?
If you are a new student, both a Windows and a VAX account should have been automatically created for you. Your username is normally the last two digits of your Social Security number plus your last name (e.g., John Smith, whose SSN is 000-00-0000,

(Figure 10.4: *continued*)

would have the username 00smith). For the password, use all nine digits of your SSN. If this doesn't work, you'll need to get a new password. See below.

I forgot my password. Can you look it up for me?
No. Your passwords are encrypted so no one can find out what they are. If you can't remember your password, you'll need to get a new one. Fill out a "Request for CUA Computer Resources" form, check "Request to Change my Forgotten Password" on the back, and send the form to the Computer Center in Leahy 200. Forms are available in the Computer Center and in the Donley Center.

I left my floppy disk in one of the computers. What do I do?
Any disks found in the lab will be left on the cork strip near the front door. You'll have a much better chance of getting your disk back if you put your name on it. In any case, the School of Nursing cannot be responsible for items left in the lab.

I saved a file on the hard disk and now I can't find it.
Anything you save on the hard disk can be read, altered, or erased by anyone else using that computer. If you want to keep a file, you should save it on a floppy disk or in your VAX account. When you log on to Windows, you set up your VAX account as drive M: when the system asks you for your password in the "Map drive to VMS cluster" box. If it's a valuable file, make two copies of it on two separate disks. If it's your complete dissertation, make three or more copies. Keep them in separate places.

The computer says that I have a virus. What do I do?
Computer viruses are small programs that attach themselves to other programs or to parts of disks. They are spread by sharing floppy disks or files. Viruses can alter files, erase files, reformat disks, and generally wreak havoc on your computer and disks. The computers in the Donley Center automatically scan floppy disks when you try to read information from them. If you get a message saying that your disk has a virus, type "C" to clean the file. If this doesn't work, see the lab staff. If one of your floppy disks is infected, chances are very good that the rest of your floppy disks are infected as well. You should scan all of them before you use them. Although the lab staff make every effort to ensure that the computers in the School of Nursing are operating properly and are free from viruses, the School of Nursing can assume no responsibility for damaged or lost material due to viruses or other problems arising from the use of the computers.

(Figure 10.4 continued on following page)

(Figure 10.4: *continued*)

I smell something burning. What is it?
It's probably one of the fluorescent light ballasts. Please turn off the lights and notify the lab staff immediately. (During the Summer of 1998, all the ballasts were replaced. This shouldn't happen any more.)

Why is it so hot/cold in here?
The heating and cooling systems in the lab have two settings: "too hot" and "too cold." You are welcome to adjust the air conditioners and windows.

I think I just wiped out the hard disk of the computer I was working on.
Don't panic. Tell the lab staff, who can re-install the software.

I think I just destroyed everything on my floppy disk.
Don't panic. See the lab staff, who might be able to repair the disk, or at least retrieve some of your files. If not, you can use your backup copy. You do have a backup, don't you?

No, I don't.
Now you can panic. You'll probably have to start over again. If it's a really valuable disk, there are companies that can restore data from damaged disks. Their recovery rate is fairly high, but they'll charge you even if they don't succeed. Prices start at around $100 and go up. See the lab staff for details.

where they will be seen by users is a must so that, for example, a student wanting to type a paper does not suddenly open the classroom door in the middle of an instruction session.

Figure 10.6 is a fictitious example of the class schedule sign posted daily just outside each of the electronic classrooms at Milner Library, Illinois State University. Rooms 164d and 213c are hands-on classrooms; 184 is a demonstration classroom that also serves as a staff meeting room. The signs are printed in color and the clip-art graphics make the signs more attractive visually. The daily quotation provides a subtle positive message about learning or libraries to students who use the signs to locate their instruction sessions.

Figure 10.5: Instruction Session Intake Form

Instruction Session Request Form

Classroom Instructor:

Department:

Telephone Number:

E-Mail Address:

Course Number and Title:

Number of Students:

Number of Instructors/Teaching Assistants:

Requested Day/Date/Time:

Library Classroom:

Teaching Librarian:

What will students be required to do after attending the instruction session?

How will student learning be assessed?

Figure 10.6: Room Schedule Sign

TUESDAY, JANUARY 23

ROOM 164D:

8:00 - 9:15	LILAC (COM 110-10)	JOHNSON
9:30 -11:00	FOUNDATIONS OF INQUIRY/SMITH	HINCHLIFFE
1:00 - 3:30	FOUNDATIONS OF INQUIRY/JAMES	TAYLOR
7:00 - 8:15	HISTORY 200/MILLER	KIRKE

ROOM 184:

10:00 -11:00	TRANSFER STUDENT GROUP	SHARP
11:00 -12:00	MILNER MEMOS	BATES
2:00 - 3:00	LIBRARY INSTRUCTION	HINCHLIFFE
4:00 - 5:00	RESEARCH COMMITTEE	WOODFIELD

ROOM 213C:

9:30 -11:00	LILAC (COM 110-17)	JOHNSON
12:35 - 2:00	LILAC (COM 100-28)	SHARP
4:00 - 5:00	SPECIAL EDUCATION 145/SALES	FULLER
7:00 - 8:00	LILAC (COM 110-69)	FULLER
8:00 - 9:00	LILAC (COM 110-57)	HINCHLIFFE

You must live feverishly in a library. Colleges are not going to do any good unless you are raised and live in a library every day of your life.

– Ray Douglas Bradbury

STATISTICS

Tracking room use creates important data to use in writing an annual review of library services and facilities utilization. More important, however, these statistics will serve as powerful evidence when the library seeks to construct an additional classroom to meet the demands that the existing classroom has created. Many electronic scheduling programs will either create statistical reports directly or allow room use data to be exported and then manipulated in a spreadsheet or database program. If you do not already have a scheduling program and you decide to purchase one, include usage reporting as a criteria for selecting a program.

If the instruction program includes sessions that are not taught in the electronic classroom, then it may be necessary to separate scheduling from statistical reporting. In such cases, individual librarians should send records for the instruction sessions that they teach to a staff member assigned to compile the statistics.

Figure 10.7 is a copy of the Library Instruction Data Sheet used at Milner Library, Illinois State University. The form is printed on noncarbon, reproducible paper—the teaching librarian keeps one copy and sends the other to the Library Instruction Coordinator. Information from the data sheet is then entered into a Microsoft Access database from which needed reports are produced. Statistical data are available from 1988 to the present, thereby easily facilitating examination of trends and changes in the instruction program.

OTHER INSTRUCTIONAL SPACES

Though not necessarily included in the design and construction of an electronic classroom per se, instructors will also need space, equipment, and services to design, produce, update, and store instructional materials (Guidelines for Instruction, 1996). These instructional spaces should also be managed by the classroom administrator and be accessible to all library staff members who teach in or maintain the electronic classroom. Alternatively, if the campus has a technology center that can be used by faculty and staff who are preparing instructional materials, instruction librarians may be able to use that facility to create their materials. However, storage space in the library will still be needed.

Figure 10.7: Library Instruction Data Sheet

LIBRARY INSTRUCTION DATA SHEET

MILNER LIBRARY
ILLINOIS STATE UNIVERSITY

Date: ____________________ Start/End Times: ____________________

Course Instructor or Contact Person: ______________________________

Course Title or Group Name: ____________________________________

Department: ___________ Course Number and Section: _____________

Number of Students: _____________ Location: ____________________

Librarian: _________________________ Database Number: __________

[Additional Librarian(s): ____]

[Classroom Assistant: ____]

Summarize instruction, notes, methods, handouts, etc.
or use for planning instruction.

White Copy: Library Instruction Coordinator Yellow Copy: Librarian
Line Number: __________ Date Entered __________ Initials: ________

Chapter Eleven

Teaching and Learning Strategies

You may recall that an electronic classroom was defined in Chapter One as a separate room that is equipped with electronic devices for instructional purposes. The focus on instructional purposes distinguishes an electronic classroom from a computer laboratory and from the reference terminals area. The exciting aspect of the definition is in its statement of purpose—for instructional purposes, for teaching and learning.

TRANSFORMING THE LEARNING EXPERIENCE

An electronic classroom provides an opportunity to change radically the way one approaches library instruction and information literacy. Instruction will likely become more responsive to learner needs, increasingly interactive, and less scripted. This change is particularly true for a hands-on classroom but is also true for a demonstration classroom. In addition, there is some evidence that students who receive hands-on instruction perform better on a post-test than those taught using lecture/demonstration only (Bren, Hillemann, and Topp, 1998: 45). In adopting new instructional technologies and strategies, your instruction program will likely move through three stages—automation, enhancement, and innovation (Gilbert, 1996: 16).

Automation involves identifying administrative functions that have been automated elsewhere and implementing a similar approach. For the library instruction program this will primarily involve administrative applications of computing technology. For example, a program might adopt electronic scheduling software to replace a printed calendar. These changes are not likely to affect student learning greatly and are not directly related to the availability of an electronic classroom.

Enhancement entails adopting technologies and applying them to core tasks. Technological enhancements to a library instruction program might be as simple as creating printed overhead transparencies to replace handwritten ones. More meaningful, however, will be applications of computing technology in an electronic classroom. For example, one might use PowerPoint (Microsoft) to create an interactive slide show presentation of information previously presented using overhead transparencies. The best applications of technology will not only replicate what could be accomplished using older technologies, but further develop those accomplishments by taking advantage of newer capabilities and enhancements.

Finally, innovation involves identifying and accomplishing new kinds of tasks. For a library's instruction program, access to an electronic classroom can offer opportunities to utilize teaching and learning methods that were difficult, if not impossible, to use in a traditional, nonelectronic classroom setting. Electronic classrooms provide librarians with the opportunity to do real-time demonstrations of databases, perhaps even in response to a student's topic, unknown before it was volunteered, and to offer practice time within the comfort of the instructional setting with a librarian available for coaching and assistance.

A WORD OF WARNING AND A GUIDING PRINCIPLE

Winston Churchill once stated: "We shape our buildings and afterwards our buildings shape us." And then we shape them again. (Brand, 1994: 3). After you teach in your electronic classroom, you will see how well this statement applies to classrooms as well as buildings. Your teaching methods and style will likely change—perhaps subtly, perhaps not so subtly. But, they will change. The challenge is to be certain that the changes are for the better.

The hidden danger in an electronic classroom is the temptation to focus on the technological tools and to put aside the conceptual frameworks that are the foundation of information competence. Keith Gresham warns that "in the rush to incorporate electronic classrooms into instructional programs, instruction librarians may inadvertently create a learning environment in which information concepts and information technologies appear to be in a state of disconnect" and thus allow "information concepts to appear, if not irrelevant, then secondary" (1997: 515). The risk of creating this disconnection is particularly strong in a hands-on classroom. In that setting an instructor can easily become overly focused on teaching students to manipulate technological tools, especially if the given tool is complex or cumbersome to use, and neglect to address fully or make explicit the conceptual knowledge that students need to develop. In such cases, the instructor is confusing means and ends and creating a learning environment in which the technological tools are the focus, rather than the means by which students and instructor accomplish learning goals. Students who learn to manipulate tools without understanding underlying concepts will not acquire the information literacy and lifelong learning skills that they need.

Attending to this concern, Gresham recommends using a *concepts-in-application* approach to teaching in an electronic classroom by "employing an instructional model that makes explicit the *inherent concepts* of the online environment at the precise time students encounter or apply the concepts while searching" (1997: 516). D. Scott Brandt (1998) makes a similar point in advocating that library instructors differentiate between information literacy, information technology, and technology skills. Such instruction makes clear the connections between technological competence and the intellectual purposes for acquiring that competence. Rather than only teaching students, for example, the mechanics of entering terms or deciphering search results in an online database, concepts-in-application instruction instead takes advantage of the opportunity (created by the need to enter search terms and decipher search results) to explore the concepts of access points and controlled vocabularies. By grounding instruction in concepts in application, librarians can provide students with both the conceptual and the procedural knowledge needed to be an effective researcher in the networked information environment.

TEACHING METHODS

A teaching method, according to William Tracey, "is the basic approach to instruction" (1992: 248). As the basic approach, a teaching method identifies the means by which the information is communicated. Instructional methods include lecture, demonstration, conferencing/collaborative learning, performance/active learning, and programmed self-instruction. Different librarians will likely prefer to use different teaching methods and will tend to use their preferred methods regardless of the students or content specific to a particular session. Challenge yourself to learn to use methods that are perhaps not your first choice but are pedagogically effective for a particular group of students or for teaching a particular instructional concept.

Lecture/Demonstration

A combination of lecture and demonstration is commonly used in both demonstration and hands-on classrooms. In most cases, while presenting concepts and procedural instructions, the instructor simultaneously performs the described activities, showing the learners what to do and how to do it, as well as when and why to do it (Tracey, 1992: 251, 253). Though an efficient means of conveying large quantities of information, the lecture/demonstration is usually a passive experience for the learners and does not engage them in active learning unless the instructor carefully plans to involve them.

Developing an effective lecture requires that you carefully structure the instructional content so that the learners can absorb the ideas being presented while also coming to understand the relationships between different points. Common organizational patterns for lectures include hierarchical, using either a classification and/or outline format or a problem-solutions format, as well as chaining, presenting a sequence or procedure (Bligh, 1998: 70–75). In all likelihood, a lecture in an electronic classroom will either follow a topical outline or present procedural information. In addition to carefully organizing the content of the main body of a lecture, you should start a lecture with an introduction that gives the framework and context for the information that will be presented, and end with a conclusion that summarizes the information that has been presented. In other words, make certain that your lecture has an introduction, a body, and a conclusion—all of which include a statement of your main points. This may seem repetitive to you as the instructor; however, the repetition will help students understand and retain the information that you present (Bligh, 1998: 88).

Instructors can involve students in a lecture/demonstration in a number of ways. One way to involve learners is to develop a presentation that solicits research topics from students and then continues in a manner that is responsive to the topics suggested by the students. An overly scripted presentation that is not responsive to students will be a particularly passive experience for students and, though they may appear to be attending to the content of the instruction, they may be thinking about other things. Additionally, a student can be asked to manipulate the instructor's computer during the lecture/demonstration. In some cases, different students could be asked to demonstrate different searches over the course of an instructional session. Another way to involve learners in a lecture/demonstration is to provide copies of instructional materials to the students during the instruction session and encourage note-taking. Alternatively, a librarian might develop a worksheet that students fill in during the lecture/demonstration based on the information being presented.

In a hands-on classroom, the instructor might also require that students perform the same searches or tasks on their computers that the instructor is demonstrating. This approach may be particularly useful when the procedure being demonstrated is complex and requires precise execution for successful completion of the activity. In such cases, the instructor must be certain to explain carefully each component of the process and pay close attention to the progress of individual students to ensure that no one falls behind. An example of this type of procedural instruction is detailed by Nicholas G. Tomaiuolo in his article "Effective Simultaneous Hands-on Drill for Basic Electronic Database Instruction" (1998).

Active and Collaborative Learning

Active and collaborative learning approaches to instruction engage students to a greater extent in the learning process and allow the learners take a leadership role in their own learning. By engaging students in their own learning, active and collaborative learning techniques facilitate both knowledge acquisition and retention. Conferencing and performance are teaching methods that involve students in active and collaborative learning experiences.

In conferencing, the instructor uses group discussion techniques to support a variety of learning objectives, including problem solving, emphasizing main points, and exploring student understanding (Tracey, 1992: 252). When used in combination with a lecture/demonstration, conferencing can create a more active and collaborative learning environment in a demonstration classroom. For example, after executing a keyword search that retrieves hundreds of citations, an instructor could facilitate a discussion in which the students identify the strategies one can use in such a situation (for example, browse the first few citations to see whether the results are relevant, identify subject headings, add additional keywords to the search statement), evaluate the options, and then select one for implementation. Using small-group discussion followed by large-group debriefing on a question can further increase the number of learners participating.

Asking questions is a good technique for starting a discussion. In *Teaching Tips*, Wilbert McKeachie (1994: 37–40) details a number of types of questions. Application/interpretation, problem, comparative, and evaluative questions can be particularly effective in an electronic classroom setting. Application/interpretation questions ask students to consider relationships, applications, or analyses. For example, how does the idea of authorship apply to a corporate Web site? Problem questions present students with a case study or hypothetical problem to address. For example, what research strategy should a marketing analyst at Company ABC use to find out about the effect of the increasing number of single-parent households on purchasing behavior of mothers? Asking learners to consider the similarities and differences among three Web search engines would be using a comparative question. Evaluative questions build on comparative questions by requiring learners to decide the relative value of the compared items. For example, which search engine is better for locating scholarly Web resources? Regardless of the question type used, it is important to remember to give students sufficient time to think after you have posed a question. Leave at least ten seconds of silence. This may seem like a very long time to you as the instructor, but it will give the students enough time to take in the question, process relevant information, and formulate an answer.

Performance as a teaching method requires the learners to perform the skill or technique being taught—learning by doing. Performance can involve independent practice, but small-group work, (or teamwork), which creates a collaborative learning environment, as well, is also effective (Tracey, 1992: 254). Performance in a demonstration classroom will be limited to those activities that students can practice without access to a computer workstation. In a hands-on classroom the equipment to support performance is readily available; however, the challenge may be to guide students to focus on the task at hand.

Conferencing and performance as teaching methods in the electronic classroom can directly address three of the "Seven Principles for Good Practice in Undergraduate Education" delineated by Art Chickering and Zelda Gamson (1987: 4–6):

- develop reciprocity and cooperation among students,
- encourage active learning, and
- respect diverse talents and ways of learning.

For additional ideas on how to use active and collaborative learning methods in your classroom, see Gillian Gremmels's chapter "Active and Cooperative Learning in the One-Shot BI Session" (1996), which details six techniques applicable to many instruction sessions, and *Designs for Active Learning* (1998), edited by Gail Gradowski, Loanne Snavely, and Paula Dempsey, which describes 54 active learning activities, many of which were designed for use in an electronic classroom.

Individualized Instruction

Individualized instruction allows multiple students to work through materials at their own pace while experiencing a carefully developed series of instructional materials (Tracey, 1992: 255, 273). In the electronic classroom, this teaching method will likely entail some type of computer-assisted or computer-based instruction. In the past, such instruction would have consisted of specially installed software programs, diskettes, or CD-ROMs. HyperCard (Apple) is still used to produce stand-alone instructional modules; however, it is primarily used in elementary and secondary education settings. In most postsecondary settings, individualized instruction is now Web-based.

The advantage of Web-based instruction is that the instructional modules are not only available in the classroom but are also accessible through any computer connected to the Internet. Because of this accessibility, there may be less emphasis on using the instructional materials during an instruction session. Instead, they can be used to supplement in-person instruction, perhaps serving as an introduction to concepts before the session or as resource for review after the session. If the classroom is primarily used for computer-based instruction, be sure to allow adequate elbow room for individuals working independently.

Web-based instruction can be created using HTML coding and nothing more; however, to create more interactive and responsive instruction, JavaScript, graphics, and quizzing features might also be added. Web-based instruction can also be created using a courseware development package, such as WebCT (WebCT, Inc.), Macromedia CourseBuilder for Dreamweaver (Macromedia, Inc.) or ToolBook (click2learn.com). Courseware software provides the instructor with a robust environment for developing instructional materials as well as mechanisms for tracking and testing student progress. "TILT: Texas Information Literacy Tutorial" (*http://tilt.lib.utsystem.edu*), "RIO: Research Instruction Online" (*www.library.arizona.edu/rio*), "Research Quick-Study: Library Research Guide" (*http://tutorial.lib.umn.edu*), and "Finding Statistics" (*www.mlb.ilstu.edu/learn/stat/home.htm*) are just a few examples of the online tutorials available on the Internet.

CLASSROOM COMPETENCIES

Many libraries, and librarians, were early adopters of technology and quickly integrated technology into the daily routines of librarianship. In some libraries, automation extended immediately into the realm of instruction, and teaching librarians quickly developed technological skill and savvy. Other libraries were slower to automate and maybe even slower to incorporate technology into teaching. Library administrators should not assume that all librarians have the necessary skills to teach an instructional session in an electronic classroom. It is especially important to avoid this assumption with respect to teaching in a hands-on classroom. Finally, even those librarians who are currently confident instructors in an electronic classroom will need to make an ongoing commitment to improving their skills as technologies change over time.

Librarians teaching in an electronic classroom must have basic teaching competencies in addition to comfort and skill in working with technology. As reported by Rao Aluri and June Lester Engle (1987: 117), in 1984 the Education for Bibliographic Instruction Committee of the former Bibliographic Instruction Section (now the Instruction Section) of the Association of College and Research Libraries identified the following proficiencies as necessary for conducting instructional activities:

- Ability to select educational objectives for specific activities
- Ability to select appropriate educational methods
- Knowledge of evaluation techniques
- Teaching ability
- Instructional media skills

These basic proficiencies can be used as a framework for understanding the skills needed in the electronic classroom. In addition to selecting the content, teaching methods, and instructional materials, the librarian teaching in the electronic classroom must have a basic understanding and comfort with networks, computer hardware and other complex electronic equipment, and a variety of software packages, as well as the ability to coordinate simultaneously the students' computing activities. In other words, library instructors must have the technical skills to operate the equipment as well as the pedagogical skills to use the technology to facilitate teaching and learning. Without these additional skills, instructors are likely to use an electronic classroom "as a lecture hall that has become complicated and annoying to use" (Chambers et al., 1992: 294).

Developing Electronic Classroom Teaching Skills

Developing competencies for teaching in an electronic classroom requires careful planning and the availability of opportunities for professional development and training, followed by ongoing opportunities for practice and improvement. When building the first electronic classroom in a library, library administrations should budget funding for initial training and professional development for the instructors who will be teaching in the new classroom. Glenn E. Meeks, Ricki Fisher, and Warren Loveless suggest that professional development costs will require a budget of five to ten percent of the total costs of installing the new technologies (1997).

Observing other librarians teaching in an electronic classroom is a simple way to begin to develop your electronic classroom teaching skills. Such observation is probably best kept informal and should be completely separate from any personnel evaluation that may be required for annual performance reviews and the like. The librarian who is observing might also offer to work with the keyboard during the presentation and/or to rove during hands-on practice time to assist with any technological difficulties that students encounter (LaGuardia and Oka, 2000: 36). An advantage to roving is that you can improve your classroom technology skills while being confident that, should a particular technological problem befuddle you, the more experienced instructor will be available to assist.

Once you have developed your skills to the point where you are comfortable teaching a class, you might ask a more experienced colleague to assist as backup for any situations that you cannot figure out during the hands-on session. The same colleague might also observe as you teach and provide feedback. For example, you might be concerned whether your spoken explanations are in sync with your typing and clicking of the mouse. As a variant on this, you could arrange to have yourself videotaped while teaching and review the video for areas of concern. Do not be discouraged, though, if you feel as if you are struggling to learn the skills needed for this new teaching environment; just as with so many skills, teaching in an electronic classroom gets easier and better with practice.

In addition to allowing for skills to be acquired through practice and observation with informal feedback, the classroom administrator should also provide formal professional development opportunities. At a minimum, all instructors who will teach in the classroom should be trained to use the equipment in the classroom. Most people will just avoid using any technology that they do not know how to use, and so, if the librarians are not trained, they will be unlikely to utilize the capabilities of the electronic classroom to the fullest extent. Beyond technical training, the classroom administrator might arrange a series of sessions in which instructors demonstrate how they use the electronic classroom and discuss the changes they have made in their instruction based on the added functionalities of the electronic classroom. The series might also include sessions during which new instructors have the opportunity to practice by presenting their planned instruction to an audience of library staff who provide feedback and support.

The Flow of an Instructional Session

Each instructional session has its own character which is greatly affected by the teaching style of the library instructor, the learning styles of the students, and the relationships between the library instructor, the learners, and, if applicable, the classroom instructor. Even so, many instruction sessions follow a general pattern. Internalizing this pattern will help you in developing your instruction skills for the electronic classroom.

Before any session starts, it is important to prepare the classroom. This process involves generally making the classroom welcoming by putting all of the chairs in place, opening the classroom door, and writing introductory information on the board, as well as checking on the technology to confirm that everything is working. Turn on all of the equipment that will be used during the session and bring up the relevant software to make certain that the computers, software, and networking connectivity are functioning. If you are not certain whether a particular piece of equipment will be used, turn it on and test it too. It is far better to have something turned on that you do not need than to spend the time to turn it on and test it during the instructional session. Finally, be certain to set out any needed print materials and handouts.

The pattern of the instruction session is generally:

(1) Welcome and introduction
(2) Demonstration and lecture
(3) Learner practice
(4) Conclusion and wrap-up

In many cases, the instruction will loop through stages 2 and 3 a number of times during the session, particularly if the class meets for more than 50 minutes. In a hands-on classroom, the emphasis will likely be on learner practice, giving learners the opportunity to be actively involved in exploring the instructional content. In a demonstration classroom, learner practice may not be part of the instruction session but instead may be assigned as homework.

Managing Instruction in an Electronic Classroom

Classroom management in an electronic setting involves orchestrating the events to serve the purposes of teaching and learning. One challenge,

Figure 11-1: Classroom Assistant Training Outline

CLASSROOM ASSISTANT TRAINING

Classroom Assistant training is coordinated by the Library Instructor Coordinator and the Training Team leader. All Classroom Assistants are required to attend training. Opportunities to practice new skills are provided during the training. Topics to be covered during training include:

Purpose and goal of the Classroom Assistant

- Purpose: To aid the teaching librarian during the presentation of individual library instruction sessions.
- Goal: To fulfill the support role as defined by the needs of the teaching librarian (keyboarding at the presentation workstation, roving around to room to provide individual assistance, passing out materials, technical support and troubleshooting, etc.)

Technical support skills for the Classroom Assistant

- Instructor (presentation) workstation setup and shutdown procedures
- Student workstation setup and shutdown procedures
- CD-ROM usage (6-disk changer)
- Control panel setup and shutdown procedures
- Document camera
- Overhead projector setup and shutdown procedures, transparencies, pens, cleaning fluid, and extra lamps
- Laser pointers

Unobtrusive student assistance

- Awareness of sight lines
- Voice modulation
- Physical movement around the room

General structure and flow of an instruction session

- Welcome
- Demonstration
- Hands-on Practice
- Conclusion

End user database concerns

- Obtaining information from search
- E-mail
- Printing (cost = $.08/page $.80/page on the color printer)
- Content: abstract, full text, how many pages will print
- Printer locations: current floor, other floors, color laser

particularly in a hands-on classroom, may be getting students to pay attention to the instructional content. Use of control/collaboration software may assist with this process. Some libraries have also designed hands-on classrooms so that a switch controls the electricity to the student workstation monitors and instructors can shut off the power to gain student attention. These approaches can be effective for preventing students from using the computers for purposes other than those being taught; however, engagement in the learning process requires more than this. The students need to be attending to the content of what they are to learn. Though engaging every student in every instruction session may not be possible, attention to motivation is important if learning is to occur. Making explicit the connection between the instruction session and the tasks that students need to accomplish, combined with presenting clear expectations and applying a pedagogy of concepts in application, should help engage learners and encourage them to focus on the instructional content.

Another challenge of teaching in a hands-on classroom, if the class size is larger than about 15 people, is providing sufficient individual assistance and technical troubleshooting during hands-on practice time. To address this problem, some libraries use team-teaching or classroom assistants. In either case, the second library staff member moves about the room during the instruction session providing individual assistance to students, performing basic technical troubleshooting and generally serving as a backup to the teaching librarian. If the classroom assistants are staff members who do not usually provide library instruction, they should be trained before being assigned to assist. The training should cover the general structure of an instruction session, technical support skills, how to assist learners unobtrusively, and user concerns about databases and computers. Figure 11.1 is the outline for the training given to members of the Classroom Assistant Team at Milner Library, Illinois State University.

Finally, because the electronic classroom contains technology by definition, and because, at some point, technology will fail to work as intended, managing instruction in the electronic classroom also requires an instructor to be able to address such failures. Useful coping strategies generally fall under technical troubleshooting, or teaching adaptations.

If a piece of equipment fails, the first step is always checking that everything is plugged in—network cables, power cords, and so on. After confirming that everything is plugged in, exit and restart the software program and/or shut off the equipment and then turn it back on. If the problem persists and time allows, try swapping parts you think are causing the problem. For example, exchange keyboards with another terminal or plug the monitor into a different outlet (Levin and Miyake). If these strategies do not resolve the problem, and if only a minimal number of terminals are affected and the instructor station is functional, direct the students with malfunctioning equipment to share workstations with other students and proceed with the instruction session. If all student workstations in a hands-on classroom are affected but the instructor terminal is still functioning, continue with the instruction session as if the session were occurring in a demonstration classroom, making necessary adjustments in the teaching methods and content.

On the other hand, if the instructor workstation is affected, the situation may be more challenging. Depending on how the instructor workstation is connected to the projection and sound systems, it may be possible to unplug the instructor's computer and then plug in one of the student computers. The instructor can then use the student computer for the demonstration. Even without an instructor workstation, if the student workstations are functioning, it may be possible to guide the learners through the instructional content without demonstrating from the instructor station. Alternatively, if no workstations are functioning, or if some demonstration by the instructor is required for students to work successfully at their own terminals, backup instructional materials will be needed. These backup materials could be diagrams drawn on a flipchart or whiteboard, or they could be handouts, overhead transparencies, or screen captures loaded into a program such as PowerPoint. Which backup material will work in a particular situation will depend on the extent of the technology failure. For example, if there is no electrical power, options will be very limited. Regardless of the approach taken, the instructor must develop the backup materials before the instructional sessions—hoping that they will not be needed but preparing in case they are.

Thinking ahead about how you will deal with technical problems during an instruction session will help you manage the stress that comes with having such problems in the middle of a class. Some instructors also find it useful to have a few mini–lessons or humorous anecdotes, maybe about library research, to share while fixing a technical glitch or waiting for technical support to arrive.

INSTRUCTIONAL MATERIALS

Handouts, computer-based slide shows, and Web pages are the most common instructional materials used in electronic classrooms. High-quality instructional materials can make a positive contribution to student learning in both demonstration and hands-on classrooms. Careful attention to both the content and design of these materials is therefore important.

Handouts are most often used in an electronic classroom to describe a resource or procedure. Selecting the content for a handout involves identifying the most important informational elements and then organizing them for presentation. Information about a resource will probably be best presented in an outline or classified format. Information about a procedure should be presented in a sequential format and the steps in the processes should be numbered (West, Farmer, and Wolff, 1991: 15–16). Handouts may also be used to assess student learning. Such handouts present practice exercises or assignments that students complete and then turn in to the instructor.

Designing handouts involves making choices about size, page orientation, white space, line width, typography and fonts, and line justification (Walsh, 1995). In general, moderation and simplicity are the best guidelines. Limit the number of fonts, variations in line spacing, types of justification, and colors used in any given handout. The one exception to the moderation guideline is the use of white space—use it liberally. By spacing text and graphics, you will help learners more easily absorb the information.

Developing computer-based slide shows also involves selecting, structuring, and displaying information; however, an added design element must be addressed—animation. Use animation to help learners focus on important information and be careful that it does not distract them. Simplicity and moderation should still be your guiding principles. In addition, remember that the slides should contain key points and phrases, not the entire text of your lecture. In all likelihood, a computer-based slide show will be used to support a lecture and will not be given to students to work through on their own, though students might be provided with a printed copy of the slides for taking notes. Generally speaking, each slide should have no more than five to seven lines of text and each line should be no more than five to seven words long.

When designing a presentation for use in the classroom, be certain to preview it in the classroom where you intend to show it. Certain font and background color combinations may not be visible unless the room is very dark, so dark that students cannot take notes. The details on some graphics may not be visible from the back half of the room. Finally, the settings on your personal computer monitor and the projection system may differ significantly, and so what appears as a beautiful color palette in your office may be headache-inducing when displayed in the classroom.

Selecting, structuring, and displaying animation should be considerations in developing Web pages as well; however, issues of interactivity, hyperlinking, and navigation must also be considered. Unlike handouts, which are primarily given to students for their own use, or computer-based slide shows, which are primarily for lecture support, webpages will likely serve a dual-purpose—to support your lecture and to be a resource for students to use on their own. Web pages must thus have a built-in navigation structure that helps learners understand how to progress through the information and how the information on one Web page is related to the information on another. The navigational structure is particularly important in Web pages that have a complex hyperlinked structure and a nonlinear organizational pattern. Finally, you will need to decide whether you wish to include interactive elements (such as self-quizzing) in your Web page.

Appendix E contains the instructional materials used at Milner Library, Illinois State University, in the library instruction sessions for Communication 110: Language and Communication. In addition to the two student handouts, one descriptive and one procedural, Appendix E also includes the information provided to the librarians teaching the sessions. Appendix F contains sample instructional materials for teaching students to evaluate information. These and other similar materials are used at Milner Library in both undergraduate and graduate instruction sessions, as well as in faculty development workshops designed to help faculty teach their students about information quality.

Chapter Twelve

Evaluation

Evaluating an electronic classroom as a teaching/learning space involves studying the room design and how it supports instruction. In reality, instructors and learners will constantly assess the space for how well it meets their needs at the moment. Evaluation is an attempt to formalize these assessments into general statements for action.

The emphasis in evaluation is on comparing how the room was designed to work (in theory) with how it does work (in practice) and with how well a classroom should work (ideally). Some of the findings from a classroom evaluation can be used immediately to improve the teaching and learning environment. Other findings must wait for action until refurbishing. Still other findings will not be acted upon in the classroom under study, but may be useful for designing future classrooms. In addition to comparing how the room functions relative to the design considerations, evaluating the classroom may also provide some evidence to determine whether the priority items selected in the planning process are truly the priority items for teachers and learners.

THE NEEDS ASSESSMENT

During the planning process, the planning team completed an instructional needs assessment. As an initial evaluation activity, review the current and future needs identified by the planning team. Check whether the classroom appears to respond to those needs and note any areas of concern. This review will give the classroom administrator a heads-up regarding what may be revealed through the other evaluation activities. On the other hand, if the other evaluation activities do not reveal any concerns in the noted areas, the classroom may be performing even better than expected or hoped.

LOGBOOK

One of the simplest evaluation tools is a classroom logbook. Ask people who use the room to record any difficulties they encounter in using the space as well as any thoughts they have about ways to improve the space. Depending on the organizational culture in your library, instructors might also be encouraged to record "room wishes" to indicate their preferences for future classroom spaces. By capturing such data in the classroom, the classroom administrator will have access to information that is usually forgotten immediately after the instructor exits the room.

Examine the logbook on a regular basis for suggested improvements that are simple and inexpensive to implement. If they will not interfere with other uses of the room, implement them. For example, instructors may comment on the hassle of having to retrieve a separate teaching workstation key from a central location and the difficulties encountered if another instructor forgets to return the key to its proper location. A simple and low-cost solution might involve rekeying the instructor console so that it opens with the classroom door key or replacing the current lock with a combination lock. If instructors observe that their comments are taken seriously and suggestions are implemented, they will be more likely to write in the logbook.

Logbook entries may alert the classroom administrator to equipment failures and difficulties that instructors will otherwise fail to mention. When an individual piece of equipment fails, other equipment of the same type might be examined for similar problems. Also watch for patterns in the comments. If a particular monitor fails repeatedly, it may be necessary to have it replaced. Lightbulbs that repeatedly burn out faster than others in the classroom may indicate a light fixture problem that should be examined. Figure 12.1 is an example of what a simple logbook page might look like.

OBSERVATION

Another evaluation method to evaluate an electronic classroom is observation. Repeated observations, however, will be necessary to determine whether events in a given instruction session are related to room design, the instructor, or the dynamics of a particular group of learners. One could observe instructors and students during a class session; however, you may wish to make other observations as well. For example, it may be informative to observe an instructor set up the classroom for the first class of the day and see how long it takes to turn on all of the equip-

Figure 12.1: Logbook Page

ELECTRONIC CLASSROOM LOGBOOK

Please record date, idea/question/problem, and your initials.

ment in a hands-on classroom. Alternatively, one could observe the process of transition between instruction sessions taught by different instructors or the process of shutting down a classroom after the final session of the day. Finally, one might also observe computer technicians, network administrators, and facilities operations workers who maintain the classroom infrastructure, equipment, furnishings, and environment. To the extent possible, a classroom should be designed in such a way that the teaching and learning needs of instructors and students do not create undue hardship for those who are charged with supporting the classroom.

Methods of observations may be very informal—watching and writing down anything that is striking or otherwise interesting—or very formal—recording the location of a given individual at regular intervals. Informal observations may provide insights into more obvious problems with the design of the classroom and general conclusions about who uses what types of technology when teaching. More formal methods will be useful for ferreting out less obvious problems. For example, by recording the location of the instructor every 30 seconds, one might discover that most of the time the instructor is seated behind the instructor workstation and not visible to the students. Observation can be done in person or through videotaping; however, it is important to remember that videotaping may be particularly unnerving to instructors and may affect their teaching. In all cases, it is best to ask for permission to observe and to explain the purpose of the observations.

Figure 12.2 is a fictitious example of an observation worksheet. For this worksheet, the location of the instructor has been recorded on a systematic basis over the course of three instruction sessions. By studying the patterns that have emerged, it appears that the instructor is getting "caught" in one side of the classroom during each class. It may be useful for the instructor to request a classroom assistant to ensure that students seated on each side of the classroom have an opportunity for individualized assistance during hands-on practice.

FOCUS GROUP

A focus group of instructors, students, and/or classroom support staff may also be an effective means of gathering information about the usability of a given classroom. A focus group requires an impartial facilitator who will pose questions and moderate discussion but not participate in the discussion itself. The classroom administrator might serve as a facilitator, but in all likelihood that person will have difficulty avoiding joining the discussion. It may be better for the classroom administrator to observe a discussion facilitated by someone else, or to receive a report of the focus group findings without having any interaction with the participants. A note on this method—it can be very time-consuming to organize a focus group because of the need to coordinate the participants' schedules.

STUDENT EVALUATION FORM

If you already distribute a student evaluation form as part of the instruction program, consider adding a question or two to the form about the classroom facilities. If you have specific concerns, multiple-choice questions may provide more precise feedback. For example, if you are concerned whether the temperature of the classroom is acceptable, students might be asked whether the classroom is too hot, too cold, comfortable, or variable from too hot to too cold. On the other hand, to gather general feedback, open-ended questions are more useful. Student responses to such prompts as "The best thing about this classroom is…" or "One thing I would change about this classroom is…" can provide valuable insight into the effectiveness of the classroom facilities from the perspective of the learners, as well as identify topics that should be addressed through multiple-choice questions on future surveys.

INSTRUCTOR SURVEY

Finally, you might consider an instructor survey as a means for uncovering what technologies instructors use and their satisfaction with the classroom. In asking about what technologies are used, list the technologies and then ask respondents to indicate their use level (never, occasionally, frequently, always) or to estimate during what percentage of class sessions they use the technologies. A similar list of technologies might be presented and the respondents asked how necessary they are (very necessary, necessary, nice to have, unnecessary, detracts from teaching and learning) or, if the list were to be of new technologies that might be implemented, how desirable they are (e.g., very desirable, desirable, nice to have, undesirable, very undesirable). Finally, instructors could be asked how satisfied they are with the technologies and the room (very satisfied, satisfied, unsatisfied, dissatisfied). (Roberts and Dunn, 1996). Tabulating the results and cross-checking use with satisfaction will give you valuable information to pinpoint any changes needed in the classroom or for topics for instructor training.

Figure 12.2: Example Observation Worksheet

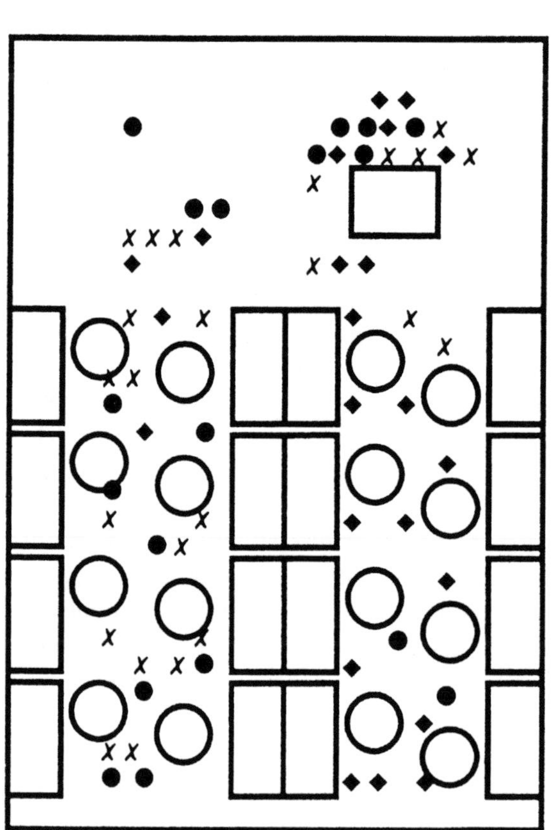

Legend:

X = Monday's Class

● = Tuesday's Class

◆ = Friday's Class

INDIVIDUAL CONVERSATIONS

Though admittedly a fairly informal approach to evaluation, the classroom administrator should also talk with individual instructors about the electronic classroom. Beyond the low-cost and low-effort advantages of this approach, such informal encounters also often reveal issues and ideas that do not emerge in formal surveys or focus groups. Paying attention to and following up on comments made in the course of conversations on other topics can also result in useful information.

Regardless of the evaluation method or methods used, remember that the goal in evaluating is to investigate how well the electronic classroom serves the needs of teachers and learners. Welcome all feedback, even that which is critical. If possible, use the evaluation results to improve your electronic classroom immediately. If immediate action is not possible or the results point to ways to make better decisions in the future, be certain to save the evaluation results so that they can be used at a later date.

Chapter Thirteen

The Future

Congratulations! You have an electronic classroom—one specifically designed to meet the teaching and learning needs of the instructors and learners at your library. During the process, members of the planning team have functioned as librarians, interior designers, facilities planners, architects, human factors engineers, systems technicians, educators, staff trainers, and translators of pedagogical needs into technological design. In all likelihood, they have done so while completing their regular duties as well. They are probably a little tired but also a bit proud of what they have a accomplished—as they should be. A pat on the back and round of applause to all for their hard work is in order. Your carefully designed, constructed, and managed electronic classroom will serve your library's instruction program for years to come. In fact, it may be so popular that you need another!

Thinking back to the beginning of this book and the discussion of "for the purpose of teaching and learning," just what will the future hold for library instruction programs?

THE EMBRACING OF INFORMATION LITERACY

Information literacy is rapidly being embraced by faculty in disciplines as diverse as engineering and education. The Association of College and Research Libraries (ACRL) is providing training materials and numerous opportunities for professional development so that librarians can become familiar and comfortable with the "Information Literacy Competency Standards for Higher Education" (*www.ala.org/acrl/ilcomstan.html*). In the near future, through a grant from the Institute for Museum and Library Services, ACRL will develop assessment tools and methods to assist librarians and faculty in evaluating student learning outcomes relative to information literacy. Best practices for information literacy programs are being identified and highlighted by the Institute for Information Literacy (*www.ala.org/acrl/nili/nilihp.html*). The National Forum on Information Literacy (*www.infolit.org*) continues its valuable work educating civic and corporate leaders about the importance of information literacy for workers and citizens. Information literacy is truly being embraced as a foundational skill of the educated person.

NEW UNDERSTANDINGS OF TEACHING AND LEARNING

Indeed, new understandings of the relationship between teaching and learning have been emerging in higher education generally. A renewed emphasis on attending to student learning, rather than on focusing solely on the delivery of instruction, has clarified the purpose of teaching (Barr and Tagg, 1995; Wittkopf, 1996). Much of the pedagogical focus is now on active and collaborative learning. Students are viewed as partners in teaching and learning, rather than as the recipients of instruction. Greater understanding of the role of experiential learning has explained the importance of providing students with opportunities to practice as well as opportunities to reflect on their practice (Gresham, 1999). Librarians have embraced these new understandings and theories and work diligently to figure out what works for the instructional situations they encounter in their daily work lives.

PROLIFERATING DATA TYPES AND FORMATS

Simultaneously with the refocusing on student learning, librarians have experienced a proliferation of information resources and data types. Print and electronic versions of the same information multiply daily. A given library may have access to *Time* or *Newsweek* in a staggering number of ways (print, microfilm, as part of subscription databases, and freely available from the publisher's Web site). Traditional print reference sources are reborn as searchable databases. Databases that previously only provided text information now incorporate graphics and multimedia files. New types of data also have been added to the everyday list of librarian concerns—statistical data sets, mapping information, and multimedia resources are no longer the sole purview of subject specialists who have developed advanced skills to manipulate such types of data. As instruction sessions become increasingly interactive and responsive to student interests, the library instructor must be prepared to encounter and skillfully manipulate multiple data types and formats.

ADVANCES IN TECHNOLOGY

Technological advances in computing equipment and networking are changing the information landscape at stunning speed. Technology planning is challenging, some say it is a contradiction in terms. One can perceive various trends though. Handheld information devices and information technology embedded into other appliances mean that people regularly encounter digital information in the course of daily life. Coupled with advances in wireless and digital networking, people are more and more connected to information resources, regardless of location. Information is truly being integrated into daily living through technology. As such, knowing how to access, select, and use information is increasingly important.

FOCUSING ON TEACHING AND LEARNING

The information and technology landscape is developing at an incredible pace. The world of librarians is changing rapidly. So, too, is the role of library instruction. Alice Harrison Bahr contends that "in this new environment, librarians have new opportunities to play a forceful, dynamic role in collaboratively designing and developing the contexts for learning strategies" (2000: 3). Faculty members and students will look to librarians for guidance in managing the information they encounter on a daily basis and for assistance in developing instructional strategies that take advantage of the capabilities of the technology. In responding to these new opportunities, keep in mind the observation of a nonlibrarian:

> No matter what librarians are called in the profession or how much more technology is used to access information through the medium of library and information resources, the most effective librarians in the new millennium will be those who empower learning and who facilitate the teaching and learning process (Simmons, 2000: 44).

The educational role of librarians is vital in today's society. As vital, as it was in 1876—if not more so—when Otis Robinson claimed that:

> No librarian is fit for his place unless he holds himself to some degree responsible for the library education of his students…All that is taught in college amounts to very little; but if we can send students out self-reliant in their investigations, we have accomplished very much (123–124).

Citizens must be prepared to seek out, critically assess, select, and use information in their personal, professional, and civic lives. No one is better prepared to assist learners in so many areas of their lives than the librarian. It is the librarian who can help one user identify industry standards for metal fabrication and then help the next select a book of short stories for use in a lesson plan for students in grade seven. In collaboration with faculty and other campus professionals, the librarian is a crucial educational partner.

Furthermore, the library is an important place. Even with wireless, portable information devices and bandwidth sufficient to accommodate streaming audio and video, the library as a place for study, research, and learning continues to be valued by thousands and thousands of individuals. The challenge, then, is to design learning facilities that meet the needs and desires of today's users while reaching forward to explore future needs and opportunities.

For the purpose of teaching and learning—regardless of what the future may bring—an electronic classroom built on this principle will serve learners for many years to come.

Appendix A

Reproducible Figures

Layout and design of a classroom is a complex process that requires being aware of the "big picture" while also attending to multiple details regarding space requirements, furniture parameters, and technology demands. This appendix will assist with the process; it provides reproducible figures for you to cut out and then move about to "try out" different classroom designs. The scale of all of the images is the same (1 inch = 1 foot).

Figure A.1: Blank Floor Space

	Blank Floor Space 4 feet by 6 feet		

Figure A.2: Aisles

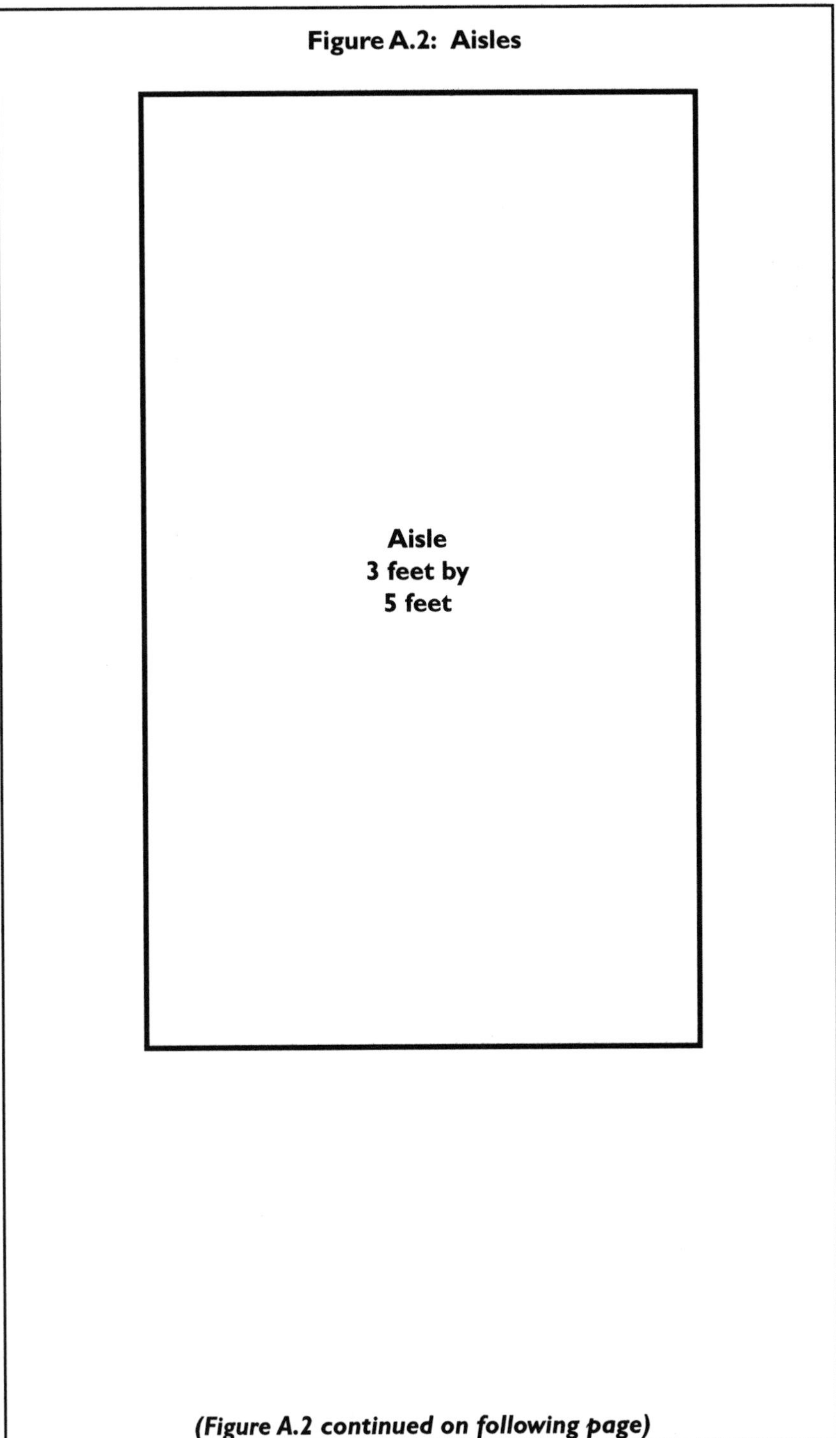

(Figure A.2 continued on following page)

(Figure A.2: *continued*)

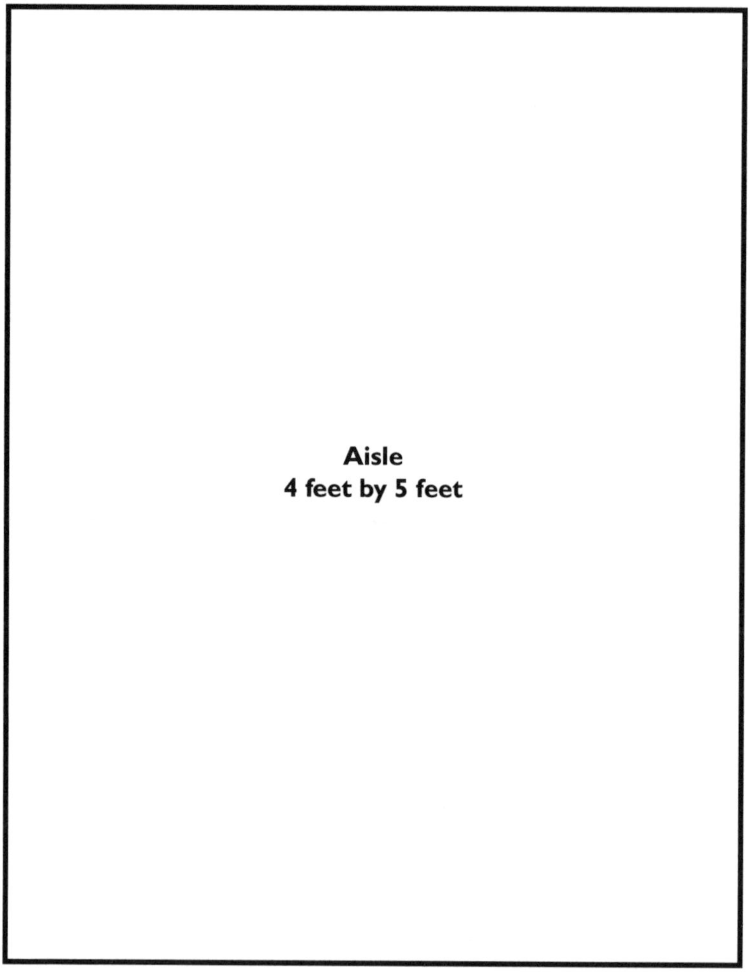

Aisle
4 feet by 5 feet

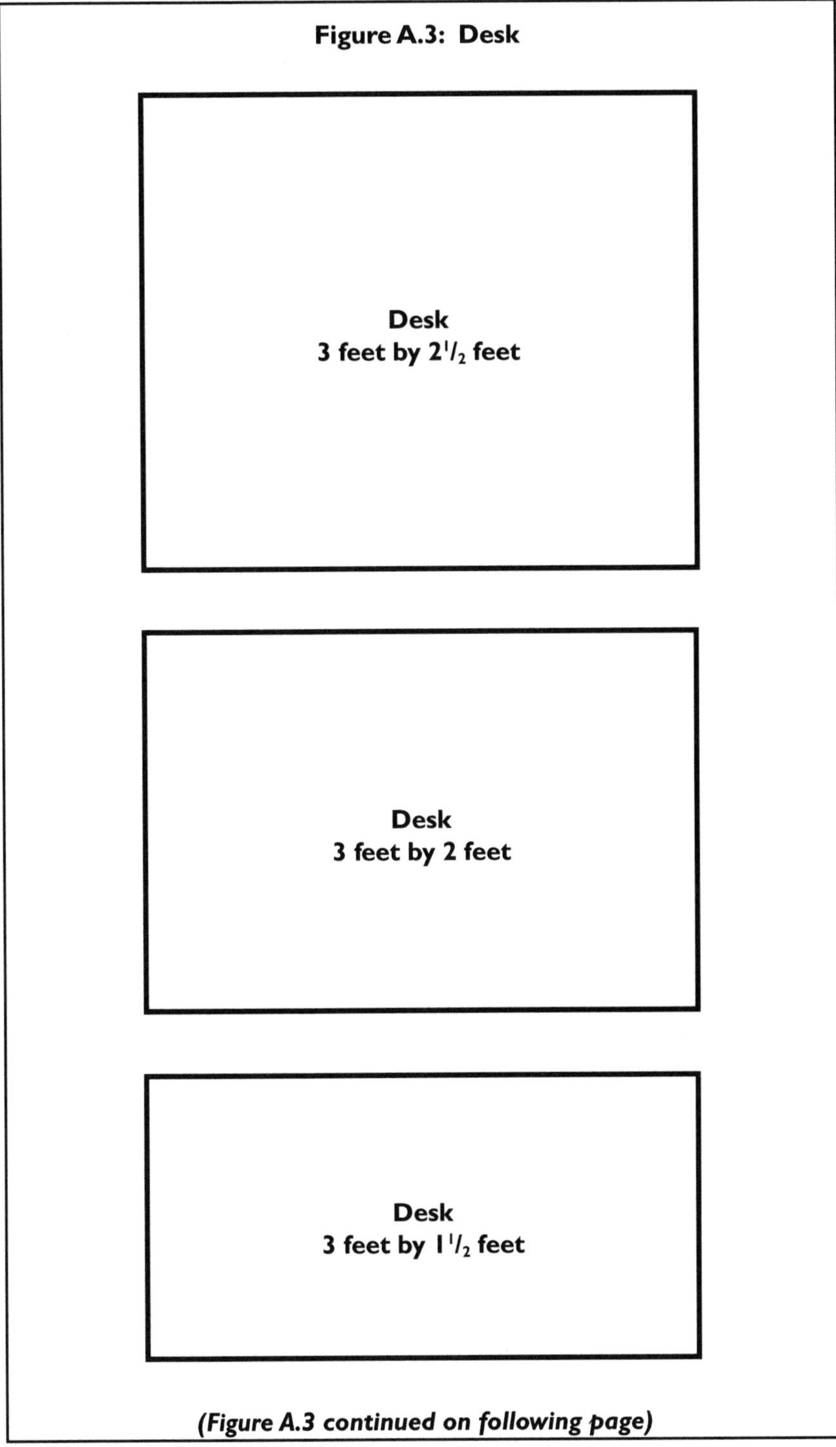

Figure A.3: Desk

(Figure A.3 continued on following page)

(Figure A.3: *continued*)

Desk
5 feet by 3 feet

Figure A.4: Equipment and Other Furnishings

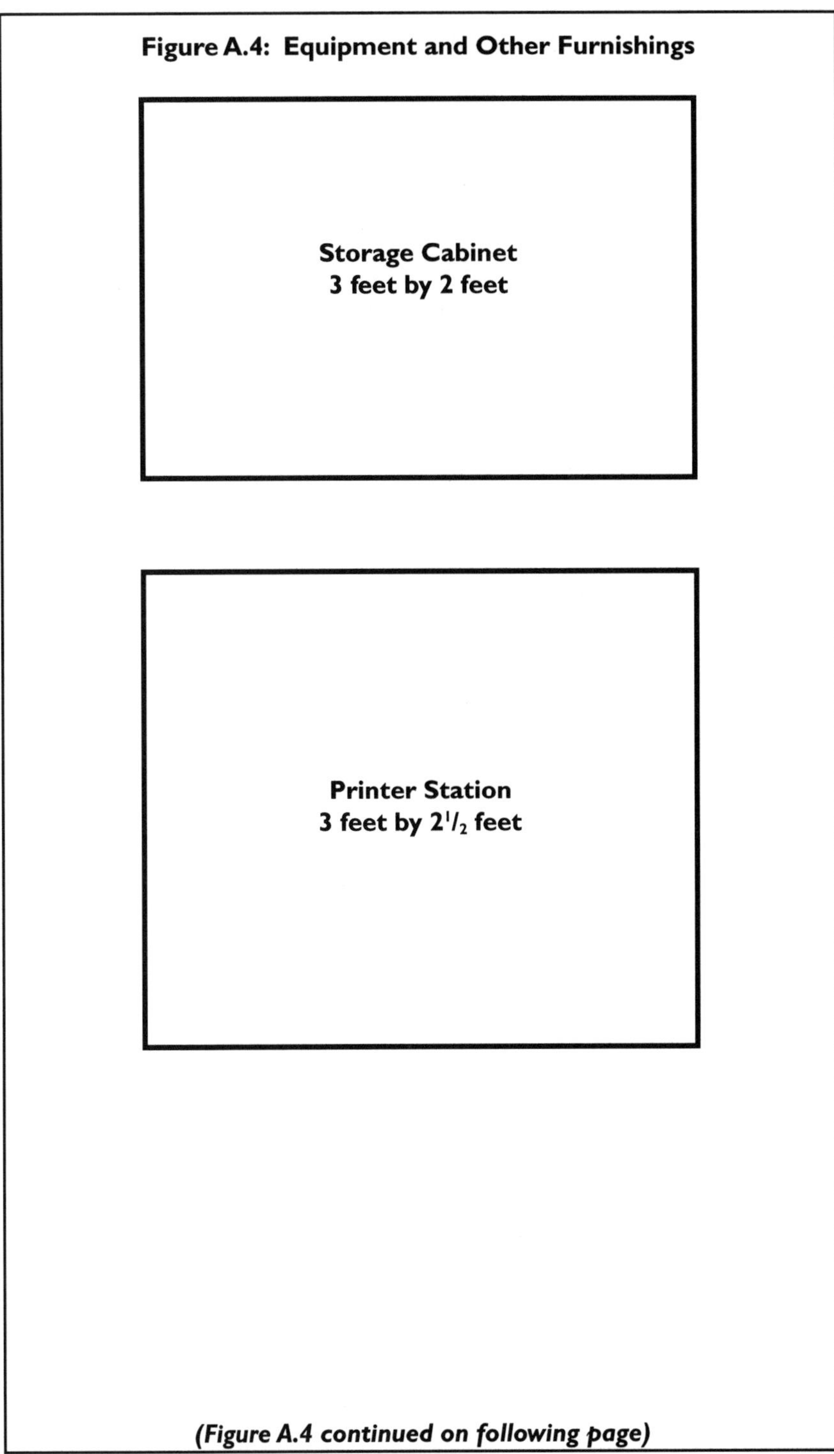

(Figure A.4 continued on following page)

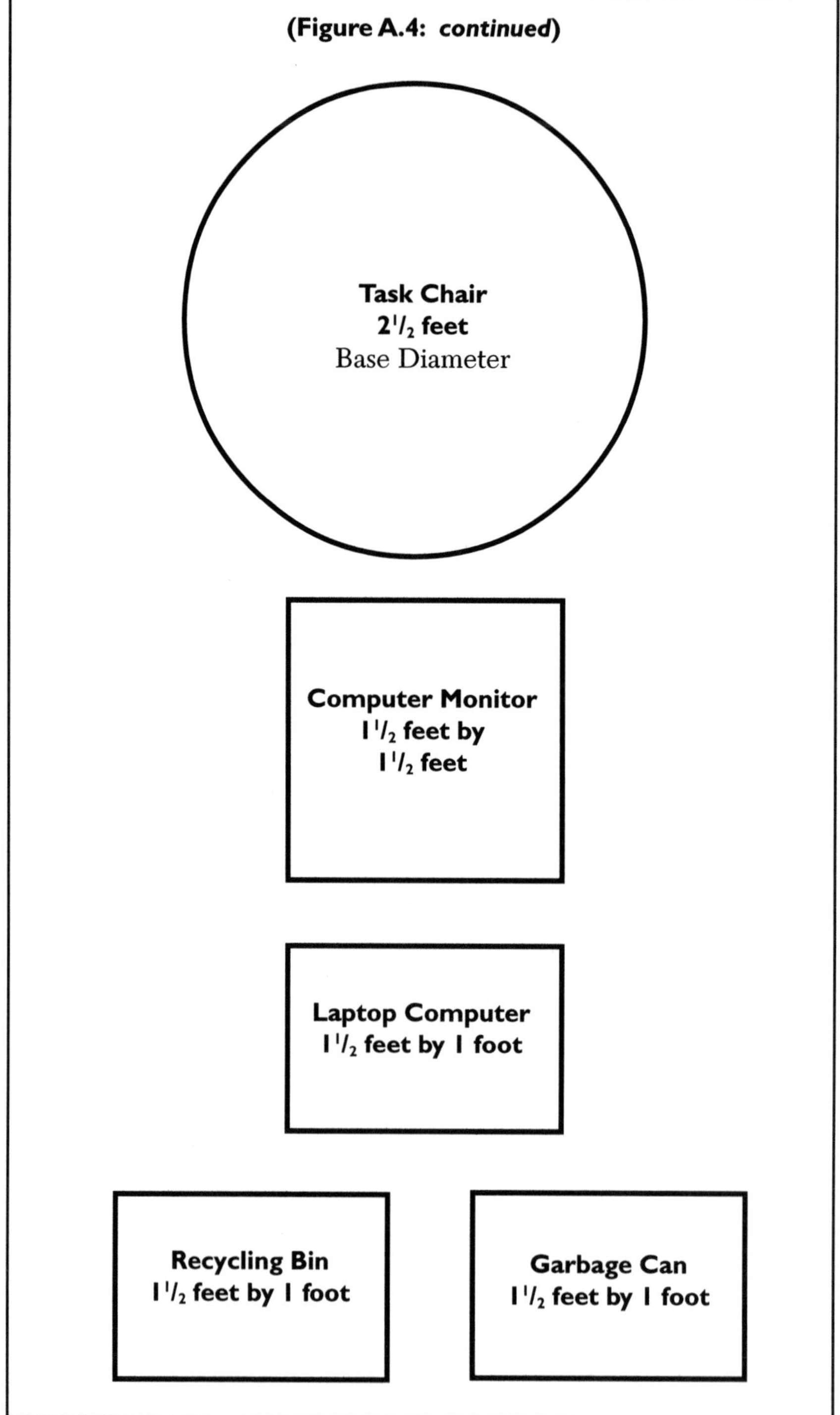
(Figure A.4: *continued*)
Task Chair
2 1/2 feet
Base Diameter
Computer Monitor
1 1/2 feet by
1 1/2 feet
Laptop Computer
1 1/2 feet by 1 foot
Recycling Bin
1 1/2 feet by 1 foot
Garbage Can
1 1/2 feet by 1 foot

Appendix B

Laws, Codes, Regulations, Standards, and Guidelines

Librarians involved in developing electronic classrooms need to be aware of the numerous codes, regulations, standards, guidelines, and laws that may affect their classrooms. This appendix identifies a number of example documents but it is not an exhaustive list of potentially applicable documents that librarians may wish to consult.

"ADA Accessibility Guidelines for Buildings and Facilities (ADAAG)." 1998. *www.access-board.gov/adaag/html/adaag.htm*. (September 16, 2000).

American National Standards Institute/Business and Institutional Furniture Manufacturer's Association. 1993. *American National Standard for Office Furnishings—General-Purpose Office Chairs—Tests*. New York: American National Standards Institute. ANSI/BIFMA X5.1–1993.

American National Standards Institute/Business and Institutional Furniture Manufacturer's Association. 1998. *American National Standard for Office Furnishings—Desk/Table Products—Tests*. New York: American National Standards Institute. ANSI/BIFMA X5.5–1998.

American National Standards Institute/Illuminating Engineering Society of North America. 2000. *Recommended Practice on Lighting for Educational Facilities: High School and College*. ANSI/IESNA RP-3–2000.

American National Standards Institute/International Organization for Standardization. 1992–2000. *Ergonomic Requirements for Office Work with Visual Display Terminals (VDTs)*. New York: American National Standards Institute. ANSI/ISO 9241.

American National Standards Institute/Photographic and Imaging Manufacturers Association. 1999. *American National Standard for Audiovisual Systems—Safe Handling and Operation of Audiovisual Equipment.* New York: American National Standards Institute. ANSI/PIMA IT7.101–1999.

American National Standards Institute/Photographic and Imaging Manufacturers Association. 1999. *Audiovisual Systems—Recommended Practice for Determining the Design of Teaching-Learning Spaces Where Audiovisual Equipment Is Used.* ANSI/PIMA IT7.100–1993 (R1999).

American National Standards Institute/Underwriters Laboratories. 1997. *Office Furnishings*. New York: American National Standards Institute. ANSI/UL 1286–1997.

American Society for Testing and Materials. 1999. *ASTM Standards in Building Codes*. Philadelphia: American Society for Testing and Materials.

American Society of Heating, Refrigerating, and Air-Conditioning Engineers. 2000. *ASHRAE Handbook*. Atlanta: American Society of Heating, Refrigerating, and Air-Conditioning Engineers.

Americans with Disabilities Act of 1990, Pub L. No. 101–336, 104 STAT. 327 (1990) (codified at 42 U.S.C. §§ 12101–12213)

Architectural Barriers Act of 1968, Pub L. No. 90–480, 82 STAT. 718 (1968) (codified at 42 U.S.C. §§ 4151–4157)

Assistive Technology Act of 1998, Pub L. No. 105–394, 112 STAT. 3627 (1998) (codified at 29 U.S.C. §§ 3001–3058)

Building Construction Cost Data. 2000. Kingston, Mass.: R. S. Means Co.

Building Officials and Code Administrators International. 1999. *The BOCA National Building Code*. Country Club Hills, Ill: Building Officials and Code Administrators International.

Cornell University. 1999. "Classroom Design Guidelines." *www.cit.cornell.edu/computer/instruct/classtech/design/*. (November 12, 2000).

McGill University. "Classroom Design Guidelines." *www.is.mcgill.ca/phyres/class_gd.htm*. (November 12, 2000).

Committee on Education, Training, and Support, Machine-Assisted Reference Section, Reference and Adult Services Division, American Library Association. 1995. "Electronic Information Sources Guidelines for Training Sessions." Chicago: American Library Association. *www.ala.org/rusa/stnd_training.html*. (September 18, 2000).

Dickens, Janis L., and David J. Tanza. 1996. *Classroom Guidelines for the Design and Construction of Classrooms at the University of California, Santa Cruz*. Santa Cruz, Calif.: UCSC Media Services.

Functional Space Requirements Committee, Buildings and Equipment Section, Library Administration and Management Association, American Library Association. 1995. *Building Blocks for Library Space: Functional Guidelines*. Chicago: American Library Association.

Guidelines for Instruction Programs Task Force, Instruction Section, Association of College and Research Libraries, American Library Association. 1996. "Guidelines for Instruction Programs in Academic Libraries." Chicago: American Library Association. *www.ala.org/acrl/guides/guiis.html*. (September 18, 2000).

Haviland, David, ed. 1994. *The Architect's Handbook of Professional Practice*. Washington, D.C.: American Institute of Architects Press.

Library and Information Technology Association, American Library Association. 1999. "Information Technology Access Assessment Checklist." Chicago: American Library Association. *www.lita.org/committe/techacc/access.html*. (September 18, 2000).

Myrick, Robert D. 1999. "Penn State Technology Classroom Design

Guidelines." *http://classrooms.cac.psu.edu/Tech/design.htm*. (November 12, 2000).

National Standards Systems Network. *www.nssn.org*. (September 16, 2000).

"Proposed Standards for Federal Electronic and Information Technology." 2000. *www.access-board.gov/sec508/508index.htm*. (September 16, 2000).

Panero, Julius, and Mertin Zelnik. 1979. *Human Dimension and Interior Space: A Sourcebook of Design Reference Standards*. New York: Whitney Library of Design.

Rea, Mark S. ed. 2000. *IESNA Lighting Handbook*. New York: Illuminating Engineering Society of North America.

Reznikoff, S. C. 1986. *Interior Graphic and Design Standards*. New York: Whitney Library of Design.

"Telecommunications Act Accessibility Guidelines." 1998. *www.access-board.gov/telecomm/html/telfinal.htm*. (September 16, 2000).

"Uniform Federal Accessibility Standards." *www.access-board.gov/ufas/ufas-html/ufas.htm*. (September 16, 2000).

Appendix C

Directory of Suppliers

This appendix provides contact information for companies and manufacturers mentioned elsewhere in the book as well as a few not specifically mentioned but useful for library classroom designers. Whenever specific products or companies are mentioned, they are intended as examples of a general type or category. No endorsement is intended or implied by inclusion in this book.

Adobe Systems Inc.
345 Park Ave.
San Jose, CA 95110–2704
800–833–6687
www.adobe.com

Ai Squared
P.O. Box 669
Manchester Center, VT 05255
802–362–3612
www.aisquared.com

Altiris
387 S. 520 W.
Lindon, UT 84042
888–252–5551
www.altiris.com

Apple Computer
1 Infinite Loop
Cupertino, CA 95014
800–293–6617
www.apple.com

Applied Computer Systems, Inc.
3060 Johnstown-Utica Rd.
Johnstown, OH 43031–9903
800–237–5465
www.acs-linksystems.com

Audience Response Systems
2148 N. Cullen Ave.
Evansville, IN 47715
800–468–6583
www.audienceresponse.com

Blackwelder's Industries, Inc.
294 Turnersburg Hwy.
Statesville, NC 28677
800–438–0201
www.homefurnish.com/blackwelders

Bretford Manufacturing, Inc.
11000 Seymour Ave.
Franklin Park, IL 60131
(800) 521–9614
www.bretford.com

Cetus Software
P.O. Box 1450
Marshfield, MA 02050
781–834–4411
www.cetussoft.com

Circle Systems
1001 Fourth Ave., Suite 3200
Seattle, WA 98154
800–366–3794
www.stattransfer.com

click2learn.com
110–110th Ave. N.E., Suite 700
Bellevue, WA 98004
800–448–6543
www.click2learn.com

Computer Furniture Direct
11619 Beach Blvd.
Jacksonville, FL 32246
800–555–6126
www.cf-direct.com

COMWEB Technology Group
155 Rte. 46
Wayne Interchange Plaza II
Wayne, NJ 07470–6831
973–890–0010
www.comweb.com

Crestron Electronics, Inc.
15 Volvo Dr.
Rockleigh, NJ 07647
800–237–2041
www.crestron.com

CrossTech Corporation
500 N.E. Spanish River Blvd., Suite 201
Boca Raton, FL 33431
800–675–0729
www.crossteccorp.com

Daedalus Group
1106 Clayton Lane, #510W
Austin, TX 78723
800–879–2144
www.daedalus.com

DataViz
55 Corporate Dr.
Trumbull, CT 06611
800–733–0030
www.dataviz.com

Environmental Systems Research Institute
380 New York St.
Redlands, CA 92373–8100
800–447–9778
www.esri.com

Fleetwood
P.O. Box 1259
Holland, MI 49424
800–257–6390
www.fleetwoodgroup.com

Fortres Grand Corporation
P.O. Box 888
Plymouth, IN 46563
800–331–0372
www.fortres.com

Fortress Technologies
4025 Tampa Rd., Suite 1111
Oldsmar, FL 34677
888–477–4822
www.fortresstech.com

Grafco, Inc.
P.O. Box 71
Catasauqua, PA 18032–0071
800–367–6169
www.grafco.com

Henter-Joyce
11800 31st Court N.
St. Petersburg, FL 33716
800–444–4443
www.hj.com

Herman Miller
855 E. Main Ave.
P.O. Box 302
Zeeland, MI 49464–0302
888–443–4357
www.hermanmiller.com

Howe Furniture Corporation
12 Cambridge Dr.
P.O. Box 0386
Trumball, CT 06611
203–374–7833

IBM
New Orchard Rd.
Armonk, NY 10504
800–IBM–4YOU (800–465–4968)
www.ibm.com

IMSI
75 Rowland Way
Novato, CA 94945
415–878–4000
www.imsisoft.com

InfoWorks Technology Company
P.O. Box 2261
Cranberry Township, PA 16066
800–465–8668
www.itcompany.com

Inline, Inc.
22860 Savi Ranch Pkwy.
Yorba Linda, CA 92887
800–882–7117
www.inlineinc.com

Innovision
8325 Lenexa Dr.
Lenexa, KS 66214
913–438–3200
www.innovision.com

Intel
2200 Mission College Blvd.
Santa Clara, CA 95052–8119
800–628–8686
www.intel.com

IntelliTools, Inc.
1720 Corporate Circle
Petaluma, CA 94954
800–899–6687
www.intellitools.com

ISI ResearchSoft
800 Jones St.
Berkeley, CA 94710
800–554–3049
www.isiresearchsoft.com

KI (Krueger International)
1330 Bellview St.
P.O. Box 8100
Green Bay, WI 54308
800–424–2432
www.krugerinternational.com

Macromedia, Inc.
600 Townsend St.
San Francisco, CA 94103
415–252–2000
www.macromedia.com

MapInfo Corporation
One Global View
Troy, NY 12180
800–FASTMAP (800–327–8627)
www.mapinfo.com

McAfee
535 Oakmead Pkwy.
Sunnyvale, CA 94086
888–622–3331
www.mcafee.com

Meeting Maker
Waltham Woods
880 Winter St., Bldg. 4
Waltham, MA 02451–1449
781–487–3538
www.meetingmaker.com

Microsoft
One Microsoft Way
Redmond, WA 98052–6399
425–882–8080
www.microsoft.com

MicroTouch Systems, Inc.
300 Griffin Brook Park Dr.
Methuen, MA 01844
800–642–7686
www.microtouch.com

Mimio
56 Roland St.
Boston, MA 02129
877–696–4646
www.mimio.com

Minicom Advanced Systems Inc.
414 North Wood Ave.
Linden, NJ 07036
888–486–2154
www.minicomusa.com

Netscape
466 Ellis St.
Mountain View, CA 94043–4042
650–254–1900
www.netscape.com

NetSupport Inc.
106 Colony Park Dr., Suite 400
Cumming, GA 30040
888–665–0808 (Sales)
www.netsupport-inc.com

Nova Solutions, Inc.
421 W. Industrial Ave.
Effingham, IL 62401
800–730–NOVA (800–730–6682)
www.novadesk.com

Novell
1800 S. Novell Pl.
Provo, UT 84606
800–453–1267
www.novell.com

Numonics
101 Commerce Dr.
P.O. Box 1005
Montgomeryville, PA 18936
800–523–6716
www.numonics.com

One Touch Systems
40 Airport Pkwy.
San Jose, CA 95110
408–436–4600
www.onetouch.com

Panja
3000 Research Dr.
Richardson, TX 75082
800–222–0193
www.panja.com

Phonic Ear
3880 Cypress Dr.
Petaluma, CA 94954
800–227–0735
www.phonicear.com

PowerOn Software
901 N. 3rd St., #305
Minneapolis, MN 55401
800–344–9160
www.poweronsw.com

Prentice Hall Inc.
Upper Saddle River, NJ 07458
800–282–0693
www.prenticehall.com

Raxco, Inc.
6 Montgomery Village Ave.
Gaithersburg, MD 20879
800–546–9728
www.raxco.com

Real Networks
PO Box 91123
Seattle, WA 98111–9223
888–768–3248
www.realnetworks.com

Robotel Electronique Inc.
3185 Delaunay
Laval, PQ, H7L 5A4, Canada
800–964–1448
www.robotel.ca/product.htm

SAS Institute Inc.
SAS Campus Dr.
Cary, NC 27513–2414
919–677–8000
www.sas.com

Sixth Floor Media
222 Berkeley St.
Boston, MA 02116
800–565–6247
www.sixthfloor.com

SMART Technologies
1177 11th Ave. S.W., Suite 600
Calgary, AB T2R 1K9, Canada
800–42–SMART (800–427–6278)
www.smarttech.com

SMARTdesks
P.O. Box 4463
Lutherville, MD 21094
800–777–7042
www.smartdesks.com

SoftBoard
16112 S.W. 72nd Ave.
Portland, OR 97224
888–763–8262
www.softboard.com

Spectrum
1600 Johnson St.
P.O. Box 400
Chippewa Falls, WI 54729
800–235–1262
www.spectrumfurniture.com

SPSS Inc.
233 S. Wacker Dr., 11th Fl.
Chicago, IL 60606
800–521–1337
www.spss.com

Stata Corporation
702 University Dr. E.
College Station, TX 77840
800–782–8272
www.stata.com

Symantec
20330 Stevens Creek Blvd.
Cupertino, CA 95014
408–517–8000
www.symantec.com

Tech Electronics, Inc.
6420 Atlantic Blvd., Suite 145
Norcross, GA 30071
800–572–4935
www.techelec.com

Techline
901 S. Lawe St.
Appleton, WI 54915
800–356–8400
www.techline-furn.com

TechSight Engineering Services
General Dynamics Defense Systems
100 Plastics Ave.
Pittsfield, MA 01201
414–494–3362
www.techsight.com

Thos. Moser Cabinetmakers
27 Wright's Landing
P.O. Box 1237
Auburn, ME 04211
800–708–9710
www.thosmoser.com

Vertiflex
3000 W. Dundee Rd. #415
Northbrook, IL 60062
800–966–5511
www.vertiflex.com

Wearing Williams Limited
1140 St. James St.
Winnipeg, MB R3H 0K7, Canada
800–954–5656
www.wearingwilliams.mb.ca

WebCT, Inc.
Six Kimball Lane, Suite 310
Lynnfield, MA 01940
781–309–1000
www.webct.com

Westing Software
144 Dominga Ave.
Fairfax, CA 94930
800–325–1862
www.westinginc.com

Appendix D

Library Classroom Web Sites

Following is just a sampling of the library classroom Web sites available on the Internet. Many institutions also have Web sites describing electronic classrooms for departmental and general use. You can locate many more Web site examples through a quick search using your favorite search engine.

Ball State University
Bracken Library
Muncie, IN
www.library.bsu.edu/internal/ala/poster.htm

Christian Brothers University
Plough Library
Memphis, TN
www.cbu.edu/library/infolab/index.html

Dakota State University
Karl E. Mundt Library
Madison, SD
www.departments.dsu.edu/library/opnclass.htm

Louisiana State University
Middleton Library
Baton Rouge, LA
www.lib.lsu.edu/classroom/schedule

Mississippi State University
University Libraries
Mississippi State, MS
http://library.msstate.edu/li/classrooms.asp

Penn State Lehigh Valley
CoLab
Fogelsville, PA
www.lv.psu.edu/jsn3/colab/

Purdue University
Purdue University Libraries
West Lafayette, IN
http://thorplus.lib.purdue.edu/library_info/departments/ugrl/lec/index.html

Radford University
McConnell Library
Radford, VA
http://lib.runet.edu/libserv/handout/multipurpose.html

Rochester Institute of Technology
Wallace Library
Rochester, NY
http://wally.rit.edu/general/facilities/bib/bib.html

Stanford University
Stanford, CA
http://dill.stanford.edu/facilities.html

State University of New York at Stony Brook
Health Sciences Center Library
Stony Brook, NY
www.hsclib.sunysb.edu/services/systems
www.hsclib.sunysb.edu/policies/pol_class.htm

Stephen F. Austin State University
Ralph W. Steen Library
Nacogdoches, TX
http://libweb.sfasu.edu/systems/default.htm#classroom

The Libraries of the Claremont Colleges
Honnold/Mudd Library
Claremont, CA
http://voxlibris.claremont.edu/hm/keck.html

University of Oshkosh
Forrest R. Polk Library
Oshkosh, WI
www.uwosh.edu/departments/llr/instruct/facilities.htm

University of Iowa
University of Iowa Libraries
Iowa City, IA
www.lib.uiowa.edu/arcade/facilities.html
www.lib.uiowa.edu/commons/vr.html

University of Louisville
William F. Ekstrom Library
Louisville, KA
www.louisville.edu/infoliteracy/Instrooms.htm

University of Memphis
McWherter Library
Memphis, TN
www.lib.memphis.edu/instr/chezinfo.htm
www.lib.memphis.edu/instr/policies.htm#center

University of Oregon
University of Oregon Library
Eugene, OR
http://libweb.uoregon.edu/instruct/classrooms.html

University of Southern California
Leavey Library
Los Angeles, CA
www.usc.edu/isd/locations/undergrad/leavey/Instruction/faculty.html

University of Southern Indiana
David L. Rice Library
Evansville, IN
www.bsu.edu/library/internal/ala/poster.htm

University of St. Thomas, Minneapolis
Charles J. Keffer Library
Minneapolis, MN
www.lib.stthomas.edu/keffer/services/comp.htm

University of Washington
Seattle, WA
www.washington.edu/uwired/services/collabs

Yale University
Yale University Library
New Haven, CT
www.library.yale.edu/ref/eclass/eclass.html

Appendix E

Sample Instructional Materials—The Research Process

The research process is a common topic for first-year library instruction sessions. The interactive nature of making a presentation in an electronic classroom with live connections to networked information resources allows the instructor to involve students in the demonstration by asking for sample search topics or research questions. Students who are learning about the process of research in a hands-on electronic classroom also have the opportunity to put into practice immediately the concepts being presented.

Following are the instructional materials used at Milner Library, Illinois State University, for the 50-minute LILAC Workshop. LILAC stands for Library Instruction for Language and Communication (Communication 110: Language and Communication), and is an attempt to use the concept of "branding" to help students and instructors understand that the instruction is customized for that particular course and is not a repetition of other instructional sessions. All materials distributed during the LILAC Workshop, as well as the materials explaining the LILAC Workshop that are distributed to the teaching assistants and faculty who teach Communication 110, are printed on light purple or white paper.

All first-year students are required to take Communication 110 in one of their first two semesters at the university. Approximately 1,500 students enroll in about 70 sections of the course each fall and spring semester. The workshop for each section is course-integrated, occurs during a regularly scheduled class period, and takes place in one of the library's two hands-on electronic classrooms. The library instruction sessions are taught in a two-and-one-half week period and involve more than ten teaching librarians.

Figure E.1 contains the information provided to the teaching librarians. "Information About and Outline for the LILAC Workshop" provides general background information, identifies needed handouts, suggests a room setup, and outlines the components of the workshop. Librarians are free to adapt the outline to meet their teaching styles and the needs of a particular group of students.

Figure E.2 is the descriptive handout "Milner Library Annotations for Chapter 6: Gathering Materials of *The Art of Public Speaking* (7th Edition)." *The Art of Public Speaking* is the course textbook which contains a very good chapter on library and Internet research. The handout is intended to help students make the connection between the chapter in their textbook, which they are assigned to read before the session, and the LILAC Workshop, and to indicate alternatives to resources recommended in the textbook but not available at Milner Library. In future years, it is hoped that this handout can be included in the student workbook for the course.

Figure E.3 is a procedural handout and is simply titled "Worksheet." The worksheet was carefully designed to incorporate features from Communication 110 course materials—specifically, the purpose statement and process reflection. Again, the goal is that students understand the relationship between the content of the LILAC Workshop and the course in which they are enrolled. The worksheet focuses on the broad concept of "research as process" while also touching on the concepts of topic refinement, types of information, popular and scholarly materials, database/research tool selection, keyword searching, and citation elements. The instructional design assumes that students will already have some familiarity with the mechanics of searching and are comfortable using a computer.

Figure E.1: Instructor Information

Information About and Outline for the LILAC Workshop
(Library Instruction for Language and Communication)
2000-2001

Background Information:

The LILAC (Library Instruction for Language and Communication) Workshop is a component of the General Education Library Instruction Program and complements the Foundations of Inquiry Library Instruction. The session is customized and unique to Language and Communication – no other classes use the worksheet and the worksheet is very specific to the speech assignments, using terminology drawn directly from the course texts. The focus is on the process of analyzing a topic and selecting appropriate information tools for researching the topic. Students are expected to bring the topics of the informative speeches that they will be giving in their Language and Communication class to the LILAC Workshop and their instructors have been asked to facilitate this. Based on past experience, the topics seem likely to be current social issues or elements of popular culture; however, they are not required to choose such topics.

Though they are no longer listed in the course packet, below are the Sample Topics for the Informative Speech that had been listed in the past (the course packet is put together by the directors of Language and Communication, not the library):

- Using the Internet
- Election year (candidate profiles)
- The Berlin Wall
- Sign language
- Passover
- Mardi Gras
- Tornado Safety
- Maya Angelou
- ISU's Circus
- Van Gogh's art
- Peace Corps
- Genetic engineering
- Setting up a webpage
- Migraine headaches
- The Grateful Dead
- ISU's International Studies Program
- History of jazz
- Birth order
- Rain forests
- Virtual reality
- Sleep disorders

(Figure E.1 continued on following page)

(Figure E.1: *continued*)

Because students are attending the session during class time, there is no need to emphasize the worksheet as "proof of attendance" – the instructor will be with the class and know who is present and who is absent.

A Classroom Assistant will be scheduled for each Session to provide technical assistance, keyboarding at the instructor station, and student assistance during hands-on working time.

Handouts:

Each student should receive one copy of each of the following:

1. LILAC Worksheet (Purple Paper)
2. Milner Library Annotations for Chapter 6: "Gathering Materials" of *The Art of Public Speaking* (7th Edition) (White Paper) – Provides locations for the resources mentioned in the library research chapter of the textbook.

Set-Up Room:

- Place piles of the handouts on the table at the back of the room for students to pick up as they enter the room. (Handouts will be found in the handout cabinet.)
- Bring up the Milner Library webpage on the instructor station or the Milner Trivia Tracks (if you choose to use the trivia show).
- Bring up the Milner Library webpage on the student workstations.
- Prop open the door to help students realize that the room is open.
- Take out copies of *Statistical Abstracts*.

Outline of a LILAC Workshop:

Introduction. <5 minutes>

1. Introduce yourself and the Classroom Assistant who is helping with the session.
2. Explain the purpose of the workshop to the students, emphasizing the relationship between the instruction session and the course assignments.

The purpose of the workshop is to assist students in developing effective research strategies for locating information sources for their Informative, Group, and Persuasive speeches.

The session will cover the following concepts:

- Selecting and analyzing a research topic.
- Selecting appropriate research tools.
- Using the research tools to retrieve information.
- Reflecting on the research process.

(Figure E.1: *continued*)

3. Mention the Milner Library Annotations to Chapter 6: Gathering Materials of *The Art of Public Speaking* (white) handout and its relationship to their textbook.
4. Explain that the students will be completing the LILAC Worksheet. The Worksheet provides an opportunity for students to begin researching the Informative Speech. Note for the students that the Worksheet only requires that they identify two sources for their Speech but that they will need a total of four sources for their Informative Speech Bibliography.

Topic Exploration and Information Analysis. <10 minutes>

1. Explain the importance of starting library research with a clear understanding of what topic one is looking for information about. Model the thought process with an example topic – either one of your own or one from the list of sample topics.
2. Ask the students to complete questions 1-3 about their own topics.

The Research Record. <30 minutes>

1. Overview the layout of the Milner Library website pointing out how to access the online catalog and the set-up of the article indexes and databases. Emphasize that, *in general*, using the online catalog or an article index or database will help them retrieve relevant information more quickly and potentially of higher quality than the information they might retrieve from the Internet.
2. Discuss the directions for the Worksheet sections – *Magazine/ Newspaper Articles*, *Scholarly/Scientific Journal Articles*, *Books*, *Statistics*, and *Additional Resources*.
3. Explain the importance of documenting the process of doing research – saves time, prevents mistakes, helps with the creation of the bibliography, etc.
4. Students should use the time remaining in the session to use the research tools they selected and complete the worksheet including the section on Process Reflection. The Librarian and the Classroom Assistant should provide coaching and assistance for students as they work on the worksheets.
5. Assure students that they can complete the worksheets using any terminal in the library or elsewhere on campus if they are unable to finish them during the session.

Wrap-Up. <5 minutes>

1. Thank students and instructor for coming. Encourage them to ask questions at any Information Desk in Milner Library whenever they are doing research.

Figure E.2: Textbook Annotations Handout

Milner Library Annotations for Chapter 6: "Gathering Materials" of *The Art of Public Speaking* (7th Edition)

LILAC: Library Instruction for Language and Communication *2000-2001*

The Art of Public Speaking (7th Edition) recommends a number of information resources in Chapter 6: "Gathering Materials" which will be helpful to you as you search for information in preparation for composing your speeches. To increase the efficiency of your research, this handout tells you where the resources recommended by your textbook are found in Milner Library. If the recommended resource is not available, at least one alternative that is available is listed for you. If you need assistance in finding the resources on this handout or have other questions about research, ask at any of the Milner Library Information Desks. The Milner Library website is at http://www.mlb.ilstu.edu.

Text Page	Name of Resource	Call Number	Milner Floor
126	Card Catalogue	No longer updated.	Floor 3
126	Online Catalogue	*Illinet Online*. Available from the Milner website.	
128	Aviation Week and Space Technology	TL501. A8	Floor 5
128	Consumer Reports	TX335.A1 C6	Floor 5
128	Ebony	AP2. E165	Floor 1
128	General Reference Center	Use Wilson Select (Milner website).	
128	Ms.	HQ1101. M55	Floor 4
128	Newsweek	AP2. N6772	Floor 1
128	Psychology Today	BF1. P83	Floor 1
128	Reader's Guide to Periodical Literature	Ref. AI3. R48	Floor 2
128	Rolling Stone	ML1. R65	Floor 6
128	Scientific American	T1. S5	Floor 5
128	Sports Illustrated	GV561. S733	Floor 1
128	Time	AP2. T37	Floor 1
128	Vital Speeches of the day	PN6121. V52	Floor 6
129	Academic Search	Use Wilson Select (Milner website).	
129	ProQuest Research Library	Use Wilson Select (Milner website).	
129	Public Affairs Information Service International	Available from the Milner website.	
130	Applied Science and Technology Index	Available from the Milner website.	
130	Art Index	Use Art Abstracts (Milner website).	
130	Business Abstracts	Available from the Milner website.	
130	Education Index	Use Education Abstracts (Milner website).	
130	ERIC	Available from the Milner website	
130	Ethnic NewsWatch	Use Academic Universe (Milner website).	
130	Hispanic American Periodicals Index	Ref. Z6953.8 .H36	Floor 4
130	Index to Black Periodicals	Ref. AI3 .I6802	Floor 4
130	Social Sciences Index	Use Social Sciences Abstracts (Milner website).	
130	Women's Resources International	Use Contemporary Women's Issues (Milner website).	
131	Atlanta Constitution	Newspaper Section	Floor 2
131	Black Newspaper Index	Use Kaiser Index to Black Resources (Ref Z1361 .N39K34 1992). Floor 4	
131	Christian Science Monitor	Newspaper Section	Floor 2
131	Editorials on File	Ref. D410. E35	Floor 2
131	Lexis/Nexis Academic Universe	Available from the Milner website.	
131	Los Angeles Times	Newspaper Section	Floor 2
131	National Newspaper Index	Use Academic Universe (Milner website).	
131	New York Times	AP2. N675	Floor 2

(Figure E.2: *continued*)

131	New York Times Index	Ref AI 21.N45	Floor 2
131	NewsBank's NewsSource	Use Academic Universe (Milner website).	
131	ProQuest Newspapers	Use Academic Universe (Milner website).	
131	The Wall Street Journal	Reference Desk	Floor 4
131	UMI's Newspaper Abstracts	Use Academic Universe (Milner website).	
131	USA Today	Newspaper Section	Floor 2
131	Washington Post	Newspaper Section	Floor 2
132	Encyclopedia Americana	Ref. AE5. E3331996	Floor 2
132	Encyclopedia Britannica	Ref. AE5. E3631995	Floor 2
132	Encyclopedia of Philosophy	Ref. B41. E5	Floors 1, 2
132	Encyclopedia of Religion	Ref. BL31. E461987	Floor 1
132	Encyclopedia of World Art	Ref. N31. E4883	Floor 2
132	Encyclopedia of World Crime	Ref. HV6017. E54241992	Floor 4
132	Grove's Dictionary of Music and Musicians	Ref. ML100. G881927	Floors 2, 6
132	Grzimek's Animal Life Encyclopedia	Ref. QL3. G7813	Floor 5
132	International Encyclopedia of the Social Sciences	Ref. H40. A2I5	Floors 2, 4
133	African American Encyclopedia	Ref. E185. A2531993	Floor 4
133	American Heritage Dictionary	Ref. PE1625. A541982	Floor 1
133	Asian American Encyclopedia	Ref. E184.O6 A8271995	Floor 4
133	Black's Law Dictionary	Re. KF156.B531979	Floor 4
133	Dictionary of Feminist Theory	Ref. HQ1115.H861995	Floor 4
133	Encyclopedia of Computer Science	Use Encyclopedia of Computer Science and Engineering (Ref. QA76.15.E481983) Floor 5	
133	Facts on File	Ref. D410. F3	Floor 2
133	Latino Encyclopedia	Ref. E184.S75 L3571996	Floor 4
133	McGraw-Hill Encyclopedia of Science and Technology	Ref. Q121.M311997	Floor 5
133	Morris Dictionary of Wold and Phrase Origins	Ref. PE1580. M61977	Floor 2
133	Oxford English Dictionary	Ref. PE1625.O871989	Floor 1
133	Statistical Abstract of the U.S.	DOC.C3.134 or HA 202	Floors 1, 2, 4, 5
133	The Computer Dictionary	Ref. TK5102. S4851998	Floor 5
133	World Almanac & Book of Facts	Ref. AY67.N5 W7	Floors 1, 2, 4
134	A Treasury of Jewish Quotations	PN6095.J4 T741985	Floor 6
134	Fire in Our Souls: Quotations of Wisdom and Inspiration by Latino Americans	Ref. PN6084.H47F1996	Floor 2
134	Harper Book of American Quotations	Ref. PN6084. A5C371988	Floor 6
134	International Who's Who	Ref. CT120.I5	Floors 2, 4
134	My Soul Looks Back, 'Less I Forget: A Collection of Quotations by People of Color	Ref. PN6081.3.M91993	Floor 2
134	Oxford Dictionary of Quotations	Ref. PN6080. O951999	Floor 2
134	The New Quotable Woman	Ref. PN6081.5.N491992	Floor 6
134	Who's Who in America	Ref. E176. W642	Floors 2,4
135	Biography Index	Ref. Z5301. B5	Floor 2
135	Contemporary Black Biography	Ref. CT120.C66	Floor 2
135	Current Biography	Ref. CT100. C82	Floor 2
135	Current Biography Yearbook	Ref. CT100. C8201	Floor 2
135	Dictionary of Hispanic Biography	Ref. CT120. C66	Floor 2
135	Jerusalem Post	Newspaper Section	Floor 2
135	Merriam-Webster's Geographical Dictionary	Ref. G103. W421997	Floor 4
135	Native American Women	Ref. E98.W8 B381993	Floor 2
135	Rand McNally Cosmopolitan World Atlas	Ref. G1019. R241978	Floor 4
135	Tokyo Shimbun	See other Floor 2 newspapers.	
135	Who's Who of American Women	Ref. CT3260. W5	Floor 4
142	U.S. News and World Report	JK1. U65	Floor 4
152	Encyclopedia of Associations	Ref. HS17. G33	Floors 2,4
155	Encyclopedia of Jazz	Ref. ML3561.J3 E55	Floor 6
160	Latino Encyclopedia	Ref. E184.S75 L3571996	Floor 4

Figure E.3: Process Worksheet

Name: ______________

LILAC

Worksheet

LILAC: Library Instruction for Language and Communication

Spring 2001

Purpose: To develop **effective research strategies for locating information sources** for your Informative (four sources), Group (ten sources), and Persuasive (six sources) speeches in *Communication 110: Language and Communication.*

Topic Exploration

1. What topic have you selected for your **Informative Speech**? If you have not yet selected a topic, what subject area would you like to explore in preparation for selecting a topic?

2. What other words or phrases might be used to describe your Informative Speech topic?

Information Analysis

3. What aspects of your Informative Speech topic would you like to explore?

- ❑ Campus/Local
- ❑ Ethical/Moral
- ❑ Economic/Business
- ❑ Psychological
- ❑ Educational
- ❑ Political
- ❑ Religious
- ❑ Scientific/Medical
- ❑ Historical
- ❑ ______________

(Figure E.3: *continued*)

Research Record

4. Find at least two relevant sources for your Informative Speech. They can be in any category or categories (Magazine/Newspaper Articles, Scholarly/Scientific Journal Articles, Books, Statistics, or Additional Resources). Record below the process that you use and what you find.

🕮 Magazine/Newspaper Articles

- Start at the Milner Library website (http://www.mlb.ilstu.edu). Click on *Databases and Article Indexes*. Under *By Subject...*, select "General Indexes" or "Newspapers Indexes" and then click on *Show Databases*. Write down the name of the database that you are going to use. (Hint: The database name is a hotlink in the right-most column.)

  ____

- Login to the database. Enter a search. Write down the keywords that you searched.

  ____

- Look at your search results. Choose a relevant item or two and write down the citations.

  ____

  ____

🕮 Scholarly/Scientific Journal Articles

- Start at the Milner Library website (http://www.mlb.ilstu.edu). Click on *Databases and Article Indexes*. Under *By Subject...*, select your topic area and then click on *Show Databases*. Write down the name of the database that you are going to use. (Hint: The database name is a hotlink in the right-most column.)

  ____

- Login to the database. Enter a search. Write down the keywords that you searched.

  ____

- Look at your search results. Choose a relevant item or two and write down the citations.

  ____

  ____

(Figure E.3 continued on following page)

(Figure E.3: *continued*)

Books

- Start at the Milner Library website (http://www.mlb.ilstu.edu). Click on *Online Catalogs*. Select *Illinet Online (Web Version)*. At the next screen, click on the *Start* button.
- Enter a search. Write down the keywords that you searched.

____

- Look at your search results. Choose a relevant item or two and write down the citations.

____

____

Statistics

- To locate statistical information, use a copy of *Statistical Abstract of the United States*. Copies of this reference book are available in the classroom as well as in the Reference Section on Floors 1, 4, and 5 (Call Number: HA 202) and at the Floor 2 Information Desk (Call Number: DOC.C3.134).

- Use the index to look up statistics on your topic. The index lists table numbers (not page numbers). Choose a relevant table and write down its name, table number, and page number.

____

____

Additional Resources

- You may also choose any resource listed on the handout: **Milner Library Annotations for Chapter 6: "Gathering Materials" of *The Art of Public Speaking* (7th Edition).**
- Look through the list on the handout. Write down the name of at least one relevant resource.

____

____

(Figure E.3: *continued*)

Process Reflection

5. Did you find the information that you need? If yes, what was the most successful part of your research strategy? If not, why do you think that your research strategy was not successful?

6. What other information do you still need to find?

7. What did you learn about the research process that will help you locate information resources for your **Group** and **Persuasive** speeches?

Helpful Information

Copies of the Publication Manual of the American Psychological Association are available from the Information Desks (Floors 1 and 2) for use in Milner Library.

Appendix F

Sample Instructional Materials—Evaluating Information

Teaching students to evaluate information has long been an important part of many library instruction programs. The differences between various types of periodicals—newspapers, magazines, trade publications, and scholarly journals, comparisons between opinion and research writing, and notions of disciplinarity are all familiar topics to the teaching librarian. In recent years, the explosion of information resources made available via the Internet has made information evaluation an even more vital component of library instruction. Faculty members who were previously uninterested in library instruction sessions for their classes now regularly schedule workshops for their students. Librarians are challenged daily to help students determine which Web sites are appropriate for their term papers and which should be avoided.

This appendix contains sample instructional materials for teaching students to evaluate information. These materials, and many others like them, are used at Milner Library, Illinois State University, in both undergraduate and graduate instruction sessions. They are also used in faculty development workshops, which are designed to help faculty teach their students about information quality.

Figure F.1 provides lists of Web sites on different topics. For each topic, some of the Web sites are high quality and very credible, some argue for or from a particular viewpoint, and some are questionable in either their facts and/or their reasoning. A few are hoax Web sites, but most are not.

Figure F.2 is an excerpt from the textbook used in the first-year critical thinking course at Illinois State University. The excerpt is taken from a chapter on doing library research. All of the classes also attend at least one to three library instruction sessions. Many instructors request that one whole class period be devoted to developing search strategies for locating information on the Web and evaluating the information found.

Figure F.3 contains a series of PowerPoint slides, which complement the textbook excerpt, that are posted on the library's internal network and can be accessed from the instructor workstations in all of the library's electronic classrooms.

Finally, Figure F.4 is an example worksheet from an active learning exercise created for a library instruction session. The class was divided into small groups and each small group was assigned to report on one of the criteria to the whole class. After a class discussion of the various criteria, a mini–lecture about how information gets posted on the Web was presented to the class.

Figure F.1: Sample Web Sites for Practicing Evaluation

CAT BEHAVIOR
Behavior Problems http://www.noodor.com/cat.htm
Increase Your Cat's Sociability http://www.catfancy.com/library/behavior/general/accept.asp
Feline Reactions to Bearded Men http://www.improb.com/airchives/cat.html
Feline Seizures and Epilepsy http://www.cs.cmu.edu/People/lowekamp/feline_epilepsy.html
Traveling With a Cat http://www.metrokc.gov/lars/animal/Educate/cassidy/Cat/cat25.htm

HOLOCAUST
36 Questions About the Holocaust http://motlc.wiesenthal.com/resources/questions/index.html
David Cole's 46 Important Unanswered Questions Regarding the Nazi Gas Chambers http://codoh.com/gcgv/gc46-ORIGI.HTML
The Holocaust: An Historical Summary http://www.ushmm.org/misc-bin/add_goback/education/history.html
The Holocaust: Have We Really Learned Anything? http://www.jdl.org/misc/learned.html
The 'Problem of the Gas Chambers' http://www.ihr.org/leaflets/gaschambers.html

CLONING
The Case for Cloning Humans http://www.best.com/~vere/cloning.htm
Cloning Myths: Debunking Science Fiction http://www.d-b.net/dti/intro1.html
GenoChoice http://www.genochoice.com/
How to Clone a Human (Version 1.1) http://www.biofact.com/cloning/human.html
Moving Toward the Clonal Man http://www.theatlantic.com/unbound/flashbks/cloning/watson.htm
Should We Clone Humans? http://dspace.dial.pipex.com/srtscot/clonhum2.htm

(Figure F.1 continued on following page)

(Figure F.1: *continued*)

AIDS
Antiretroviral Drug Interactions in the HIV-Infected Patient http://www.iapac.org/clinmgt/avtherapies/arvinteract.html
Rethinking AID$ Web site http://www.virusmyth.net/aids/index.htm
True But Little Known Facts About Women and AIDS http://147.129.1.10/library/research/AIDSFACTS.htm
Frequently Asked Questions on HIV/AIDS http://www.cdc.gov/hiv/pubs/faqs.htm
The Cure that Failed http://www.duesberg.com/tbcure.html

SECONDHAND SMOKE
The Data That Went Up In Smoke http://www.smokers.org/html/resource/rarchive/articles/002.html
Has The CDC (Centers For Disease Control And Prevention) Misinformed the Public in Order to Advance a Political Agenda? http://www.smokers.org/html/resource/rarchive/articles/007.html
Health Hazards of Tobacco: Some Facts http://www.who.int/archives/ntday/ntday96/pk96_3.htm
Role of the Media in Tobacco Control -- World No-Tobacco Day, 1994 http://oncolink.upenn.edu/cancer_news/1994/smoke_media.html
Secondhand Smoke (SHS), Also Known as: Environmental Tobacco Smoke http://www.epa.gov/iaq/ets.html
Tobacco and Health http://www.starscientific.com/frame_pages/health_frame.htm

Figure F.2: Textbook Excerpt on Information Evaluation

Can I Trust What I've Found?

Obviously, a man's judgement cannot be better than the information on which he has based it.

– Arthur Hays Sulzberger

You've found some information for your assignment. Now comes a very important step: deciding whether or not you can really rely on the information you have found. Not all information is created equal. (This is true of all types of information, but especially of websites.) Anybody can write anything. Ultimately, it's up to you to evaluate what the person has written to decide if it's something you can rely on (and something you want to use for your assignment), or if it's something that belongs in the waste basket. Listed below are some useful things to look at when making this decision. Some of these things may not apply to your particular assignment. You may also think of other ways of evaluating the information for your particular assignment that are not on this list. Nevertheless, this list will provide you with a useful starting point.

Coverage (How accurate and up-to-date is it?). In order to determine the value of the information, you will need to understand the information. Consider:

- What conclusions are presented?
- What premises/claims are presented?
- Does the evidence support the premises/claims and conclusions?
- Is the information that is provided complete?
- How does this resource compare to other resources on the same topic?
- Are facts and claims of truth documented through footnotes or other appropriate references?
- Are there factual or typographical errors in the information?
- Are there any biases in the information?
- How current is the information?

Author/Creator. Particularly with respect to scholarly information, the authority of the person who created the information is important in determining the credibility of the information. Consider:

- Who created the information?
- What is the reputation of the creator? Is the creator a reputable and reliable scholar or writer?

(Figure F.2 continued on following page)

(Figure F.2: *continued*)

- Is the creator an expert on the topic?
- Is organizational affiliation or contact information given?

Audience. The audience is of particular concern with respect to scholarly information. Consider both the intended and unintended audiences for the information.

Purpose. Consider the purpose of the information. Ask yourself: Given the coverage of the resource, what does the creator want the audience to do, know, think, feel, etc.? In some cases, the purpose of the information may be less than virtuous, for example, if the information is propaganda.

Relevancy. Finally, and most importantly, consider whether the information that you have found is relevant to *your* research. High quality, scholarly information will not meet your information needs if it is off-topic. On the other hand, even obviously biased information may be relevant to a particular research project.

Excerpt from: Lisa Janicke Hinchliffe and James Huff. 2000. *Foundations of Information* in *The Foundations Book: A Reference Book for Foundations of Inquiry and Other Courses* (Second Edition), Kenton Machina, Ed. Boston: Pearson Custom.

Figure F.3: Evaluating Information PowerPoint Slides

Evaluating Information

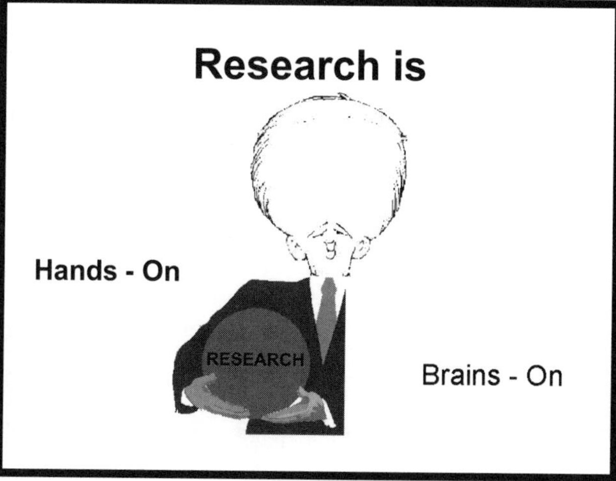

(Figure F.3 continued on following page)

(Figure F.3: *continued*)

Evaluating Information

- Automatic Daily Experience!
- Process of Determining the Value.

Library Environment

Resources are...

- carefully reviewed and selected by librarians.
- produced through the traditional publishing process.
- organized and well developed.
- finding tools are available.

(Figure F.3: *continued*)

Internet Environment

Resources are ...

- **created and added by anyone.**
- **usually not reviewed before they are made available.**
- **not well organized.**
- **finding tools are not**
- **well developed.**

Comprehension and Analysis

Factors to Consider

- **Coverage**
- **Author**
- **Audience**
- **Purpose**

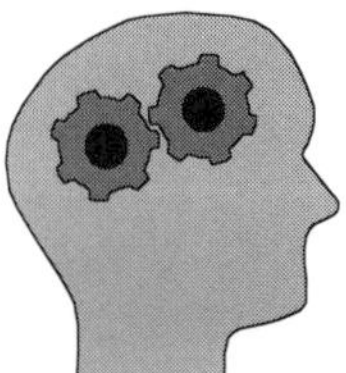

(Figure F.3 continued on following page)

(**Figure F.3:** ***continued***)

Coverage

- Main ideas?
- Overarching, unifying idea?
- How much information provided?
- Documentation?
- Contradictions?
- Errors?
- Date?

Author

- Who?
- Reputation?
- Expert?
- Contact Information?
- Organizational affiliation?
- Host website?

(Figure F.3: *continued*)

Audience

- Intended
  - — Scholars?
  - — Students?
  - — General Public?
  - — Children?
  - — Expert?
- Unintended
  - — Scholars?
  - — Students?
  - — General Public?
  - — Children?

Purpose

The author wants the audience to

- — do what?
- — think what?
- — feel what?

(Figure F.3 continued on following page)

(Figure F.3: *continued*)

Relevancy
• Possible Considerations
—Agreement with Your Own Conclusions
—Illustrates One of Your Points
—Example to Argue Against
—Background Information
• Often the Most Difficult Evaluation Step

MILNER LIBRARY
ILLINOIS STATE UNIVERSITY

Foundations of Inquiry
Library Instruction Program
Lisa Janicke Hinchliffe and Jan Johnson
Milner Library
Illinois State University

Figure F.4: Evaluating Information Worksheet

Name: ____________________

Worksheet

Scenario: You decide that you want to investigate the research question "What environmental factors were most significant in bringing about the Dust Bowl?" By happenstance you overhear someone mention that the levels of Dihydrogen Monoxide were very influential in the events that occurred. Through an Internet search engine you find the following website:

http://www.dhmo.org/facts.html

You remember that the library chapter in *The Foundations Book* titled "Foundations of Information" suggested criteria for evaluating websites and decide to put the website to the test. Use the criteria from the chapter (listed below for your convenience) to determine whether the website is a credible source. Write a short summary of your evaluation for each criteria. Then, decide whether you would use the website to write your paper and list reasons for your decision.

Criteria:

Coverage: What are the premises and conclusions presented? How accurate and up-to-date is the information?

Authorship: Who is the creator or sponsor of the website? How credible is the creator/sponsor?

Audience: Who is the intended audience for the website?

Purpose: What does the creator/sponsor of the website wish for the website's audience to do or think?

Relevancy: Is the website relevant to the research topic?

Decision: Would you use this website in your paper? What are the reasons for your decision?

Appendix G

Case Studies: School, Public, and Special Library Examples

A great majority of the published works on electronic classrooms are about classrooms in academic libraries, and this book is no exception. However, just like user instruction programs, electronic classrooms can be found in all types of libraries—academic, school, public and special. Fortunately, most of what is known about electronic classrooms in academic libraries can also be applied to other library settings. To increase the usefulness of this book, this appendix contains three short case studies—one for a school library, one for a public library, and one for a special library. After the case study, what follows are worksheets from the main part of the book, filled out for the circumstances described in the case study.

SCHOOL LIBRARY CASE STUDY

Matt is the new library media specialist at District Junior High School. When he interviewed, he was impressed by the computer classroom down the hall from the library. He was happy to learn that the principal intended to build a second classroom in the library itself. The principal wants Matt to have a written proposal for consideration at the school board meeting in two months. Although state curriculum standards require that eighth-grade students demonstrate computer competence, the school board is not as convinced of the importance of technology skills as a basis for lifelong learning as the principal is. Matt must not only design the classroom but also compose a compelling rationale for the role of technology in building critical thinking and information literacy skills. Matt asks the library media specialists at District Elementary School and District High School to work with him on the proposal. He also seeks input from a number of teachers at District Junior High—the computer skills instructor, the writing teachers, and, of course, the social studies teacher who is always talking about the latest technologies.

Figure G.1: School Library — Instructional Needs Assessment Worksheet

Consideration	Present	Future
Teachers	*School Library Media Specialist. Some classroom teachers interested in technology.*	*School Library Media Specialist – collaborative implementation with classroom teachers.*
Instructional Methods	*Lecture and demonstration with minimal hands-on.*	*Focus on hands-on active learning with lecture and demonstration as needed for guidance.*
Instructional Content	*Locating books. Using encyclopedias. Internet searching when computer classroom is available.*	*The research process – integrating print and electronic resources. Technology literacy.*
Instructional Materials and Technologies	*Use library materials to demonstrate. Handouts.*	*Handouts. Library materials. Web pages.*
Limitations	*No regular access to an electronic classroom. Not meeting state curriculum technology standards.*	*Time constraints in developing collaborative working relationships.*
Trends	*Increasing emphasis on technology literacy in state standards. Increasing use of resource-based learning.*	*State standards continue to evolve. Resource-based teaching expands.*

(Figure G.1: *continued*)

Consideration	Present	Future
Learners	*District Junior High School students.*	*Junior High School students – with a focus on grades seven and eight.*
Instruction Session Format	*Course-related and open workshops.*	*Sequential and course-integrated as well as open workshops.*
Where	*In the School Library Media Center. In the computer classroom when possible (only late afternoons).*	*In the School Library Media Center and the Media Center Electronic Classroom.*
When	*During class library time. After school.*	*During class library time. After school.*
Extent	*About 50 class sessions and five after school workshops each semester.*	*About 75 class sessions and five after school workshops each semester.*

Figure G.2: School Library—Classroom Tour Comments Worksheet

Classroom:	*Electronic Classroom at District High School*
Purpose:	*Hands-on information literacy training sessions. Also functions as an open computing laboratory when not in use for instruction sessions.*
Equipment:	*Instructor workstation (computer, monitor, keyboard, mouse, overhead projector, and videocassette player), projector on cart, screen in front right corner of room, white boards at front of room, 12 student workstations (computer, monitor, keyboard, mouse). All computers are iMacs.*
Software:	*Apple Works, Netscape, and Photoshop. Games are on computers but student use is carefully monitored.*
Room Layout:	*Rows, Parallel (Middle Aisle). Instructor workstation in front left corner. Entrance at rear.*

(Figure G.2: *continued*)

Likes:	**Dislikes:**
Software carefully selected to support the classes that are taught in the room and to support student homework assignments. *The secondary use of the classroom as an open computing laboratory maximizes the school's investment in technology and computing resources.* *Students must reaffirm their understanding of the Acceptable Use Policy each time the log on to a computer.*	*Room layout seems to inhibit discussion and students working together in small groups; however, the space is used very efficiently.* *Switching the placement of the projection screen and the instructor workstation would improve the flow of instruction. Instructor often appears awkward when gesturing toward screen.* *Whiteboard space is limited. Back wall could also have whiteboards which would be especially useful for the brainstorming exercises students do in small groups.*

Other Comments: *Maroon and cream color scheme is both soothing as well as reflective of school colors.*

Observer: *Matt*

Figure G.3: School Library—Electronic Classroom Interaction Matrix

	Classroom	Instruction Staff	Building Entrance	Reference Area	*Grade 8 Hallway*	*Computer Classroom*
Classroom		*V*	*X*	*D*	*V*	*D*
Instruction Staff	2, 3, 4		*N*	*V*	*N*	*D*
Building Entrance	1, 5 (Security)	1, 2		*U*	*N*	*U*
Reference Area	2, 4	2, 4	1		*D*	*D*
Grade 8 Hallway	2, 4	2, 4	1	2, 4		*D*
Computer Classroom	2, 3	2, 4	1, 5 (Security)	2, 4	2, 4	

PUBLIC LIBRARY CASE STUDY

Susan is the head of information services at City Public Library. The community recently voted in favor of a referendum to remodel part of the library building. The proposed electronic classroom has a great deal of public support and a local company has even agreed to underwrite the costs of the equipment for the classroom. At the current time, the library is not able to offer an information literacy training sessions. The new classroom will also be used by the city offices of the city for staff training. While the community is supportive and excited about the project, the information services staff is less so. Concerns about scheduling, damage to the equipment, and inappropriate Web surfing abound. Susan decides to involve the entire information services staff on the planning team to make certain that everyone has an opportunity to participate in planning the facility. She hopes that as they participate in the design process, their fears will be allayed and the classroom will eventually be a success. The library director supports Susan's decision. The board of trustees is excited about the idea of offering computer training in the library and requests a monthly update on the status of the electronic classroom project.

Figure G.4: Public Library—Instructional Needs Assessment Worksheet

Consideration	**Present**	**Future**
Learners	*Community. (Adults and children.)*	*Community. (Adults and children.)*
Instruction Session Format	*One-to-one.*	*One-to-one. Group workshops.*
Where	*Point of use.*	*Point of use. In the classroom.*
When	*Whenever library is open.*	*Whenever the library is open, considering early morning/late evening sessions for working adults.*
Extent	*Not tabulated.*	*One-to-one will not be tabulated. Ten sessions/month in classroom.*

(Figure G.4: *continued*)

Consideration	Present	Future
Teachers	*Library staff.*	*Library staff. Maybe community volunteers.*
Instructional Methods	*Hands-on tutoring.*	*Hands-on tutoring. Lecture and demonstration with discussion.*
Instructional Content	*Online catalog. Reference books and other library materials.*	*Online catalog. Library materials. Research process. Computer skills.*
Instructional Materials and Technologies	*Handouts.*	*Handouts. Computer-based slide shows. Webpages.*
Limitations	*No classroom. No space in library that can be used for groups. Staff attitudes.*	*Sharing space with city administrative offices. Classroom furniture must accommodate adults and children.*
Trends	*Community demand for instruction.*	*Increasing demand for computer and information literacy skills at all ages.*

Figure G.5: Public Library—Classroom Tour Comments Worksheet

Classroom:	*"The Access Point" at Urban County Free Library*
Purpose:	*Community laboratory and training facility. Sessions taught by librarians and community computer trainers. Available for outside reservations. Also serves as open computing laboratory when not in use for scheduled sessions.*
Equipment:	*Instructor workstation (computer, monitor, keyboard, mouse), projector mounted on shelf on back wall of classroom, whiteboards on all walls, printer station, and 10 learner workstations (computer, monitor, keyboard, mouse).*
Software:	*Microsoft Office, Microsoft Internet Explorer. Games installed on three of the learner workstations. Utilizes Fortres 101 to prevent settings from being changed on the computers.*
Room Layout:	*Boardroom/Seminar*

(Figure G.5: *continued*)

Likes:	**Dislikes:**
Fortress 101 allows users freedom in exploring the computer while preserving the original settings. *Room layout allows the instructors to easily use the whiteboards for brainstorming and writing out directions.* *Library staff welcome community groups and individual users. Staff receives ongoing technology training so that they are comfortable with the technology and comfortable showing library users how to use the computer tools.*	*No videocassette player so instruction cannot incorporate video-based instruction.* *Teens monopolize the computers that have access to games.* *Too many chairs – one set for adults and one for children. It would be better chairs that stack so that stools for children can be moved out of the way for adult sessions and vice versa.* *Need new erasers for whiteboards.*

Other Comments: *Color scheme incorporates too many bright colors. It is distracting. Appreciate that the instructor workstation includes an adjustable chair.*

Observer: *Susan and the Information Services Staff*

Figure G.6: Public Library—Electronic Classroom Interaction Matrix

	Classroom	Instruction Staff	Building Entrance	Reference Area	*Children's Room*	*Circulation Desk*
Classroom		*D*	*V*	*U*	*D*	*V*
Instruction Staff	*2*		*U*	*D*	*U*	*N*
Building Entrance	*2, 5 (Outside Groups)*	*1*		*U*	*U*	*V*
Reference Area	*1*	*2, 4*	*1*		*N*	*N*
Children's Room	*1, 2, 5 (Child Safety)*	*1*	*5 (Child Safety)*	*1, 2*		*N*
Circulation Desk	*2, 5 (Oversight)*	*2*	*2*	*2*	*1, 2*	

SPECIAL LIBRARY CASE STUDY

John is an information specialist at Company Service Industries. During a recent strategic planning process, the directors of the Information Resources Center and the Human Resources department discovered that both units have been seeking funding and space to create a small, hands-on training room. Senior administration has agreed to fund a shared classroom if the two units can agree on a design and policies for use. John has been assigned to work with Pat, a training specialist from Human Resources and Development, to create a proposal for an electronic classroom. After initial discussions, it seems that the needs and instructional approaches used in both units are very similar. Though compromises will no doubt be necessary, John and Pat at both confident that the shared classroom will be a success. As a first step, John and Pat agree to share their written planning documents with one another.

Figure G.7: Special Library—Instructional Needs Assessment Worksheet

Consideration	**Present**	**Future**
Learners	*Library users in the company.*	*Library users in the company.*
Instruction Session Format	*One-to-one.*	*One-to-one. Small group workshops.*
Where	*In the Information Resources Center.*	*In the Information Resources Center. In the Training Room.*
When	*During regular work hours. When possible, as requested, in evenings.*	*Same.*
Extent	*Tabulated as a reference encounter.*	*One-to-one tabulated as reference encounter. Two workshops/week.*

(Figure G.7: *continued*)

Consideration	Present	Future
Teachers	*Information Resources Center staff.*	*Information Resources Center staff.*
Instructional Methods	*One-to-one tutorials.*	*One-to-one tutorials. Hands-on workshops with lecture/demonstration and active learning.*
Instructional Content	*Information resources. Online databases.*	*Same plus project and knowledge management software training.*
Instructional Materials and Technologies	*Handouts. Files on company intranet.*	*Same plus individualized, interactive tutorials available on the Training Room computers.*
Limitations	*No classroom. Not enough computer terminals.*	*Challenges of sharing classroom with Human Resources – scheduling, etc..*
Trends	*Increasing number of company managers prefer to do their own database searching.*	*Continued emphasis on end-user searching and full-text document delivery online.*

Figure G.8: Special Library—Classroom Tour Comments Worksheet

Classroom:	*"The Knowledge Edge" at The Future Company.*
Purpose:	*Interactive, hands-on training for account managers and knowledge brokers.*
Equipment:	*Ten classroom workstations (instructor and learners bring their own laptops from their offices), all workstations connected to projection system through collaboration software, wireless network, whiteboards on front and back walls.*
Software:	*Microsoft Office, Microsoft Project, Microsoft Internet Explorer, Netscape, Adobe Acrobat Reader, Dreamweaver, Photoshop, ProCite, SPSS, and ARCView. Other software available on request.*
Room Layout:	*Generally, clusters; however, tables are modular and can be easily moved into the configuration desired by a particular group or needed for a specific activity.*

(Figure G.8: *continued*)

Likes:	**Dislikes:**
Very flexible instruction space. The ability to arrange the tables as needed for a particular activity allows the instructor to be creative in planning a variety of learning experiences. *Each person learns on their own laptop and is able to immediately incorporate new skills into existing projects.* *Instruction environment is de-centralized and any learner can become an instructor through the collaboration software.* *Plethora of software.*	*Training sessions became a bit chaotic when it was not clear who was directing the session.* *One person's laptop stopped functioning mid-way through a session because of software installation conflicts (the laptop had two unique software packages that had not been tested with the new system. There are no back-up laptops.* *Not every group returned the tables to their "default" locations and so it sometimes took a great deal of time to set up the room for a new training session.*
Other Comments: *Learners clearly enjoyed the ability to shape the learning environment to their learning styles. Instructors had to let go of some control over the flow of the sessions.*	
Observer: *John*	

Figure G.9: Special Library—Electronic Classroom Interaction Matrix

	Classroom	Instruction Staff	Building Entrance	Reference Area	*Human Resources*	*Technical Support*
Classroom		*D*	*N*	*D*	*D*	*D*
Instruction Staff	*2*		*N*	*D*	*N*	*D*
Building Entrance	*1, 2, 5 (Theft)*	*1, 2*		*U*	*N*	*N*
Reference Area	*2, 4*	*2, 4*	*1*		*N*	*D*
Human Resources	*2*	*2*	*1, 2*	*1, 2*		*D*
Technical Support	*3*	*3*	*1, 2*	*3*	*3*	

References

Adams, Laurel. 1995. "Designing the Electronic Classroom." In *Teaching Electronic Information Literacy: A How-To-Do-It Manual,* edited by Donald A. Barclay. New York: Neal-Schuman.

Aiken, Milam W., and Delvin D. Hawley. 1995. "Designing an Electronic Classroom for Large Courses." *T.H.E. Journal* 23, no. 2 (September): 76–77.

Allen, Robert L., J. Thomas Bowen, Sue Clabaugh, Beth B. DeWitt, JoEllen Francis, John P. Kerstetter, and Donald A. Reick. 1996. *Classroom Design Manual.* 3d ed. College Park, Md.: Academic Information Technology Services, University of Maryland.

Aluri, Rao, and June Lester Engle. 1987. "Bibliographic Instruction and Library Education." In *Bibliographic Instruction*, edited by Constance Mellon. Englewood, Colo.: Libraries Unlimited.

Applin, Mary Beth. 1999. "Instructional Services for Students with Disabilities." *Journal of Academic Librarianship* 25, no. 2 (March): 139–141.

Arlitsch, Keith. 1998. "Building Instruction Labs at the University of Utah." *Research Strategies* 16, no. 3: 199–210.

Association of College and Research Libraries. 2000. *Information Literacy Competancy Standards for Higher Education.* Chicago: Association of College and Research Libraries. *www.ala.org/acrl/ilcomstan.html.* February 5, 2001.

Bahr, Alice Harrison. 2000. "Introduction." *Future Teaching Roles for Academic Librarians*, edited by Alice Harrison Bahr. New York: Haworth Press. Also published in *College and Undergraduate Libraries* 1999, vol. 6, no. 2: 1–4.

Bankard, Kathy. 1997. "How to Optimize Projection Technology: Using Fonts, Graphics, and Color to Maximize the Effectiveness of Your Presentation." *Syllabus* II, (November/December): 32–35.

Barclay, Donald A. 2000. *Managing Public Access Computers: A How-To-Do-It Manual for Librarians*. New York: Neal-Schuman.

Barclay, Donald, ed.. 1995. *Teaching Electronic Information Literacy: A How-To-Do-It Manual.* New York: Neal-Schuman.

Barr, Robert B. and John Tagg. 1995. "From Teaching to Learning." *Change* 27, no. 6 (November /December): 13–25.

Barrett, Edward. 1993. "Collaboration in the Electronic Classroom." *Technology Review* 96, no. 2 (February/March): 50–55.

Bauer, David. 1999. *The "How To" Grants Manual: Successful Grantseeking Techniques for Obtaining Public and Private Grants*. Phoenix: Oryx Press.

Baule, Steven. 1997. *Technology Planning*. Worthington, Ohio: Linworth Publishing.

Baumann, Melinda. 1996. "Creating and Maintaining Electronic Classrooms: The Virginia Academic Library Experience." *Virginia Libraries* 42 (January–March): 8–10.

Bazillion, Richard J., and Connie L. Braun. 1995a. *Academic Libraries as High-Tech Gateways: A Guide to Design and Space Decisions*. Chicago: American Library Association.

———. 1995b. "Building Virtual—and Spatial—Libraries for Distance Learning." *CAUSE/EFFECT* 18, no. 4 (Winter): 51–54.

Bielefield, Arlene, and Lawrence Cheeseman. 1999. *Interpreting and Negotiating Licensing Agreements: A Guidebook for the Library, Research, and Teaching Professions*. New York: Neal-Schuman.

Blackett, Anthony, and Brenda Stanfield. 1994. "A Planner's Guide to Tomorrow's Classrooms." *Planning for Higher Education* 22, no. 3 (Spring): 25–31.

Bligh, Donald. 1998. *What's the Use of Lectures?* Exeter, England: Intellect.

Boschmann, Erwin. 1995. *The Electronic Classroom: A Handbook for Education in the Electronic Environment*. Medford, N.J.: Learned Information.

Boss, Richard W. 1987. *Information Technologies and Space Planning for Libraries and Information Centers*. Boston: G. K. Hall Publishers.

Bragman, Ruth. 1987. "Integrating Technology into a Student's IEP." *Rural Special Education Quarterly* 8, no. 2: 34–38.

Brand, Stewart. 1994. *How Buildings Learn: What Happens After They're Built*. New York: Penguin Books.

Brandt, D. Scott. 1998. "Compartmentalizing Computer Training." *Computers in Libraries* 18, no. 1 (January): 41–44.

Brase, Wendell. 1989. "Design Criteria for Effective Classrooms." *Planning for Higher Education* 17, no. 1: 81–91.

Brawner, Lee. 1992. "The Roles of the Building Consultant and the Planning Team." In *Libraries for the Future: Planning Buildings that Work*, edited by Ron G. Martin. Chicago: Library Administration and Management Association, American Library Association.

Bren, Barbara, Beth Hillemann, and Victoria Topp. 1998. "Effectiveness of Hands-on Instruction of Electronic Resources." *Research Strategies* 16, no. 1: 41–51.

Brottman, May, and Mary Loe, eds. 1990. *The LIRT Library Instruction Handbook*. Englewood, Co.: Libraries Unlimited.

Brown, Carol R. 1995. *Planning Library Interiors: The Selection of Furnishings for the 21st Century*. Phoenix: Oryx Press.

Burmark, Lynell. 1997. "Presentation Tools for the Classroom and Library/Resource Center." *Media and Methods* 33, no. 4 (March/April): 6, 8, 10.

Butler, H. Julene. 1993. "Library Instruction in an Electronic Classroom." In *What Is Good Instruction Now? Library Instruction for the 90s*, edited by Linda Shirato. Ann Arbor, Mich.: Pierian Press.

Buyer's Guide to Presentation Products. 1999. Minneapolis: Bill Communications.

Chambers, Jack A., John Q. Mullins, Brenda Boccard, and David Burrows. 1992. "The Learning Revolution: Electronic Classrooms." *Interactive Learning International* 8, no. 4 (October–December): 291–295.

Chenault, Brittney. 1998. "Electronic Classroom Policies." *www.moorhead.msus.edu/chenault/epolicies.htm*. (September 18, 2000).

———. 1999. "SMART Board Changes Library Instruction." *Library Instruction Round Table News* 21, no. 4: 21–22.

Chickering, Art W., and Stephen C. Ehrmann. 1996. "Implementing the Seven Principles: Technology as Lever." *AAHE Bulletin* 49, no. 2 (October): 3–6. *www.aahe.org/technology/ehrmann.htm*. (September 19, 2000).

Chickering, Art W., and Zelda F. Gamson. 1987. "Seven Principles for Good Practice in Undergraduate Education." *AAHE Bulletin* 39, no. 7 (March): 3–7.

Clabaugh, Sue. 1992. "Classroom Design: Upgrading Aging Classrooms and Building New Ones Right." *Ohio Media Spectrum* 44, no. 3 (Fall): 46–49.

Cohen, Joel A., and Mark H. Castner. 2000. "Technology and Classroom Design: A Faculty Perspective." In *Teaching with Technology: Rethinking Tradition*, edited by Les Lloyd. Medford, N.J.: Information Today.

College and University Media Review 6, no. 2 (Spring 2000).

"ComputerShopper." *www.zdnet.com/computershopper*. (September 12, 2000).

Conway, Kathryn. 1993. *Master Classrooms: Classroom Design with Technology In Mind*." Research Triangle Park, N.C.: Institute for Academic Technology. (Updated at *www.unc.edu/cit/iat-archive/publications/conway/conway.html*)

Conway, Kathryn, Steven L. Epstein, Steve Griffin, David R. Luttell, and Jack Wilson (panelists). 1994. *Classroom Design with Technology in Mind* [satellite broadcast, videocassette recording]. Raleigh, N.C.: Institute for Academic Technology. Information available online at *www.unc.edu/cit/iat-archive/publications/broadcasts/feb94.html*.

Coppola, Jean F., and Barbara A. Thomas. 2000. "A Model for E-Classroom Design Beyond 'Chalk and Talk.'" *T.H.E. Journal* 27, no. 6 (January): 29–36.

Cramer, Michael D. 1994. "Licensing Agreements: Think Before You Act." *College and Research Libraries News* 55, no. 8 (September): 496–497.

Day, C. William. 1997. "Technology for Older Schools." *American School and University* 69, no. 10 (June): 54.

Deasy, C. M. 1985. *Designing Places for People: A Handbook on Human Behavior for Architects, Designers, and Facility Managers*. New York: Whitney Library of Design.

DePaoli, Lenore. 1995. "Flooring as an Element of Design." In *Designing Communication and Learning Environments*, edited by Diane M. Gayeski. Englewood Cliffs, N.J.: Educational Technology Publications.

Designing a Computer Classroom: Getting Started. 1992. Research Triangle Park, N.C.: Institute for Academic Technology.

Deines-Jones, Courtney. 1999. "Training Professional and Support Staff Members." In *Accessible Libraries on Campus: A Practical Guide for the Creation of Disability-Friendly Libraries*, edited by Tom McNulty. Chicago: Association of College and Research Libraries, American Library Association.

Dominick, Jay. 2000. "Wireless on Campus." *Syllabus* 14, no. 4 (November): 19–22.

Dowler, Lawrence, ed. 1997. *Gateways to Knowledge: The Role of Academic Libraries in Teaching, Learning and Research*. Cambridge: MIT Press.

Doyle, Robert. 2000. "Establishing Multimedia Standards for University Classrooms." *College and University Media Review* 6, no. 2 (Spring): 33–42.

Duggan, Brian. 1994. "A Measured Approach to Microcomputer Lab Design." *Tech Trends* 39, no. 4 (September): 24–28.

Erdreich, John. 1999. "Classroom Acoustics." "ISSUETRAK: A CEFPI Brief on Educational Facilities Issues." *www.cefpi.org:80/issue/issue9.pdf*. September 19, 2000.

Farber, Evan Ira. 1984. "BI and Library Instruction: Some Observations." *Reference Librarian* 10 (Spring/Summer): 5–13.

Feinman, Valerie J. 1994. "Library Instruction: What Is Our Classroom?" *Computers in Libraries*. 14, no. 2 (February): 33–36.

"Finding Statistics: Tutorial and Worksheet." *www.mlb.ilstu.edu/learn/stat/home.htm* February 5, 2001.

Finkel, Coleman. 1984. "A Checklist for Evaluating a Training Facility." *Successful Meetings* 33, no. 6: 94–102.

Fraley, Ruth A., and Carol Lee Anderson. 1990. *Library Space Planning: A How-To-Do-It Manual for Assessing, Allocating and Reorganizing Collections, Resources and Facilities.* New York: Neal-Schuman.

Freifeld, Roberta, and Caryl Masyr. 1991. *Space Planning*. Washington, D.C.: Special Libraries Association.

Gayeski, Diane M., ed. 1995. *Designing Communication and Learning Environments.* Englewood Cliffs, N.J.: Educational Technology Publications.

Gilbert, Steven W. 1996. "Making the Most of a Slow Revolution." *Change* 28, no. 2 (March/April): 10–23.

Gilbertson, Denny, and Jamie Poindexter. 2000. "Distance Education Classroom Design." *www.uwex.edu/disted/rooms/county.htm*. September 18, 2000.

Glogoff, Stuart. 1995. "Library Instruction in the Electronic Library: The University of Arizona's Electronic Library Education Centers." *Reference Services Review* 23, no. 2 (Summer): 7–12, 39.

Gradowski, Gail, Loanne Snavely, and Paula Dempsey, eds. 1998. *Designs for Active Learning: A Sourcebook of Classroom Strategies for Information Education*. Chicago: American Library Association.

Green, Samuel S. 1876. "Personal Relations Between Librarians and Readers." *American Library Journal* 1: 80.

Gremmels, Gillian S. 1996. "Active and Cooperative Learning in the One-Shot BI Session." In *New Ways of "Learning the Library"—and Beyond,* edited by Linda Shirato, Elizabeth R. Bucciarelli, and Heidi Mercado. Ann Arbor, Mich.: Pierian Press.

Gresham, Keith. 1997. "Electronic Classrooms: Linking Information Concepts to Online Exploration." *RQ* 36, no. 4 (Summer): 514–520.

———. 1999. "Experiential Learning Theory, Library Instruction, and the Electronic Classroom." *Colorado Libraries* 25, no. 1 (Spring): 28–31.

Guidelines for Instruction Programs Task Force, Instruction Section, Association of College and Research Libraries, American Library Association. 1996. *Guidelines for Instruction Programs in Academic Libraries.* Chicago: American Library Association. *www.ala.org./acrl/guides/guiis.htm.* September 18, 2000.

Hart, Ian. 1996. "Building the Perfect Classroom, or the Labors of Sisyphus." *College and University Media Review* 2, no. 2 (Spring): 11–21.

Hart, Russ A., and Roger Parker. 1996. *Technological Challenges: Designing Large Compressed Video and Multimedia Classrooms.* ERIC Reproduction Service No. ED 392 402.

Hawkins, Beth Leibson. 1993. "Training Rooms Keep Organizations Up and Running." *Facilities Design and Management* 12, no. 6: 52–55.

Hawthorne, Pat, and Ron G. Martin, eds. 1995. *Planning Additions to Academic Library Buildings: A Seamless Approach.* Chicago: Library Administration and Management Association, American Library Association.

Heaton, Paul C. 1995. "Heating, Ventilating and Air Conditioning." In *Designing Communication and Learning Environments,* edited by Diane M. Gayeski. Englewood Cliffs, N.J.: Educational Technology Publications.

Helander, Martin G., and Thiagarajan Palanivel. 1992. "Ergonomics of Human-Computer Interaction." *Impact of Science on Society* 42, no. 1: 65–74.

Hinchliffe, Lisa Janicke. 1994. "Planning an Electronic Library Classroom: An Annotated Bibliography." *http://alexia.lis.uiuc.edu/~janicke/Abstracts.html.* (September 18, 2000).

———. 1998. "Resources for Designing Library Electronic Classrooms." *MC Journal: The Journal of Academic Media Librarianship* 6, no. 1 (Spring). *http://wings.buffalo.edu/publications/mcjrnl/v6n1/class.html.* (September 18, 2000).

Holt, Raymond M. 1989. *Planning Library Buildings and Facilities: From Concept to Completion.* Metuchen, N.J.: Scarecrow Press.

How To Design Training Rooms. 1989. INFO-LINE Series No. 8912. Alexandria, Va.: American Society for Training and Development.

Howden, Norman. 2000. *Buying and Maintaining Personal Computers: A How-To-Do-It Manual for Librarians.* New York: Neal-Schuman.

Imhoff, Kathleen R. T. 1996. *Making the Most of New Technology: A How-To-Do-It Manual for Librarians.* New York: Neal-Schuman.

Jacob, M. E. L. 1990. *Strategic Planning: A How-To-Do-It Manual for Librarians*. New York: Neal-Schuman.

Jafari, Ali. 1990. "Designing and Engineering a Teacher-Friendly High-Tech Classroom." *Ohio Media Spectrum* 42, no. 4 (Winter): 22–26.

Jafari, May, and Anthony Stamatoplos. 1996. "Promoting Active Learning in the Electronic Classroom: Making the Transition From Presentation to Workshop." *New Ways of "Learning the Library"—and Beyond,* edited by Linda Shirato, Elizabeth R. Bucciarelli, and Heidi Mercado. Ann Arbor, Mich.: Pierian Press.

Jay, M. Ellen, and Hilda L. Jay. 1994. *The Library/Computer Lab/Classroom Connection: Linking Content, Thinking and Writing*. New York: Neal-Schuman.

Johnson, Doug. 1997. *The Indispensable Librarian: Surviving (and Thriving) in School Media Centers*. Worthington, Ohio: Linworth Publishing.

Keown, Cheryl. 1999. "A Learning Curve." *American School and University* 71, no. 12 (August): 116–119.

Kerstetter, John P. 1986. "Designing Classrooms for the Use of Instructional Media: A Planning and Specifications Checklist." *Media Management Journal* 6, no. 1 (Fall): 25–28.

Kettinger, William J. 1991. "Computer Classrooms in Higher Education: An Innovation in Teaching." *Educational Technology* 31, no. 8 (August): 36–43.

Kirk, Thomas G., James R. Kennedy Jr., and Nancy P. Van Zant. 1980. "Structuring Services and Facilities for Library Instruction." *Library Trends* 29, no. 1 (Summer): 39–53.

Knirk, Frederick G. 1987. *Instructional Facilities for the Information Age.* Syracuse, N.Y.: ERIC Clearinghouse on Information Resources. ERIC Reproduction Service No. ED 296 734.

———. 1992a. "Facility Requirements for Integrated Learning Systems." *Educational Technology* 32, no. 9 (September): 26–32.

———. 1992b. "New Technology Considerations for Media Facilities: Video Technologies and Space Requirements." *School Library Media Quarterly* 20, no. 4 (Summer): 205–210.

Konya, Allan. 1986. *Libraries: A Briefing and Design Guide.* London: The Architectural Press.

Kotlas, Carolyn. *Computer Classroom and Laboratory Design: Bibliography*. Updated online at *http://www. unc.edu/cit/guides/irg-03.html*

LaGuardia, Cheryl, and Christine K. Oka. 2000. *Becoming a Library Teacher*. New York: Neal-Schuman.

LaGuardia, Cheryl, and Stella Bentley. 1994. "We Teach the Networks

Electric: The Networked Library Classroom." *In 15th National Online Meeting Proceedings—1994: New York, May 10–12, 1994*. Medford, N.J.: Learned Information.

LaGuardia, Cheryl, Michael Blake, Lawrence Dowler, Laura Farwell, Caroline M. Kent, and Ed Tallent. 1996. *Teaching the New Library: A How-To-Do-It Manual for Planning and Designing Instructional Programs*. New York: Neal-Schuman.

Laird, Dugan. 1984. "Demand the Trivial! Yells an Unhappy Trainer." *Successful Meetings* 33, no. 6 (June): 97–102.

Lance, Kathleen. 1995. "Designing Electronic Classrooms." *Colorado Libraries* 21 (Winter): 37–38.

Ledford, Bruce R., and John A. Brown. 1992. "A Case Study in Acoustical Design." *International Journal of Instructional Media* 19, no. 2: 127–140.

Leed, Karen B., and James R. Leed. 1987. *Building for Adult Learning*. Cincinnati: Leed Design Associates.

Lehman, Donna, and Charlene Loope. 1998. "Classroom for the New Millennium: Design, Use and Management of a Library Instruction Multimedia Room." In *Theory and Practice,* edited by Linda Shirato, and Elizabeth R. Bucciarelli. Ann Arbor, Mich.: Pierian Press.

Leighton, Philip D., and David C. Weber. 2000. *Planning Academic and Research Library Buildings*. Chicago: American Library Association.

Levin, James A., and Naomi Miyake. "Care and Repair of Your Computer: A Top-Down Strategy for the Novice." *http://faculty.ed.uiuc.edu/j-levin/how-computers-work/levin-miyake.html* (November 5, 2000).

Libutti, Patricia O'Brien, and Bonnie Gratch, eds. 1995. *Teaching Information Retrieval and Evaluation Skills to Education Students and Practitioners: A Casebook of Applications*. Chicago: American Library Association.

Loomis, Jim. 1995a. "Lighting Design." In *Designing Communication and Learning Environments,* edited by Diane M. Gayeski. Englewood Cliffs, N.J.: Educational Technology Publications.

———. 1995b. "Projection Screens." In *Designing Communication and Learning Environments,* edited by Diane M. Gayeski. Englewood Cliffs, N.J.: Educational Technology Publications.

MacDonald, Brad S. 1998. "CLASS ACT: Designing a Portable Approach to Multimedia Library Instruction for the Remote Classroom." *Research Strategies* 16, no. 2: 127–133.

Martin, Ron G., ed. 1992. *Libraries for the Future: Planning Buildings that Work*. Chicago: Library Administration and Management Association, American Library Association.

McAdoo, Monty L. and Joan Tease 1997. "Notebook Computers: To Buy or Not?" *American Libraries* 28 (September): 84.

McCarthy, Richard C. 1999. *Designing Better Libraries: Selecting and Working With Building Professionals*. Fort Atkinson, Wis.: Highsmith Press.

McDermott, Irene E. 1998. "Solitaire Confinement: The Impact of the Physical Environment on Computer Training." *Computers in Libraries* 18(1): 22–27. Also available online at *www.infotoday.com/cilmag/jan/story1.htm*.

McDonald, David. 2000. "Coordinating Classroom Technology Projects to Address User Needs." *College and University Media Review* 6, no. 2 (Spring): 105–24.

McGovern, Gail, Amy Bernath, Kenna Forsyth, Laura Kimberly, and Kathleen Stacey. 1997. *Program Planning: Tips for Librarians*. Chicago: Continuing Library Education Network Exchange Round Table, American Library Association.

McKeachie, Wilbert J. 1994. *Teaching Tips: Strategies, Research, and Theory for College and University Teachers*. Lexington, Mass.: D. C. Heath.

McNulty, Tom. 1999. "Disability in Higher Education: An Overview." In *Accessible Libraries on Campus: A Practical Guide for the Creation of Disability-Friendly Libraries*, edited by Tom McNulty. Chicago: Association of College and Research Libraries, American Library Association.

Meeks, Glenn E., Ricki Fisher, and Warren Loveless. 1997. "Implementation Costs for Educational Technology Systems." *ISSUETRAK: A CEFPI Brief on Educational Facilities Issues*. *www.cefpi.org:80/issue/issue7.html*. September 19, 2000.

Merritt, Mark. 2000. "What Are They Thinking?" *Presentations* 14, no. 4 (April): 86–89.

Miller, Marsha. 1997. "Hands Off My Hands-on: The Trials and Tribulations of Adding an Electronic Classroom to Your Library Instruction Program." *Indiana Libraries* 16, no. 1: 13–20.

Miller, Michael. 1999. "Design Considerations for Computer Classrooms". Presented during the 1999 Library Instruction Round Table Program, Technology in Action: Getting the Most from Your Electronic Classroom. American Library Association Annual Conference, New Orleans. Powerpoint slides online at *www.lib.umich.edu/ummu/miller/index.htm*.

Moore, Gary T., and Jeffery A. Lackney. 1994. *Educational Facilities for the Twenty-First Century: Research Analysis and Design Patterns*.

Milwaukee: Center for Architecture and Urban Planning Research, University of Wisconsin-Milwaukee.

Moran, Thomas. 1987. "The Ideal Computer Lab from Floor to Ceiling." *Tech Trends* 32, no. 2 (March): 18–20.

Mucciolo, Tom. 1998. "When Planning, Don't Forget These Six Room Setup Tips." *Presentations* (August). Article available online at: *www.presentations. com/deliver/room/1998/08/23_sn_when.html.*

Niemeyer, Daniel. "Smarter College Classrooms Home Page: A Complete Source of Classroom Information for Colleges, Architects and Facilities Planners." *http://classrooms.com*. (September 18, 2000).

Norman, Kent, and Leslie E. Carter. 1994. "An Evaluation of the Electronic Classroom: The AT&T Teaching Theater at the University of Maryland." *Interpersonal Computing and Technology: An Electronic Journal for the 21st Century* 2, no. 1: 22–39.

Oberman, Cerise. 1996. "Library Instruction: Concepts and Pedagogy in the Electronic Environment." *RQ* 35 (Spring): 315–323.

Pederson, Ann. 1995. "Teaching Over an Interactive Video Network." In *The Impact of Technology on Library Instruction*, edited by Linda Shirato. Ann Arbor, Mich.: Pierian Press.

Peterson, Billie. 1999. "Tech Talk [Control Software]." *LIRT News* 21, no. 3 (March): 13–14.

Pine, Devera. 1989. "Action Learning." *Psychology Today* 23, no. 7/8: 25–26.

Porter, Lynnette R. 1997. *Creating the Virtual Classroom: Distance Learning with the Internet*. New York: John Wiley.

Porter, Randall C. 1999. "Reaching Out." *American School and University* 71, no. 12 (August): 120–121.

Presentations.com. *http://presentations.com*. (September 16, 2000).

Price, Michael A. 1991. "Designing Video Classrooms." *Adult Learning*, 2, no. 4 (January): 15–19.

ProjectorCentral. *www.projectorcentral.com*. (September 12, 2000).

QuickStudy: Library Research Guide. *hhtp://tutorial.lib.umn.edu*. February 5, 2001.

Research Committee, Library Instruction Round Table, American Library Association. 1999. Library Instruction Teaching Tips: Technology in the Classroom. *http://Diogenes.Baylor.edu/Library/LIRT/lirttech.pdf*. (September 18, 2000).

Research QuickStart. *http://research.lib.umn.edu/*. (September 18, 2000).

Riley, Peter C., and Louis C. Gallo. 2000. "Electronic Learning Environments: Design Considerations." *T.H.E. Journal* 27, no. 6 (January) 50–54.

Ring, Donna M. and Patricia F. Vander Meer. 1994. "Designing a Computerized Instructional Training Room for the Library." *Special Libraries* 85, no. 3 (Summer): 154–161.

"RIO: Research Instruction Online." *http://www.library.arizona.edu/rio/.* February 5, 2001.

Roberts, Geoffrey A., and Phillip M. Dunn. 1996. "Electronic Classrooms and Lecture Theatres: Design and Use Factors in the Age of the Mass Lecture." Paper presented at EdTech '96: Biennial Conference of the Australian Society for Educational Technology, Melbourne, Australia. ERIC Reproduction Service No. ED 396 743.

Robertson, Michelle M. 1992. "Ergonomic Considerations for the Human Environment: Color Treatment, Lighting and Furniture Selection." *School Library Media Quarterly* 20, no. 4 (Summer): 211–215.

Robinson, Otis H. 1876. "Proceedings: First Session." *American Library Journal* 1:123–124.

Rohlf, Robert H. 1986. "Library Design: What Not to Do," *American Libraries* 17, no. 2 (February): 100–104.

Ross, Tweed W., and G. Kent Stewart. 1993. "Facility Planning for Technology Implementation." *Educational Facility Planner* 31, no. 3:9–12.

Sales, Gregory C. 1985. "Design Considerations for Planning a Computer Classroom." *Educational Technology* 25, no. 5 (May): 7–13.

Salomon, Gavriel. 1990. "The Computer Lab: A Bad Idea Now Sanctified." *Educational Technology* 30, no. 10 (October): 50–52.

Schneiderman, Ben, Ellen Yu Borkowski, Maryam Alavi, and Kent Norman. 1998. "Emergent Patterns of Teaching/Learning in Electronic Classrooms." *ETR&D* 46, no. 4: 23–42.

Scholz, Ann Margaret. 1996. "Purdue University Libraries Electronic Classroom." In *New Ways of "Learning the Library"—and Beyond,* edited by Linda Shirato, Elizabeth R. Bucciarelli, and Heidi Mercado. Ann Arbor, Mich.: Pierian Press.

Schoomer, Ella. 2000. "Classrooms 2000: Innovative Approaches to Classroom Technology." *College and University Media Review* 6, no. 2 (Spring): 19–31.

Sellers, Don. 1994. *Zap! How Your Computer Can Hurt You—And What You Can Do About It*. Berkeley, Calif.: Peachpit Press.

Silvers, Donald E. 1994. *The Complete Guide to Kitchen Design with Cooking in Mind.* Tarzana, Calif.: NMI Publishers.

Simmons, Howard L. 2000. "Librarian as Teacher: A Personal View" In *Future Teaching Roles for Academic Librarians*, edited by Alice Harrison Bahr. New York: Haworth Press. Also published in *College and Undergraduate Libraries* 1999, vol. 6, no. 2: 41–44.

SMARTdesks. 2000. "Plans Online—Table of Contents." *www.smartdesks.com/poltoc.htm*. (September 18, 2000).

Smith, Lester K., ed. 1986. *Planning Library Buildings: From Decision to Design*. Chicago: Library Administration and Management Association, American Library Association.

Southard, Ruth. 2000. "Technology: New Trends in Higher Education and Facility Design Implications." *College and University Media Review* 6, no. 2 (Spring): 11–19.

Stewart, G. Kent. 1993. "Avoiding Negative Physical Environment Impact from Budget Limitations." *Educational Facility Planner* 31, no. 3: 19–21.

Stierman, John P. 1992. "A Hands-on Approach: The Missing Ingredient in Online Searching Instruction." *Illinois Libraries* 74, no. 6 (December): 513–516.

Strasser, Dennis. 1996. "Tips for Good Electronic Presentations." *Online* (January/February):78–81. *www.onlineinc.com/onlinemag/JanOL/strasser.html.*

Teach, Beverly. 2000. "Through the Editor's Lens." *College and University Media Review* 6, no. 2 (Spring): 7–10.

Teaching Methods Committee, Instruction Section, Association of College and Research Libraries. 2000. "Classroom Control Systems." *www.libraries.rutgers.edu/is/projects/control.html*. (March 24, 2000).

Terlaga, Kory L. 1990. *Training Room Solutions: A Guide to Planning the Learning Environment*. Trumbull, Conn.: Howe Furniture Corporation.

Thorne, Kaye. 1998. *Training Places: Choosing and Using Venues for Training*. London: Kogan Page.

"TILT: Texas Information Literacy Tutorial." *http://tilt.lib.utsystem.edu/*. (September 18, 2000).

Tomaiuolo, Nicholas G. 1998. "Effective Simultaneous Hands-on Drill for Basic Electronic Database Instruction." *Research Strategies* 16, no. 2: 135–145.

Tracey, William R. 1992. *Designing Training and Development Systems*. New York: AMACON.

Ucko, Thomas J. 1990. *Selecting and Working with Consultants: A Guide for Clients*. Los Altos, Calif.: Crisp Publications.

Van Horn, Royal. 1997. "Electronic Classrooms: Design and Use." *Phi Delta Kappan*, 79, no. 3 (November): 254–255.

Vasi, John, and Cheryl LaGuardia. 1992. "Work Areas, Part I: Ergonomic Considerations, User Furniture, Location." *CD-ROM Professional* (March): 44–46.

———. 1994. "Creating a Library Electronic Classroom." *Online* 18, no. 5: 75–84.

Video Development Initiative. 2000. "Video Conferencing Cookbook." *www.vide.gatech.edu/cookbook2.0/printit.html*. (September 18, 2000).

Walsh, Mary Jane. 1995. "Graphic Design for Library Publications." In *The Impact of Technology on Library Instruction*, edited by Linda Shirato. Ann Arbor, Mich.: Pierian Press.

Warner, Dorothy A., John Buschman, and Robert J. Lackie. 1999. "Getting Blood from a Stone." *College and Research Library News*: 60, no. 7: 536–541.

Weisberg, Michael. 1993. "Ergonomic Guidelines for Designing Effective and Healthy Learning Environments for Interactive Technologies." *Interpersonal Computing and Technology* 1 (April). *http://tlc.nlm.nih.gov/resources/publications/ergo/ergonomics.html* (September 16, 2000).

West, Charles K., James A. Farmer, and Phillip M. Wolff. 1991. *Instructional Design: Implications from Cognitive Science*. Englewood Cliffs, N.J.: Prentice Hall.

Wiggins, Marvin E. 1996. "Planning Electronic Classrooms: Beginning, Expanded and Enriched."In *New Ways of "Learning the Library"—and Beyond,* edited by Linda Shirato, Elizabeth R. Bucciarelli, and Heidi Mercado. Ann Arbor: Pierian Press.

Wiggins, Marvin E., and Donald H. Howard. 1993. "Developing Support Facilities for BYU's Bibliographic Instruction Program." *Journal of Academic Librarianship* 19, no. 3 (July): 144–148.

Wilson, D.L. 1993. "Universities Wrestle with the Design of Tomorrow's High-Tech Classroom." *The Chronicle of Higher Education*, 39, no. 28: A19–A20.

Wilson, Linda. 1996. "Assistive Technology for the Disabled Computer User." *www.unc.edu/cit/guides/irg-20.html*. (November 9, 2000).

"A Wireless Infrastructure." 2000. *Syllabus* 14, no. 4 (November): 22.

Wittkopf, Barbara. 1995. "Planning an Electronic Classroom." *Research Strategies*. 13 no. 2: 66–68.

———. 1996. "Learning Paradigm." *Research Strategies* 14 (Spring): 66–67.

WorkSpace Resources. *www.workspace-resources.com*. (September 19, 2000).

Wright, Carol, and Linda Friend. 1992. "Ergonomics for Online Searching." *Online* 16, no. 3 (May): 13–15, 17–20, 22–27.

Wurman, Richard Saul. 1992. *Follow the Yellow Brick Road: Learning to Give, Take, and Use Instructions*. New York: Bantam Books.

Young, Rosemary M., and Stephana Harmony. 1999. *Working with Faculty to Design Undergraduate Information Literacy Programs: A How-To-Do-It Manual for Librarians*. New York: Neal-Schuman.

Index

About the Author

Lisa Janicke Hinchliffe is the Library Instruction Coordinator and Assistant Professor at Milner Library, Illinois State University. Her experience in designing electronic classrooms began with an independent study project during library school. In her current position, she oversees three electronic classrooms (one demonstration and two hands-on) and serves on the university's Classroom Technology Support Services Advisory Committee. Lisa also does independent consulting work related to electronic classroom design and information literacy instruction.

In addition to electronic classrooms, Lisa is interested in how people use, learn to use, and misuse information. Her research is currently focused on undergraduate students and the transition from high school to college. She presents and publishes often to both library and nonlibrary audiences. Lisa is active in the Instruction Section of the Association of College and Research Libraries and founded the Central Illinois Library Instruction Group. Lisa has master's degrees in both library science and educational psychology from the University of Illinois at Urbana-Champaign and an undergraduate degree in philosophy from the University of St. Thomas, Minnesota.

Lisa can be contacted at Lwhinch@ilstu.edu or Janicke@alexia.lis.uiuc.edu, or through her personal Web page (*www.lis.uiuc.edu/~janicke/lisa.htm*).